YES, MA'AM!

RUNNING THE THIN BLUE LINE

Our story —
p. 157
Michael Vanna

OFC. SUSAN BICKETT

YES, MA'AM! Running the Thin Blue Line

© Susan L. Bickett. ALL RIGHTS RESERVED.

Authored by Susan L. Bickett
Foreword by Tracy C. Ertl

      Published by TitleTown Publishing
      Green Bay, Wisconsin
      www.titletownpublishing.com

No part of this book may be reproduced in any form or by any means, electronic or mechanical, including photocopying, recording, taping, or by any storage and retrieval system, without the written permission of Susan Bickett or TitleTown Publishing.

Editing by Tracy C. Ertil and Erin Walton
Interior design by Euan Monaghan
Cover design by Travis J. Vanden Heuvel
Cover photo © TitleTown Publishing. ALL RIGHTS RESERVED

Publisher's note:
This story, including names, characters, places, and incidents, is based on true events. Some names and identifying details have been changed for privacy reasons. The author alone bears responsibility for any remaining errors in the text, which are wholly unintentional.

ISBN (hardcover): 978-1-949042-11-5
ISBN (paperback): 978-1-949042-10-8
This title is also available in electronic and audiobook formats.

PUBLISHER'S CATALOGING-IN-PUBLICATION DATA
Bickett, Susan
YES MAAM/ BICKETT
1st edition. Green Bay, WI: TitleTown Publishing, c2018.

Proudly Printed in the United States of America
10 9 8 7 6 5 4 3 2 1

DEDICATION

to Lisa A. Sterr for helping me become a police officer

to my police family for keeping me alive as a police officer

to Tammie M. Andrews for helping me become a *retired* police officer

Thank you **all** for the best ride of my life!

PRAISE FOR *YES, MA'AM!*

In *Yes, Ma'am!*, author and fellow officer Susan Bickett invites us into her life on the beat, giving first-hand accounts of the good, the bad, the happy, the sad. At a time in our country's history when law enforcement is often demonized and treated as the enemy, this book is especially relevant and vitally important in our line of work.

SGT. JOSEPH IMPERATRICE
DETECTIVE SQUAD, 1ST PRECINCT (WORLD TRADE CENTER) | NYPD
PRESIDENT & FOUNDER | BLUE LIVES MATTER - NYC

Yes, Ma'am! is a well-written, first-hand account of what a day in the life of a law enforcement professional looks like in Midwest America, as seen through the eyes of a female officer. Officer Bickett should be very proud of this book; a book written by a good cop, for cops.

HON. STEVE COOLEY
DISTRICT ATTORNEY | LOS ANGELES COUNTY (2000-2012)
RESERVE POLICE OFFICER (RET.) | LAPD
CO-AUTHOR | *BLUE LIVES MATTER: IN THE LINE OF DUTY*

Yes, Ma'am! is a record of the trials and triumphs of a female officer at a time when roles and acceptance for women in policing were changing. I know this, as I, too, served during this period, observing first-hand the difficulties faced by our sisters in blue in a time of gender bias, in a male-dominated profession. I also noted the considerable strengths and opportunities brought to our efforts to serve and protect by many of these women. They selflessly put up with the ignorance and disrespect on both sides of the badge and paved the way for the current generation to serve in all areas of law enforcement, making our agencies and society that much better from their presence. This is the story of an exemplary woman who led the way, simply serving others the best she knew how, and, as a result, demonstrating the value and courage of our sisters in blue.

RANDALL W. WILSON
SR. POLICE ADVISOR | INT'L. NARCOTICS/LAW ENFORCEMENT AFFAIRS
DEPUTY CHIEF-DEFENSIVE TACTICS SECTION | ICITAP
POLICE SGT, TRAINING SUPERVISOR, HEAD DEFENSIVE TACTICS INSTRUCTOR
AUTHOR | *BLUE FISH IN A DARK SEA: POLICE INTELLIGENCE IN A COUNTERINSURGENCY*

A NOTE FROM THE PUBLISHER

Police and telecommunicators are the blue family and have their own authentic language and culture. It's direct and sometimes brutal, as there is no time to sanitize and soften blows. *Yes, Ma'am!* was edited but left in the authentic voice of a cop, not a professional writer. It could have been raised to eloquence but then we would lose the "boots-on-the-ground" that makes it real. It was our choice to keep the pages true to what police officers experience, hear, see, touch and smell. With that comes their in-the-moment language, assessments and the reality of what an officer must do and survive. As Susan explains, they live in a continual "tag, you're it" world.

Some of the material in *Yes, Ma'am!* is not suitable for children, and not for teenagers unless accompanied by context and discussion.

Readers will ride through a baby autopsy, descriptions of finding deceased bodies, instances of having to search people, exposures including sexual intercourse, and, at times, foul language.

Godspeed to our women and men in blue, all of them-past, present and future.

TitleTown Publishing
www.TitleTownPublishing.com

OFC. SUSAN L. BICKETT

**BLESSED ARE THE PEACEMAKERS,
FOR THEY WILL BE CALLED CHILDREN OF GOD.
MATTHEW 5:9**

Best known for her numerous foot chases through Titletown USA, Susan L. Bickett served 18 years as a police officer with the Green Bay Police Department.

Challenging at times, Bickett enjoyed patrolling the streets of her hometown. She especially loved the many opportunities to make a positive impact on people that being a peace officer afforded her; never forgetting where she came from – dispatch.

Armed with a passion for keeping citizens safe, Bickett was a full spectrum cop, making a difference; whether that was hunting bad people or making routine traffic stops to promote safer driving habits. An active member of the local community, Bickett became a fixture at Shop With a Cop, school career days, and many other neighborhood programs. Bickett took great pride in wearing the badge and made it a priority to try and set the example by being a positive role model.

Susan is now enjoying a well-earned retirement, sharing time with family and friends in the city she served for over two decades.

CONTENTS

FOREWORD..1

INTRODUCTION..3

EARNING MY BADGE..7

THE ROUTINE..27

THE TONES..161

THE UNBELIEVABLE...177

EXCLUSIVE PREVIEW of BLM................................215

FOREWORD

Tracy C. Ertl

"COME ON BABY, COME ON BABY," he repeated earnestly, out of breath.

It was a baby boy. Their only baby boy. My caller was his daddy trying to help him to start breathing again. "Come on baby, come on baby", I would listen to, on and off, for almost three years. I made a copy of the 911 call and scrutinized it endlessly trying to figure out how I could have better saved him and his family from the anguish of the loss.

His name was Jacob and I only know that because I watched the newspaper obituaries for several days. Then I could finally learn about him and the family grieving the short amount of time they had him here on Earth. He was a S.I.D.S victim, one of many I have grieved through during my twenty-six years as a 911 dispatcher.

One of the police officers on that call was my friend and former dispatch colleague, Susan Bickett. Suz and I "rode" night shift together in dispatch along with Tom Roberts, who would also go on to work out in the field as a police officer. We all started within three months of each other and we moved through all the alternating terror and boredom of nights, together. We had and have an unbreakable bond. Blue family.

The afternoon of Jacob's death, Suz came into the station to check on me at the end of the shift. Her perspective was clear and true; a sentiment also shared by my husband. "Trace, people often come to you dead. You didn't lose that baby. He was gone when the call came in. You saved the father." Through Suz's eyes, the eyes of a police officer, I was given a 360-degree view of calls.

I studied all officer notes entered into calls but in particular, those of Bickett and Roberts. I knew them as well as family and, in their notes, I could almost hear them at times working with people in the community. I developed an absolute adoration for the work of my blue family, not just in the 911 center but out in the field as well. My passion grew extraordinarily for the team that is comprised of dispatch AND field responders. That passion remains today; in large part due to what I have *heard* my second family encounter, manage and save, on the road.

Courage, persistence, humility, hope, empathy, conviction and yes, humor, are all hallmarks of the best on the road. In YES MA'AM, Bickett takes readers on the road with her, forever 222A. She brings us in the squad, but more importantly into the valiant heart that is uniquely that of a police officer. In YES MA'AM, police officers, all of them, are humanized. Bickett, with her pickle-filled lunch cooler in her squad, gives us the laughter and the tears that belong to a beat cop.

It has been an honor to originally serve the Green Bay Police Department and all law agencies served by Brown County Public Safety Communications. In my dual role now as a publisher, I have the incredible honor and responsibility to add breathe and a face to what are often just squad numbers and a name on a metal chest plate. I will protect you on the road and champion you, honestly, as long as air fills my lungs.

God-speed, Ofc. Susan Bickett, as you enjoy the retirement you deeply earned. You made it, my friend.

Publisher & Dispatcher,
Tracy C. Ertl

INTRODUCTION

Rebecca Crandall

IT WAS A COLD FRIGID FEBRUARY NIGHT, Valentine's Day 1999. I had been on my own for two months, a cop for a total of 6 months. Fresh out of recruit school and training, I was a rookie ready to change the world. What I did not realize at the time was the fact that the world was going to change me.

Normally people are celebrating this festive occasion with their loved ones with chocolates, flowers and a nice dinner out. Learning to miss holidays would be my first lesson as a beat cop. Family comes second, and work comes first. It is a sacrifice I would never adjust to, because you can't get those years or holidays back.

I was working the afternoon shift, 14:15-22:45 on the city's west side. It was a district that I knew well, as I grew up in the area. This made getting to calls easier for me in the beginning because I did not have to look up where I would be driving. I could concentrate more on what I was going to do when I arrived. Dispatch would give me the basic information on a call. The entire time I was driving to the scene, I would role play what to say in my mind. Sometimes I would even say things aloud as if to be rehearsing how it would sound coming out of my mouth.

I had just left the West Side Garage after fueling up my squad. My innocence as a new cop was left there, never to be recovered. The dispatcher's voice called my number - 222A. I was dispatched to the report of a car-pedestrian accident at Franklin Middle School, with unknown injuries. What luck, I thought to myself, as I was only two blocks away. I quickly activated my emergency lights and siren and was at the scene within seconds.

I could clearly see a white pickup truck on the roadway with a blonde female behind the wheel. She was frozen in place. There was a circle of children all around the truck, many decked out in Valentine's Day pink, red and the innocence of white. Hundreds of crying children. It was and is a sound I will never get over as long as I live. I heard the combination of shrill screams; choking on snot and rapid, loud breathing. I ran up to the large, assembling, shuddering group, telling them to clear the way. After all, the police were here to save the day; the police…me. As I approached closer, I viewed the children leaning on each other; some collapsed on the ground crying and still others, looking confused and shocked.

Everything went into slow motion for me. When I got up to the truck, there was a lifeless body lying under it – a little girl, wearing dress clothes. It was the Valentine's Day dance at the school this night. I came by her side and saw that she had blood coming out of her mouth and ears. A man was kneeling beside her and told me he was a fireman. I got on my radio as I ran to my car to get a blanket from the trunk. I told the dispatcher to send rescue.

When I arrived back at the young girl, her eyes were fluttering. I told all the kids to get up on the curb or go into the gym that had now opened for the hundreds of them gathered. I knelt down next to the girl and silently said an *Our Father* over her as I waited for the rescue squad to arrive. In that moment, I wondered why it was taking so long; thrust into the shoes of other callers, who feel that same eternity when in reality it is mere minutes. Other officers were arriving and taking over the duties of gathering witnesses. When rescue arrived and did a "load and go", I knew this would be my first fatality of many.

The driver of the white pickup truck was still sitting in the driver's seat, hands clenched to the wheel with the vehicle still in gear. She was in shock, looking straight ahead. She was afraid to move for fear of the truck rolling. I helped her get the vehicle into park and shut off. Completely traumatized, she was barely able to get in my squad car to stay warm.

This was the beginning of a long night of paperwork, but far worse, the beginning of the deadening of my emotions as a person.

I was a cop now.

I went home that night and had several drinks and replayed the entire scene over and over in my mind. This is not something I had ever seen in my life. I thought, *how do these cops do this day after day and not have it affect them?* I learned that it does.

The vision of this twelve-year-old angelic child with her insides oozing out of her, eyes fluttering, dying on the cold concrete. The sound of hundreds of crying children around the vehicle. It would stay with me my entire career.

The next day I went back to work and found one of the older patrol women. I knew she had been around for a long time and was on the critical incident team. I had a candid conversation with her about what I had seen and how I was feeling about it.

I was actually questioning if this truly was the career path I wanted to be taking. She told me that in my career I would probably not see or work a scene like that again. However, she told me I would never get used to seeing the things I would be seeing. She said after a while, it would fade and that I would come to terms with it, like making friends with it. The re-living of this scene went on for days. I tried to never speak of the day again, until now. And no, that wasn't the only call like this that I would go on. And no, I never did make friends with it, eighteen years later.

Happy Valentine's Day, Rebecca Crandall.

YES MA'AM

EARNING MY BADGE

THE 911 COMMUNICATIONS CENTER

WHEN YOU FIRST START ANY JOB, you are like a sponge, taking in everything you can and just trying to fit in. The images of what a cop should be like have been ingrained in us from TV and what we see on the streets. These are so far from the truth it is ridiculous. It is nothing like that at all and it takes some time to realize that the heroes you looked up to on TV or your neighborhood cop are just people. The larger than life superheroes are regular ordinary people doing extraordinary things every day. Here are some stories to show how human we really are and the sense of humor you must have to get through it.

To start my career and get my feet wet I took a job as a dispatcher at the 911 communications center in Green Bay to put myself through college. This job provided a lot of training in learning the ins and out of police work from another angle, and plenty of stories too.

When I started as a dispatcher for 911 I was taking calls, working the front desk and the dreaded teletype. Back in the day, teletype was the worst, most stressful part of the job. It actually made me physically sick just thinking about sitting in that spot. I know there were several others who felt the same way. Not only was the job itself enough to keep you on your toes, you also had to keep your eyes on some of your coworkers. Other people would constantly try to trip you up into making a mistake and then show their skills to bail you out of the situation. Sometimes even the officers would purposely do things to make you look like an idiot on the radio. I started this position at the same time as Dispatcher Everett. Between the two of us, we would be the jokes of the radio room for many years. It sucks being the new guy in a room full of know-it-alls. Eventually I got out on the road as a cop and she stayed there. The teletype position was assisting officers run every person they came in contact with over the radio. Imagine a huge beer party with dozens of people, each one of those names of people had to be phonetically spelled to you over the radio by the officer on scene to be run through the system.

The first part of the job was learning the phonetics: Adam, Bravo, Charlie, David, Edward, Frank, George, Henry, Ida, John, King, Lincoln, Mary, Nora, Ocean, Paul, Queen, Robert, Sam, Tom, Union, Victor, William, X-ray, Young, Zebra. Sounds easy, but when you are learning and listening, you can get screwed up big time. Working the teletype meant you would type the names into a call on one computer and then you type them into a different computer that runs the name for warrants. The entire time the cop on the other end of the radio is asking you, "do you have anything back yet?" Now multiply this by dozens of cops making requests at the same time.

The results were printed so you could look through all the hits. These are names that closely resemble the person run through the system, any alias names that resembled the name or anyone who had used this name before. The results could be a mountain of paper for one name; and these guys were running dozens at a time. Stress? Yes! In addition to names you also had to run license plates for cops while you were doing all of the above in a similar way. To make it interesting, some of the seasoned cops would find it particularly funny to "stump the chump."

Sometimes a cop would drive through a parking lot and run every plate in the lot on a busy Friday or Saturday night, not for any particular reason other than to bury the teletype operator. In reality it would cause officer safety issues with other cops who were out with real criminals who may have felony warrants. We ran them in the order they came in, which meant if some cop was playing this game ran all these plates before a cop who was doing serious police work, well then, he had to wait until you read back every frickin' plate in a bar parking lot for some imbecile who thought this was funny. It wasn't funny, and it created a lot of undo stress. In the beginning, one particular cop would run a plate that came back to a man name Harry Dick. He found great humor in running the plate often, sometimes nightly and having you say that name over the air, even asking you to repeat the name again. These guys know who they are and throughout my career as a cop, I was always a bit removed from them.

Call takers at 911 are the true first responders of a call. They get the information from the caller and make sure it goes into the call for the dispatcher to get to the cops. It is a thankless job. It's a given when you get everything in the call right. But if you mess up even a little bit, the cops are all over you about it. I guess, having seen both sides of the fence it is a little easier to forgive the errors and realize we are all human. Not to mention you are only as good as the caller that is calling in the emergency. Sometimes the callers are hysterical, don't know where they are, what direction they are going, can't give a description of who they saw or can't even describe what is going on. As a dispatcher, you give out the information you got, and as a cop you get what you get. Many times, I would hear cops asking for additional detailed information over the radio and I would always think, *don't you think the call taker already asked that?* Some cops can be so arrogant and superior, even to the ones who have their backs. I can tell you I always respected and appreciated what those girls do up there.

Most cops have their favorite dispatchers, you just know when you hear that voice on the radio it's going to be a good day. They are all good, otherwise they wouldn't have the job; but some have that calming effect needed on the radio to keep things even. Sometimes a dispatcher gets all jacked up and it shows in their tone of voice, this in turn gets the cops jacked up which is not needed when the situations are serious. When you think about it you are trusting these dispatchers and call takers with your life and family. I had several favorite dispatchers with that soothing voice of calmness who would keep the calls moving along smoothly. Don't get me wrong, everyone up there has their off days, but for the most part, the communications center rocks. Sometimes they are the ones to come up with the funny stuff. One of my favorites of all time is Dispatcher Anderson who said "fuzzy anus" over the air as the street name of Phasianus, (Faze e an us). No winter storm would be complete without several cars going into the ditch and her saying the vehicle was "down in the pickers" over the radio. Just a little comic relief for an otherwise stressful job.

Some funny things happened in that radio room while Everett and I were working the night shift. The job was what I had to do to go to cop school during the day and what she had to do to take care of her three kids while her husband worked days. Everett had what we called a lot of Everettism's, things that could only happen because she was Everett. Many nights I knew she had been up with her kids all day and hadn't slept much. The early morning, three a.m. was always the hardest part of the night. The drunks were already home tucked in and the average Joe wasn't up yet. This was the lull in action and when you're tired, a lull is a bad thing. When that 911 line would ring at this hour you always knew it was something bad. Who calls 911 at 03:00? No one should be awake at this hour, and those who were always meant disaster, usually a stabbing or a shooting or something unthinkable to those who were tucked snug in their beds. When the 911 line rang at this hour, it always gave me a pit in my stomach. One particular night, we were both dragging ass. The lights in the room were dim and everyone was settled in for the down time. The line rang and to be honest, I was tired too. Everett answered it as she always did, "911, what is your emergency?" She was sitting about twenty feet from me. I could see on the light up panel the line was open, and it appeared someone was talking to her. This went on for several minutes, but I noticed she wasn't typing anything and no call had been entered. I got up and walked over to her to see what was going on. She was fast asleep with the caller still talking to her. I nudged her to wake up and the first thing she said was "911, what is your emergency?" Yikes. Thankfully the person on the other end was not really having an emergency and was just intoxicated. This event made me realize how things can get lost in the shuffle and accidents happen, even at 911.

Everett was my friend in that room, she and dispatcher Rivard, who also went on to become an officer. It was a great place to learn the ropes of the department, the people, the geography and just a complete sense of police. Even though she wasn't trying to be Everett was our comedy relief. Every day it seemed there was some blunder that would make us laugh. I think for the most part she did these things because she was running on no sleep. She stayed up with her kids all day until her husband got home from work, then she made supper, and finally she would sleep for two-three hours a night. After my shift I stayed up for school and then could go home in the afternoon and go to bed. It was a grueling schedule to say the least for anyone. Everett was one of those people who always tried to make people happy. We always had a connection; we were both people pleasers. She is one of those friends who I may not see for weeks or months and can pick up right where we left off like no time has passed.

NOW THAT'S A ROACH

I was working the night shift in the radio room and as I said before, it makes for some really long nights when you are up all day. We were allowed to read in the room providing the material we were reading was job or cop related. This is how I did most of my homework for cop school. To be honest when I read it makes me tired, so I didn't do a lot of reading. There were several other 911 call takers in the room, as well as a cop who was a dispatcher, a supervisor, and a fire dispatcher. My most memorable fire dispatcher was Gus, a very interesting man with an obsession with trains. He kind of reminded me of my Dad. I spent many nights conversing with him when the nights were slow. He was one of those guys who liked to talk and talk, which helped pass the night away if it wasn't busy. Of course, if it was busy we did our jobs, but there was a lot of long winter nights spent in that room.

There was a smoking lounge inside the Police Station in the basement and some of the dispatchers and 911 operators would go down there for smoke breaks. We were entitled to two fifteen-minute breaks and a half hour lunch. I usually saved all my breaks and lumped them into a one-hour break. I usually took this break in the wee hours of the morning like 03:00; I would go down into the women's locker room where there was a cot and a blanket and take a nap. I would set my alarm on my watch for fifty minutes, leaving enough time to splash some water on my face and get back to work. My friend Everett did the same thing, she usually went around 04:00. We made a deal with each other; if one or the other didn't make it back up to the room within the hour that meant we slept through our alarm. If this happened, we would call the women's locker room in hopes the ringing of the telephone would wake her up. And if all else failed someone would run down there and go inside and give you a good shake.

This particular night I woke up to my watch alarm and was walking through the basement to head back upstairs. I always like taking the steps, I hate elevators. I am a bit claustrophobic and the elevator at the station had lots of issues, like making ridiculous sounds and it jumped around a lot which I don't like. I was coming down the main hallway past evidence. I could smell the odor of raw marijuana, it has a very sweet smell. This was always an indication that someone had just done a major drug bust and placed the marijuana into the evidence area. As I rounded the corner and was heading for the stairs, still half asleep, I looked up the stairs. I was on the bottom step and the biggest cockroach I have ever seen was on the top step. He was the size of a computer mouse with long whip tentacles about six inches long. I think if I hadn't been so shocked I would have let out a little scream, but I just froze. I did an about face and got on the elevator. I reported it to my supervisor. I found out the next day that the entire station had to be bug bombed because the drug unit cops had brought in personal property of the suspects and it was loaded with cockroaches.

THE NORTHLAND HOTEL

One of the most historic hotels in Green Bay is the Northland Hotel. It was the most elegant hotel of its time. I remember as a young kid going to stamp shows in the grand lobby at the hotel. It had a revolving door off Pine St that led into a marble lobby with giant marble pillars that reached to the second-floor balcony overlooking the lobby. There were two huge crystal chandeliers that hung down into the room. It was breathtaking in its day. Over the years the hotel, like everything else in this town, had been let go. In the 1970's with the redevelopment of downtown, the grand lady was turned into Port Plaza Towers; a facility that housed the low income, mentally challenged, and disabled in the community.

During my training as a 911 dispatcher I was excited to go on a ride-along with one of the officers on the afternoon shift. I had only been in a police car once when I was a kid, but never like this; up close and personal, in the front seat. I rode with Officer Van, a brassy blond woman who had earned the reputation of being a tough cop. It was a cold winter night; the radio was not very busy. We had been driving the streets of Green Bay for several hours, talking about what it was like to be a cop, cop stories, cop questions, cop, cop, cop. This was all I thought about back then. I am sure I drove everyone I ever rode with crazy. We were finally dispatched to a call at Port Plaza Towers. I hadn't been in this wonderful old place in many years. The call was for a deceased male. I thought, *oh what fun! A dead body call.* As we walked off the elevator on the third floor a strange aroma came from down the hallway. Officer Van nodded her head and said, "yup that's the smell."

Most people think of the movies and the crime scene investigation Hollywood has portrayed. What you don't see on the television is the scene in 3-D, the sounds, the smells and the horrific sights of blood and body fluids all over. We walked into room 310. The temperature of the room was eighty degrees, it was hot. The apartment smelled of stale cigarettes, beer, and decaying human body. There was a male lying face down on his tile kitchen floor with a pool of blood surrounding his head. He was completely dressed in blue jeans, a blue flannel shirt and blue socks. As we entered the room, Officer Van handed me some rubber gloves and told me not to touch anything. The male had been found by the apartment manager who said he had not seen him in a few days.

I walked around the apartment looking for any clues of foul play. Officer Van pointed out a broken ashtray just off the kitchen and said based on where it landed, the male was probably carrying it when he went down. She told me we would have to wait for the medical examiner (ME) to come before rolling him over to see his front of his body. I laughed about it at the time, wouldn't the police look bad if they wrote off the death as medical and when the ME rolled him over there was a knife sticking out of his chest. The smell of the decaying body is a smell I will never ever forget. This was my first encounter with this type of situation, but definitely not my last. I was looking at photos in the living room when I came across a wedding photo, a bride, groom and wedding party. As I walked up to it I thought, *hey I know that couple.* I looked at the wedding party, there I was standing two girls away from the bride. The reality of the situation hit me like a ton of bricks, this was Mr. Crooks, the dad of one of my close girlfriends from high school. I never said a word to Officer Van and when the medical examiner arrived he did not find a knife when they rolled him over. Just the bloody, decomposing face of a man I had known for years. I attended his funeral two days later. I never spoke of the situation with my friend Jill. From that day on, I hated going on calls at Port Plaza Towers and especially *check the welfare* calls.

GRADUATION FROM COLLEGE

I didn't know what I wanted to be when I grew up. When I graduated from high school in 1980 I wanted to join the military. Unfortunately, my mother didn't think that was a good idea. Mom's logic was, what kind of man is going to want to be with a military wife? Hmm, I guess that backfired a bit. I was young and respected my mother's opinion, so I didn't join the military.

I worked as bookkeeper at a bank, a dispatcher at a trucking company, and a customer service rep at a paper company. But my appetite for something more than sitting at a desk shuffling papers kept calling me. I had always wanted to be in uniform. Those crisp lines, the medals and badges and a name tag pinned to my chest. I had to be in uniform.

Making the decision was hard. I had a house, car payment and bills. I kept thinking in the back of my mind, *if I don't do it now, I never will, and I'll be an old lady in a rocking chair, kicking myself for not going for it, and blaming someone else for my regrets.*

That's it, I pulled the pin. I resigned from my customer service job, registered at Northeast Wisconsin Technical College (NWTC) in Green Bay for the Criminal Justice program and took a job working as a security guard at a meat packing plant. A year later I applied for a position as a 911 dispatcher at the Green Bay Police Department. After a long, grueling hiring process, I was finally offered the job. For the next two years I worked full time during the night shift at the communication center, went to school full time during the day shift, and slept full time during the afternoon shift. It was a long, hard road filled with many sleepless days and many long hours at school and work, but I did it. Finally, the day arrived, I was graduating from college! This was a huge achievement in my life. My parents' philosophy as I grew up was very old school: girls get married and boys go to college. I have two brothers and two sisters and of five siblings, my younger brother and I are the only ones with a college degree. It may have taken me until I was thirty-years-old, but I finally did it!

To celebrate I rented a local tavern, Boondocks, to throw a party with some free beer and pizza. I invited my family, friends, and many of the police officers I had met while working as a 911 dispatcher. I was still working as a 911 dispatcher and trying to get a position as an officer, so I wanted to put my best foot forward and make a good impression. It was a beautiful, hot summer night and many people came to celebrate, share conversation, and have lots of laughs. My youngest brother, Mark, and the rest of my siblings were all there. Mark is one of those guys who believes the more he drinks, the smarter he gets, and the dumber you get.

The night went on and the beer was flowing. Then one of my most embarrassing moments as a cop happened. I had been talking to a group of eight cops, seasoned cops who had been around for many years. They were telling old time cop stories, I was soaking it up like a sponge. I couldn't get enough information about my new profession, I listened and watched their every move. It was so exciting to get to know the do's and don'ts before getting hired. I wanted to have a leg up on the competition when it came to the interview process, and this was surely one way to gain some experience, by listening.

My brother Mark, who installs windows and siding for a living, joined us. He had already been celebrating for a while and was in his drunk know-it-all mindset. It would have been one thing for him to quietly sit back and listen to these funny, factual and humorous stories being shared, but he couldn't help himself. My drunk brother took it upon himself not only to correct the officers on their traffic stop techniques, but he also gave them lessons on the proper way to perform a traffic stop. I could have died on the spot. I could see some of the guys looking at each other and thinking, *who is this moron?* As diplomatically as I could I went and got one of his friends and had him challenge Mark to a game of pool; anything to get him away from my future comrades. Then I went into damage control apologizing for his arrogance and blamed it all on the beer. How embarrassing!

MY SWEARING IN

As a 911 dispatcher, I was paid well, received good benefits, wore a uniform and a badge, but I wanted *that* badge, *that* dark blue uniform and everything that it stood for. I applied for a position as a police officer twice during the these next few years and made the list both times. The first time they didn't hire enough people to get to my number. The second time I was hired. I had dreamt about this day for years! I was dressed in my dress uniform complete with long sleeves, tie, the white gloves, the eight-point hat, clean as a whistle, pressed and ready. My parents were there for the ceremony, along with the entire administration of the police department. The Chief, Deputy Chief, all the captains, lieutenants, sergeants, I mean we are talking brass up the ass here. There were more gold stars and bars in the room than you could imagine, and it was all for me! I could not have been prouder than that moment. The Chief gave a brief biography of my background, then pinned a shiny new silver badge on my chest, right there for the whole world to see. I did it, my dream come true day!

We had a reception with cake and coffee after the pinning ceremony. I was mingling with several of the top brass; I had already known many on the force during my years as a 911 dispatcher, the Captain of Internal Affairs, the Captain of Patrol and several other top-ranking captains. As I am standing there on the proudest day of my life, my mother joins the circle. She asks which one of the captains would be in charge of me now. Captain Tradesman told her he was. Here comes the mother moment. In front of everyone she asks him if he can make sure that I don't get sent on any dangerous gun calls until I get the hang of it. I could have crawled out of that room on all fours. Captain Tradesman put his arm around her and said, "don't worry, we will take good care of her." I can laugh about it now. I would learn very early on in my career not to tell my mother anything about my day or my calls. She would never understand the dangers I was in every day and I realized all she did was worry about me and pray every day. She prayed for me every day anyway, she didn't need details.

OFC. SUSAN BICKETT

To be a Police Officer you have to have a passionate desire to help people & a fierce determination to seek Justice. Courage, fortitude, physical stamina, & a tolerance for long, lonely nights. Having a clearly defined sense of self, scrupulous honesty & comfort with alienation. It means wrestling with demons in nightmares that sometimes come true. This is my Daughter Susan's Life. I'm so proud of her & Pray Our Lord is Watching over her.

I Love You!
Mom

MY FTO'S

As a rookie, you are assigned to a field training officer (FTO) to show you the ropes. Officer Tremble was my first FTO. His nickname was JT. He is the cop who taught me the basic do's and don'ts. Not the Defense and Arrest Tactics (DAAT) stuff, the street-smart stuff. The most important thing he ever taught me was, *watch the hands.* The hands are what could kill you. Always know where they are and never let them go into any pockets for any reason. He also taught me to watch license plates. The fine art of looking at a plate and capturing the entire plate in one glance, not letter by letter or number by number, the whole plate all at once. Another tip was don't pussy foot around in putting someone in cuffs if you know you're going to arrest the person. The longer you wait to get them in cuffs the more time they have to decide how to assault you or plan their escape. He also showed me how to memorize faces.

One time during my training, our department was looking for a guy who was wanted for attempted homicide. Prior to leaving headquarters we printed out a photo of the guy. I studied it real hard in the car before heading out. I placed the paper photo between my vest and my shirt. I would periodically pull it out and just look at it. This technique paid off. We were at a traffic light waiting for it to turn green. A vehicle came around the corner and I looked at the driver. There he was, the guy in the mugshot. We called for more units and stopped the car. I got to take my first wanted person into custody.

Officer Brogan was my second FTO. He taught me how to laugh and find humor in a situation. One story in particular stands out in my training with him. We went to a family disturbance between a mother and her two daughters on E. Walnut Street. The dispatcher said the two sisters were fighting over their mother's ring. Upon arrival, one of the girls was bleeding from her hand and the other had her front teeth knocked out. Through our investigation I learned that the mother had given daughter #1 a diamond ring to pawn for drugs. Daughter #2 saw daughter #1 wearing it on her finger. In an attempt to get the ring off her finger daughter #2 had to bite a wart off daughter #1's finger to obtain the ring. She was successful, but had her front teeth knocked out in the process. Family love. Officer Brogan was a bit of a prankster to say the least. He taught me the only way to handle this job was to find some humor if possible. One of his signature lines that he used whenever possible was "I just got off Laverne and am about to Mount Mary." There are two streets in Green Bay that intersect, Laverne and Mount Mary. When you think about it that is pretty damn funny to say over the radio.

Officer Landers was my third FTO. He was a rough and tough cop who followed the rules to the letter. Or so I thought. He was a tough grader and very much into the DAAT and procedures. One night we were car-to-car with another patrol officer. The guys were talking about football and stuff. The parking lot we were parked in was icy. Landers was driving, and I was in the passenger seat observing. As we pulled away from our parking spot the back end of our squad slid over and struck the front end of the other squad car. When we got out to look at the car there was a small dent in each vehicle. He didn't report it and I never said anything. I truly believe he was testing me to see if I would break that thin blue line. I never did, but I wanted to. This incident changed the way I looked at him throughout my career. It's that integrity thing. Once you jeopardize it, you can never get it back. I never looked at him the same way again. I never jeopardized my own integrity for anyone.

When I was out of training and on my own I was sent to back him up on a traffic stop. The vehicle was pulled into Lindy's Grocery Store on University Ave. When I arrived his good buddy Officer Ward was already there but didn't show in the system as being there. Landers told me to drive around the back of the store and wait for further instructions. I waited there for about a half hour and finally asked over the radio if everything was okay. I was told I could clear. When I drove back around front Landers and Ward were talking car-to-car. I imagined they were making fun of me to see how long I would sit there before I would say anything. Landers was a captain when I retired.

The city is divided into zones. Each officer is assigned a zone to cover for the day, typically it is the same every day. The officer got to know the good, the bad and the ugly in that area; the crime patterns and people. I was assigned to the west side middle zone, 222A, during the afternoon shift for my first eight years. It was an area I was very familiar with having lived on the west side all my life. This made getting to calls easier in the beginning;

I did not have to look up where I would be driving to. I could concentrate more on what I was going to do when I arrived there. When I had enough seniority to make day shift, I was assigned the downtown zone 141, today that is referred to as 1C1. It is a high crime area and very busy. Typically, officers do not go on calls alone, two cars are dispatched to any call where there is a suspect or the possibility of danger.

FNG PARTIES

Becoming a cop takes time and hard work, imagine this as I walk you through it. It begins by obtaining a two-year associates degree from a technical college or a four-year bachelor's degree from a college. After that you apply at every possible opening you can find. In Brown County and Green Bay, you are required to take a written test of two hundred questions relating to police work. Then you wait. The hiring process consists of a thorough background investigation and when I say thorough, I mean thorough. They talk to your neighbors, all your former employers, all your references, everyone who knows anything about you. They run a credit check, DMV check, and of course a criminal history check. Then it's on to the physical agility test. You are required to navigate an obstacle course where you run, jump through a window that is four feet high, climb over a six-foot-high board on a board fence, run over a bridge, go through the tire obstacles, climb a rope, drag a ninety pound dummy, run up a flight of stairs, jump a creek and when completed hold a gun on a target in a circle without touching, all in sixty seconds.

The obstacle course is where many of the woman get washed out because they do not have the upper body strength to pull themselves up over the six-foot-high board on the board fence. If you don't get over the fence, you don't pass; that is what happened to most of the female candidates coming through the process. If you pass, then it's on to an oral interview panel, which I compare to sitting in front of a firing squad. Maybe it's not that bad, but it is a table of six people, made up of police captains, alderman and local business professionals. You walk into this room and an entire table of people are facing you. As you sit in a chair in front of them, you answer questions on the spot as they fire them at you. It is very intimidating and nerve racking. This oral interview last about thirty minutes. If you pass that, it's on to the psychological evaluation. My evaluation took place in Milwaukee.

You drive down to Milwaukee and meet with a psychiatrist who has you answer another written two hundred question test and then he interviews you for about an hour. Again, an intimidating process. If you pass that, then it's on to the lie detector test at the police department.

Many people have this preconceived idea about this test, but the reality is, if you are truthful you have nothing to worry about. You are first asked to answer a series of yes or no written questions. For example, have you ever stolen anything in your life? Have you ever lied on an official government document? Have you ever smoked pot? Have you ever done drugs? Questions like that, so the idea is not to try to fool the machine or those giving the test, it is just to be honest. Yes, I had stolen some money once when I was a kid. No, I never lied on my taxes or driver's license (government documents). Yes, I smoked pot and yes, I did drugs. You don't get the opportunity to explain, it is just yes or no, plain and simple. After you answer the questions on paper, they get you set up with wires to the lie detector machine. Well let me tell you, this thing is going to measure your heart beat and pulse. You're already going to be jacked up from being so damn nervous. I got all wired up and they started asking me the questions I had just answered. I answered each one and after each one the two Captains running the test would write notes in their notebooks. When they got to the question, *did you ever smoke pot?* I could not resist adding a little something to my answer. I said, "I grew up in the 1970's, of course I smoked pot." Both Captains got a little smirk on their face and then the one Captain said, "I take that as a yes." I replied, "yes." Just to clarify for the record, no I was not a druggy. I tried pot a couple of times in high school and I tried a little speed once, caffeine pills. And I snorted a line of cocaine once just to try it, but honestly that is it. Anyway, after you pass the lie detector test, then it's on to the physical.

This is the last step in the hiring process. The department sends you to a doctor to be given a complete physical. If you are fit for duty, you are now hired. Then it's off to a fourteen-week recruit school. In my case, it was driving to Appleton Monday through Friday all summer for school. Once you pass that, then it is another fourteen weeks on the job training with a field training officer. When, and if you pass all of the prior qualifications and tests, you are now a cop!

This begins with a one-year probation period. If you mess up you can be let go, just like that. This year can be stressful for a lot of cops; this is your time to prove yourself to the rest of the cops out there and show you have what it takes to do this job. Many times, some of these young guys would get out there and couldn't cut the mustard. If you made it through this year of probation, then it was obligatory to celebrate with an FNG Party; "Fucking New Guy Party." It was kind of like hazing, looking back. Once you made it through your year, the officers would keep on you constantly until you had this party. It was part of the culture, free beer and food for an entire twenty-four-hour period, and as the FNG you had to attend for the entire event. Twenty-four hours in the bar of your choice. I had my FNG Party with two other cops who were hired around the same time I was. This was common practice as well since one of these parties could cost hundreds of dollars, having them together was the way to go for most new cops; mine cost me about two hundred bucks.

Back in the early days of these parties, guys would get so stinking drunk it wasn't even funny. But as the culture changed, the drunk cop parties were no longer acceptable, or at least not for me. I only went to a few of these parties and for good reason. I didn't want to end up in IA, Internal Affairs. One of the last parties I went to, one of the new cops thought it was a good idea to get all liquored up and show some of his friends his duty weapon. I was standing in the bar with Officer Westland when this new cop pulled out that gun and started waving it around. We both hit the door as fast as we possibly could. I guess that just goes to show, alcohol makes smart people make bad choices, even if you're a cop. One added note, he was let go for obvious reasons.

BEFORE MY TIME

When I started at the PD, I was a bit of a sponge, always taking in all I could. There were many stores about days gone by. As a young officer it was hard to believe how far policing had come based on many of the stories I had heard. Before there were portable police radios officers had to check in at a call box. A call box was a metal box mounted to a street pole that contained a telephone. The officer would have to call in for his assignments or to get his calls. Back then officers walked a beat, mostly in the Downtown and Broadway districts. This made for some long cold nights of pulling doors and doing building security, but mostly of trying to stay warm on those freezing cold winter nights. Officers who walked the beat had keys to all the buildings in their district and often times would go inside to make sure everything was alright inside, but mostly to stay warm.

One night, Officer Sawyer was on the downtown beat. It was snowing and cold and the furniture store on Main Street provided not only a place to warm up, but also a place to sit down and take a load off for a few minutes. She let herself in using her key. The recliner in the front window sure looked comfortable. She climbed up in and before long she was fast asleep. This was three o'clock a.m. and back then nobody would be driving by anyway. I could just imagine driving by the store window and looking over to see an officer sleeping in a recliner in the front window. I can only imagine Officer Sawyer's reaction when she woke up to daylight and saw cars passing the store. She often told this story as well as another favorite. One night she went inside an empty semi-trailer parked behind a business to get out of the cold and wind. Again, she fell asleep inside the trailer only to wake up and realize her shift was over and she had not called in for hours. They had even sent officers to look for her. This story ended with a good laugh when she reported in to the day shift captain after she had been working the night shift. Officer Sawyer was also famous for stopping at a red light in a marked squad car at Main and Webster, one of the busiest intersections downtown and falling asleep with the car in drive. She was never sure how many green lights she sat through but was finally awakened by a concerned citizen who had pulled up behind her waiting for her to go. I would imagine the citizen thought she may have had a medical problem. She told me she woke up and just took off.

Officer Charles was another one of my favorites. She was a tough old broad and had earned a reputation of not taking any shit from anyone, including the male officers who thought women didn't belong in policing. I recall going on calls with her. She had a way with words and could hold her own that's for sure. She was one of those people who could tell people to eat shit and at the end of the conversation, they would thank her for it. Most often she would have a lit cigarette as she went on her calls. Imagine that in today's world.

Officer Moore was also on the downtown beat. This was at a time when they had one-way radios. Dispatch would come over the radio and tell the officer to call in for an assignment. Officer Moore said he would go to the Northland Hotel where he knew the desk clerk quite well. He would give his radio to her and tell her if anyone called his number over the radio to ring his room and he would call in. He would go up to his room and go to sleep. Wow.

Officer Dooley had an annual Christmas Party for both on and off duty officers. Every squad in Green Bay would be at the party and yes, the officers were drinking. When the radio went off, they would draw straws to see who would be going to the call. Back then there wasn't much happening on a night like Christmas Eve, but can you imagine having an officer respond with beer on his breath? In today's world you would be fired.

After our shifts we would have regular beer drinking. Often it would be in the parking lot, all of us standing over a cooler of beer, recapping the night's events. We would crush the cans and throw them on top of the roof of the station. This was still happening when I first started but it ended shortly after when the maintenance man received a report of the fans on top the roof malfunctioning and he discovered piles of cans up there.

Another famous event was called EOSS, which stood for End of Stuart Street. This was a dead-end road down by the Fox River where everyone would hang out and drink beer. This is something I never did but heard many stories about the shenanigans that went on at these parties. One being several officers throwing dynamite into the river and watching all the carp surface to the top. This was so hard for me to believe, but so many officers told me about it, it had to be true.

INDUCTION INTO THE CLUB

I have been thinking lately about "the thin blue line." Lately, many of the officers at the department are getting called out for bad behavior, including bullying or as I called it in my day, hazing. We were all hazed in one way or another, and some were hazed worse than others. It was almost like an initiation into the club, the good old boys club that is. You shut your mouth about it and pretty much had to suck it up. Being a narc would only land you with a bad name with the guys and the possibility of being chopped off at the knees, if you know what I mean.

There is nothing worse than yelling for cover on the radio and no one shows up or they respond very slowly. And if you said anything about the questionable events that went on, it would only make it worse. We are not talking about teasing here. I think sometimes the sick humor of several, was their way of dealing with the bad stuff. I am not sure because I was never a bully, but I sure did see and hear a lot of it going on. I was also on the receiving end many times in my career. Just shake it off and keep moving forward, do your job and don't worry about what others are doing, sooner or later it will catch up with them, and it has for some.

THE ROUTINE ...OR AS ROUTINE AS POLICE WORK CAN BE.

The Tools of the Trade

OLD HICKORY

*A*N OFFICER'S DUTY BELT WEIGHS ABOUT TWENTY POUNDS. We call it a tool belt. All officers carry a gun, extra ammunition, two sets of handcuffs, OC (pepper spray), a radio, a flashlight, a taser and a baton. Old school batons are what most people call a billy club, a black wooden stick that we call Old Hickory. I had one but opted to use the newer version, a retractable metal baton. It took up less room on the belt and was much smaller in size to carry around. For many years I used this retractable baton. I had recently attended a training session on batons and decided that I would give Old Hickory a try since it was proven to be more effective and more intimidating. I switched out my retractable on my belt and put a baton ring on my left side for Old Hickory.

My first day with Old Hickory at my side I was working the afternoon shift and was dispatched to a report of a disturbance on Imperial Lane. This area was known to have disturbances nearly on a daily basis; it was a tough crowd out there. The Imperial neighborhood is made up of many sets of apartment complexes in a two-block radius. Most are low income housing which let's face it, attracts a larger crime element. The report today was a disturbance among several males in the parking lot at one of the apartments. I was sent with two other cops for a total of three of us going. That is a rule of dispatching, always send more than you think you need to even the odds, the cops can always be called off.

When you are driving to a call many things go through your head. You are taking in all the information being sent over the radio and trying to get through traffic. People think cops can just turn on their light and siren and go whizzing through traffic any old time. That is not true, cops have rules to follow as well. The only time officers can use their lights and siren is when there is a true emergency. In other words, the risk of life, serious injury or substantial property damage. Many times, people have asked me why cops turn on their lights to go through red lights. It is not because they are late for break as some might suggest. Most often a cop puts on his lights and goes through a traffic light to get to some call which requires a silent response, such as a robbery in progress, or burglary in progress. You certainly would not want the suspect to hear those sirens coming from blocks away. Traffic is always an issue. I am not sure why people forget that in driver's education they learned to move to the right when there are lights and/or sirens coming your way. It is very simple, move to the right, right? Stopping in the center traffic lane and expecting the officer to go around you on the right is not going to happen. As an officer we are trained to stay out in the center lane and if you block the center lane then we have to take the oncoming lane. We will never go into the curb lane for safety reasons, when we get to an intersection we want to be in the most visible position for all cars to see. If an officer has nowhere to go because you didn't pull to the right, then it's time to go over the island and that is not fun.

On this particular day, I was driving emergency lights and siren to a physical disturbance in the parking lot on Imperial Lane. When I got about a block away, I turned off my siren but still had my emergency lights on as I coasted into the area. Officer Barker arrived about the same time I did. Just as I was pulling my squad car up to the parking area, a gold Lexus came flying out of the parking lot, squealing its tires and traveling at a high rate of speed. It was reasonable to think this was probably one of the suspects trying to flee the scene before officers arrived. The only problem with his plan was that we were there already.

I called out with the license plate as it sped past me and drove after the car. The car drove about a half block and then pulled into another apartment driveway and sped to the back of the lot. It stopped, all the doors opened, and four guys got out and started running behind the apartments. I boxed the car in and went after them. Several other officers who were monitoring the radio were also arriving on scene. The thing about a foot chase is everyone wants to be in on it when they happen, no cop ever wants the bad guy to get away. I started calling out locations to get a perimeter set up. This meant we were getting officers in locations to box in the person or persons, so they were trapped in a contained area. I had two of the subjects in sight and two of them had run off between other buildings. These two were now behind The Press Box Bar which is all fenced in. Over the chain link fence they went, and so did I. The next thing I remember I was hanging upside down with my feet in the air. Old Hickory, was still on my belt and caught in the fence, leaving me hanging upside down and stuck in the fence. I yanked that stick off my belt, threw it to the ground and kept on running. Lt. Lane was up on Lime Kiln Road; I chased my two suspects right into him. Enough units had arrived and all four were taken into custody without anyone getting injured.

Here's the funny thing, these four guys were not even the males involved in the disturbance to begin with. They were homicide suspects from Colorado and were driving a stolen car from Minnesota. One more thing, I went back and picked up Old Hickory and placed it back in my locker, I only used it one day in my entire career, but what a day it was.

SQUAD CARS

People often ask if officers are assigned squad cars. The answer is no, not officially. But when an officer finds a squad they like, it basically becomes theirs for that shift every day. It's kind of like an unwritten rule that you don't take someone else's favorite number squad, and everyone had one. This squad selection was done mostly by seniority, which meant officers waiting around for a particular squad at the beginning of their shift. This practice was okay if it wasn't busy. When it was busy, my thought was always to get in a squad and go.

Because officers basically always took the same squad, many practical jokes could be played on specific officers by other officers. For example, spraying OC into the vents on the car so when the oncoming officer would turn the blower on he would instantly be OC'd in his own squad. The worst one was leaving things pushed up under the front seat, like dead fish. That smell is impossible to get out even after the fish has been located and disposed of.

Squad cars came equipped with a radar gun. I would often see a rubber band around the trigger and wondered what that was all about. After doing a little investigating of my own, I learned that night shift officers would go park down a dead-end road and turn on their radar gun. Setting the radar gun on the dash and rubber banding the trigger would then alert the officer when someone was driving up on them. This allowed for the officer to take a little siesta on those long cold winter nights.

One thing about squad cars that most of the young rookies learn very early on is while you may think you are a superhero in the Batmobile, the fact of the matter is that it is still just a car. It really has the same limitations as any other car. You can't hit a curb at twenty-five miles per hour and think the tire or rim is going to be intact. You also can't drive through two feet of water without frying the engine, just saying.

ROUGH TOUGH BARS

Back in the day The Broadway district was known for having a lot of bars, and most attracted some pretty rough clientele. For example, the Lion's Den on S. Broadway had a sign on the back of the bar with a picture of a gun that said, "We don't call 911." Ginny's Heart of Broadway was another bar you did not go into without the backup of at least a couple of cops. These people definitely did not like cops and weren't afraid to let you know about it. The toughest bar was a little hole in the wall called the Ninth Street Tap. It was located on Ninth Street just off the south end of Broadway. They never called the police and if they did you knew they had big trouble. It was a biker bar and they knew how to take care of their own crap. I was sent on a call there with Officer York.

We were sitting under the viaduct by the Old White Store when the call came out; it sounded like things were going pretty intense there. The dispatcher said several males were tearing the place up and one guy got hit with a bar stool. We took off in our squads and arrived to see a male out in front of the bar bloody and swinging a pool stick. He luckily dropped it when he saw us, or this call could have been a lot worse. I got out of my squad and Officer York did the same. Based on the information given this bloody male was our suspect that had taken a few licks from several of the patrons before finally deciding to leave on his own. He was highly intoxicated and agitated and I figured he would not be going peacefully with us. I was right. When we approached him, he called us a few choice names and tried walking away from us. Officer York grabbed him and attempted to get his hands behind his back and the fight was on. I jumped in to assist in getting this guy into cuffs. Other units had been called to come and assist but had not arrived yet. Officer York had him from behind and I was holding his one arm. I pulled out my OC spray and pointed it point blank at the suspects face and began to spray. The only problem is the guy moved his head off to one side and I ended up spraying my partner, Officer York right in the eyes while he was still holding the suspect. Oops. Luckily backup arrived and took over and the suspect was cuffed and brought to jail. I volunteered to do the statements and report since I felt so bad that I had OC'd my partner. He found a water hose and proceeded to run it over his face for a while. Sorry York!!

TASER TASER

The Taser. For me it replaced my baton on my belt. I had never once used my baton the entire time I was a cop and I only had it out of my locker once in my career. When the taser came out as a new tool we could put on our belt, I was all in. This tool proved to be very effective in the right conditions. As officers we all received taser training. Like most of our tools, the taser had to be used on the officer so we each knew how it felt. All I can say is the thing works. You can fight your way through the pain of OC spray. The taser makes it impossible to fight and puts you on the ground. Although I carried a taser for many years, I only used it once.

I was called to a family disturbance on St. Agnes Drive. We received a report that a male and female were fighting in the house. I had been at this house before and knew the male who lived there. He was a big guy with a big mouth and could be difficult to deal with. In other words, it was always wise to bring extra cops just in case he got out of hand. As two other squads and I pulled up about three houses away, the dispatcher said that the caller just reported the male bolted out of the back door. It had also been reported that teletype had run the male's name and there were warrants out for his arrest. I ran to the back of the house with another officer and saw him running toward S. Military Avenue. One of the other officers on the call had made contact with the female at the residence who had been beaten up pretty badly by the male. Another officer in the area had been on S. Military Avenue and corralled the male before he was able to cross the roadway.

This sent the male running back toward the residence. I was surprised to see him coming back toward us. I was thinking he did not realize we had already arrived at the residence as it appeared he was going to make an attempt to get back inside. I was at the corner of the house when he appeared in the backyard. I emerged from my position and pulled my taser out and ran toward him ordering him to the ground. He continued running toward the back door. I announced if he did not stop I was going to tase him. He did not stop and began to open the back screen-door. I pulled the trigger on my taser. The male entered the house and slammed the door. I had just tased a screen door. That was the one and only tase in my career.

Officer Matthews and I were called to a residence on the far west side for a male who was acting delusional and hallucinating. The caller was his wife; she reported to dispatch the male had PTSD, was schizophrenic and off his medications. Upon arrival at the home the wife said the male had taken a large knife and went down into the basement.

Officer Matthews and I entered the basement. As we were walking down the steps, I could hear what sounded like grunting noises coming from a laundry area. I loudly announced to the male to come out from the room. He did not. I shined my flashlight into the laundry room where I could clearly see him on top of the washing machine in a crouched position. The male had a look in his eyes similar to the photographs you see of Charles Manson. He was drooling, foaming at the mouth and growling like an animal. He had a rather large knife in his one hand and had cut his arms with it several times, blood was running on to his clothing.

Officer Matthews had her taser out and through nonverbal communication it was clear, she would do the tasing. I had my gun out just in case the taser didn't work; that does happen sometimes. We entered the room and she yelled at him to drop the knife. He didn't and she tased him. The moment seemed to be in slow motion as I watched him seize up, causing the knife to drop to the concrete floor. He followed doing a summersault off the washer. He landed head first, cracking his head on the concrete. At least he didn't land on the knife. I moved in and handcuffed him. Blood was gushing out of his head and he would need medical attention, but at least he did not kill himself or either of us. This was a pretty good result considering the circumstances we had to deal with.

MDT MESSAGES

An MDT is an onboard computer in every squad car. The dispatcher gives the call over the police radio and also sends it to you via computer. On the computer screen, you get the call address, cross streets, caller information, the call type and a narrative of what is being called in. This is also where either you or your teletype operator can type in the names of the people for possible warrants and to document who you dealt with on the call. At the end of each call, the officer who handled the call types the notes into the call for a summary.

But there is one more function of the MDT; the ability to talk to either headquarters or car-to-car by typing messages. It is supposed to be used for sending out things like an attempt to locate a person, or updates on cop related stuff. Sometimes in the old days, this means of message sending was the way to convey jokes about other officers and/or supervisors. It is not wise to piss off your supervisor because they have the ability to go back into the system and read all of your messages. This is exactly what happened to a couple of cops early on in my career.

They made fun of a supervisor and every one of their messages were pulled from the system. Yes, they had made fun of a supervisor, but they did much more than that. Apparently, they had been socializing and conducting personal affairs over the messaging system. Today we would call it sexting. However, this was over the police communications system. Needless to say, neither of these officers worked at the department after this discovery. This was a valuable lesson to see early on in my career and I taught it to the many officers I trained. Never write something on the computer that you wouldn't want the chief to read or to have plastered on the front of the Green Bay Press-Gazette, because both could happen as it did in this case.

SENDING IN THE DOG

This call started out with a dog, a basic animal call, and ended with a different kind of dog altogether. I was dispatched to a report of a small dog running through traffic on E. Walnut Street. I drove to the area and there he was, a little fluffy dust mop looking dog; some kind of yorkie-doodle or shih-tzu-poo, anyway a small cute dog. I always keep a doggy treat in my bag for this type of occasion. As I tried to lure the animal into the back seat of my squad car, I called for the animal control officer to respond to take over. I ran around back and forth across the street chasing the little critter until it finally ran into a fenced in backyard. By chance it was where the dog lived, however I didn't know that yet.

Officer Henry arrived, and we made several attempts to capture the dog with little success. That's when the back door of the house opened, and a female came outside claiming the dog was hers. As standard procedure I asked the female her name because we were going to write her a written warning for animal running at large. That's when the female said she wasn't the dog owner and went back inside and sent out a guy who then claimed to be the owner. This told me two things, the female really was the dog owner and she had something to hide and she didn't want to be identified. I did not let on that I had any suspicions of her hiding her identity. I spoke with the male who gave me his identification and I ran his name for warrants.

Officer Henry had pulled her truck up and started filling out the animal written warning. I told her I didn't believe he was the owner and asked her to stall as much as possible with this guy until I could get another unit to come and do a little more investigating. Once I had a cover officer I told the male I did not believe he was the dog owner and asked him the female's name. He told me he didn't know her name, as if I was going to believe that. I knocked on the door and another female answered the door, who told me she was the mother of the house. I asked her who the female who had just come into the house was. She acted like she had no idea what I was talking about. I informed her that a female had just entered the home and asked her who owned the dog. I think I caught her off guard and she blurted, "that's my son's girlfriend's dog. Her name is Angela Skenandore." I ran the name of the dog owner. Bingo, she had a felony warrant out for her arrest.

I told the mother of the home, I needed to talk to Angela. The mother said she was not in there, she may have run out the front door. I asked her if I could come in and check. She said, "by all means come right in." I think sometimes people think they are smarter than the cops. Maybe they think we are not going to look everywhere; perhaps some don't, but I was never that kind of cop. I have said this before, I will dog you until I find you. I went through the entire house, main level, basement and upstairs and did not find her. That left the dreaded attic.

I hate attics. The attic is always full of boxes and junk that people don't use but want to save. They are hotter than hell in the summer, freezing in the winter, dark and full of insulation and spiders. The worst attics are those that you enter from a square in the ceiling; it's not a good idea to stick your head into a hole when you don't know what is on the other side. The attic at this house had a nice set of steps leading up to it. Because I was pretty certain that Angela was up there, why not call in the K-9 to search? I called for Officer Reed and his dog, Venus. Venus is the toughest police dog I have ever worked with; his handler, Officer Reed is pretty tough too. Once they arrived I explained to Officer Reed what I had going on.

We all walked to the top of the stairs. It is protocol for the K-9 handler to announce loudly there is a police dog and it will bite you if you don't come out now. Officer Reed said this three times. I often wonder what part of "the dog is going to bite you" people don't understand. A smart person would believe the warning and given the opportunity would surrender at that point. Apparently, Angela did not believe this. Officer Reed sent in Venus. It is always intriguing watching the dog at work. He first made a big loop around the attic with his nose up in the air, then he made a loop back and stopped for a minute, just sniffing, he then walked in and out of boxes and around a bunch of junk lying about. There was a board laying over some insulation. Venus started pawing at it frantically. Officer Reed said one more time, "the dog is going to bite you. Come out now." She didn't. Venus grabbed the board with his teeth, pulled it off Angela, grabbed her by the arm with his teeth and gave her a good chomp. Angela started yelling to call off the dog and Officer Reed did. I handcuffed her and took her out to my car. I asked her why she didn't come out when she knew the police dog was there. What do you think she told me? As expected, her answer was, "I didn't think he'd find me."

THE CHASE

In the last 10-42 from CCO Barber she brought up the one thing I was noted for was the chase. I was known as the hound dog of the department. Often times detective supervisors would call me in and give me the name of someone and tell me to find the person. I always did, no matter what it took to get the job done. In my career I had many people run from me, but I would always find them. It may have been that day or the next or the following week, but I would dog them until I had them. That was something I took pride in.

As a young rookie my first real chase was in a car. I was working the far east side running radar on Nicolet Drive by the Eagle's Nest Supper Club. The speed limit is thirty-five miles per hour there, but because it is so far out drivers think they can hammer it down. Most cars are doing between fifty and sixty miles per hour in this area. On this particular Sunday afternoon, I was running radar on vehicles heading out of town. I saw a black Monte Carlo coming at me at a high rate of speed, I locked the radar gun on the vehicle at seventy-five miles per hour; forty over! As the car sped past me I could see it was a young male driver. I pulled out after him with my red lights and siren blaring. I have to admit my heart was racing a bit and my adrenaline was pumping. As I floored my squad car to catch up to him, I realized he was moving away from me at a rapid pace. I had not even called headquarters with the stop yet because I was busy trying to catch this car. Looking back this was probably not the best idea, and I had just left the city limits. Policy says you don't leave the city unless you have permission from a supervisor. I kept on him and called out with the stop at Nicolet and Fischer Road which is in Brown County, but we were far from stopped yet. I really have no idea how far it was before this guy finally stopped and pulled over. Looking back, I imagine he was hiding his drugs or concealing something in his car and was buying time.

I seriously thought about breaking away from chasing him and putting him on my *I will get him next time list.* But then he pulled over. I was out in the boonies with no cover for miles. The thought did go through my head as to how stupid this was and now what was I going to do? I got out of the car and made contact with the driver, a twenty-two-year-old white male who was shaking like a leaf on a tree. When I asked him why he did not stop for me right away he told me he didn't realize I was even behind him. I did what I would do many times after that and played along like I believed him. I call it the Barney Fife; playing dumb so the bad guy thinks you're a moron until you can get his name run through the teletype and see who you are dealing with and allowing time for your cover officer to get on scene. Today, I returned to my car and found that this kid was clear and valid, he wasn't wanted and had a license. I decided to cut him a break, I wrote him a quick ticket and sent him on his way. I was as nervous as he was. Had that same event happened later in my career, I would have done things a bit different.

It was a Packer Sunday and the game was scheduled for noon. I did not work the games although the money was good. I had back issues for some time and I elected not to work the games standing on the cold concrete. Besides that, I would always say "you can't pay me enough to deal with seventy thousand drunk assholes." At 11:30 the crew who were going to work the game were coming off the road and their replacement officers were still getting logged on. This meant there was a very limited number of officers on duty at this particular time to answer calls.

As luck would have it, right at this time I observed a blue Ford Taurus speeding down E. Walnut St. Not just ten over, he was speeding closer to fifty in a twenty-five mile per hour zone in a residential area. As I sped up to catch up to him to get the plate he made a hard left onto S. Roosevelt St. I activated my red lights and siren and the vehicle pulled to the west curb in the two hundred block. I had that *feeling*. Some cops call it the sixth sense, others call it the Spidey sense. Whatever you call it, I knew this was going to be a cluster call. As a cop you learn to trust the *feeling*. I immediately called for backup. The closest cover car was coming from the far west side, I had about ten minutes to kill before anyone would be there to help me when things went south. I always ran the vehicle plate on my squad computer before getting out of the car just in case there was a warrant on the owner or the vehicle was stolen. In this case it came back to a local twenty-year-old male.

Knowing my cover was a ways out yet, I approached the car and did my Barney Fife, bullshitting around with the driver and playing dumb. The driver seemed really nervous. He told me he was test driving the vehicle and the vehicle owner was in the passenger seat. I asked the driver for identification. He gave me an Illinois photo ID card which meant he most likely did not have a valid driver's license. I asked him if he had a license and he told me no. I then asked the passenger for identification. He told me he didn't have any. That was my first red flag dealing with him. When I looked at the male I knew he was not twenty-years old like the registration said. I walked to the passenger side of the vehicle and had him roll his window down. I asked for his name and date of birth since he claimed to be the vehicle owner and the driver was not valid. The second red flag was raised when, he started his name with "um" and then gave me a name. I knew he wasn't who he said he was. In hindsight I should have stayed at the door, but I wanted to go back to my car and search this alias name. I wanted to find out who he really was. I told both males to stay in the vehicle.

As I turned to start walking back to my car, the passenger side door whipped open and the passenger bolted from the vehicle westbound in between two houses, I immediately gave chase and started calling out my location into my radio, which was in vain because there were no units to help me and I could not go searching for a bad guy alone. I last saw him duck in between some garages on Doty Street and then he was gone. I went back to the Ford Taurus. The driver was still sitting in the driver's seat. I was shocked. I figured he would have run the other way and been gone. Finally, my cover arrived and could stay with the driver who claimed he had no idea who the passenger was.

I went to my squad car and did some investigating in our records files. He was James Brown with seven felony warrants. I sent out an attempt to locate to the new units just starting the shift. I issued the driver a citation for operating without a license and let him go. I did an inventory on the vehicle and located a stolen laptop in the back seat. The trunk of the car was loaded with expensive tool boxes, I figured these were most likely stolen too. My lieutenant arrived, and I told him what had happened. He agreed with me that all of the items in the car would be placed in evidence until the rightful owners came forward. The car was also impounded for the vehicle owner to come and claim. I spent most of the rest of the day looking for this male at every address he had ever been associated with. I did not find him. The next day, the vehicle owner, who happened to be the suspect's son, came to the police department looking for his car. He showed his title and identification proving he was in fact the owner and I released the vehicle to him. A short time later he came back to the department asking for his dad's tools. Since he admitted they were not his, I told him only the legal owner could pick them up. I knew he wouldn't, but it felt good to beat the bad guy at his own game once in a while. I kept this guy's mug shot in my briefcase until I finally learned of his whereabouts and he was arrested. It took me three years to find him.

I was on patrol on the afternoon shift. At 21:00 I was dispatched to the Valley Green Apartments on Shawano Ave for a report of a domestic disturbance. The caller was the mother of two small children reporting the father of the kids was at the apartment demanding she turn the children over to him. Child custody disputes are very common for officers, they happen daily. As I was responding, the dispatcher reported the father had actually taken the children in the car and was leaving out of the parking lot in a dark green Pontiac Grand Prix. I was just pulling up on Shawano Avenue. There it was, the car was leaving westbound on Shawano Ave. I activated my lights and siren. The vehicle did not stop. It sped up and turned northbound on Fellows Street and back into a subdivision in that area. What luck, this was the area I grew up, there would be no loosing me back here. I knew exactly where we were, hundred blocks, street names, I had him now; or so I thought. He got onto Westplain Drive then turned onto Bond Street. I was waiting for another unit to get near me to close in. I watched as he turned the corner onto Steven Street. I made the corner and he was gone, vanished into thin air. I got up to Boland Road thinking maybe he could have made it that far without me seeing him. I saw no tail lights, no nothing.

Then dispatch reported a citizen on Steven Street had called 911 to say a car just blacked out and pulled into his garage and a male ran from the vehicle. I responded to the address. There was the car, still running in this citizens garage with two babies abandoned in the back seat. The coward left his kids and ran off into the night. The mother was called to come get her children. The car was impounded. It took me several days, but I located the driver and gave him several tickets. I also referred a charge to the court for abandoning his children.

Officer Paulson had just gotten back from Iraq. He had been an officer for about three years before he was deployed for two years. Whenever an officer is off the road for an extended period of time they have to ride with a field training officer for a few days to get reacclimated. I was called in by the training captain and asked to refresh Officer Paulson on his paperwork and computer skills. What I didn't know at the time was that administration thought he may have been suffering from some PTSD from his time at war. That information would have been nice to have going into this particular night.

We were traveling westbound on W. Mason Street when a report of a vehicle all over the road, a drunk driver, came out. A description was given and the last direction of travel. A blue Chevrolet Impala shouldn't be too hard to find if it was all over the road like the caller said. We turned onto W. Mason Street from Twelfth Ave and spotted a blue Chevy Impala, and sure enough it is all over the road. Officer Paulson activated the emergency lights and siren. We were heading westbound, luckily the traffic light at S. Oneida Street was green and the one at Ridge Road as well. He then made a left turn and then a quick right onto Shirley Street. The Impala finally pulled over and stopped. We called out with the plate and approached the vehicle.

It was definitely a drunk driver. As a training car we only count as one officer, we had to wait for a backup unit to run this male through field sobriety tests. This is where Paulson screwed up. As a trainer and speaking from experience I have always asked for the keys. I would rather chase someone on foot than having a drunk operator pulling away and driving a two-thousand-pound deadly weapon. The other thing about asking for the keys is if the operator won't give them to you, you know you have a person on your hands who is probably not going to cooperate with you. When we got back to the car to run the guy's name and wait for our cover, I said to Paulson, "You should have taken the keys." The words no sooner came out of my mouth and the vehicle pulled away from the curb and took off. Damn, here we go.

The vehicle pulled onto S. Locust Street and then eastbound on W. Mason Street and we took off after him. The Impala blew through a solid red light at S. Ridge Road which isn't the worst because it's a "T" intersection. But when he blew through the solid red light at S. Oneida Street with cars narrowly striking his vehicle and our squad, I said to Paulson, "that's enough, terminate." Paulson had this deranged look on his face and was fixated on the Impala, he acted like he hadn't heard a word I said. We were traveling about eighty miles per hour and there were cars everywhere. I grabbed him by the right arm and shook him and repeated, "terminate." He kept right on going, down the ramp to S. Ashland Avenue and northbound on what felt like two wheels. The guy then made a left-hand turn onto the railroad tracks westbound, Paulson did as well and across S. Oakland and into the train yard we went. The Impala finally stopped when it hit one of the train stops on the tracks. Thank God, the drunk was stopped, and nobody got hurt, well except for Paulson, he lost his job.

I was working the far east side with Officer Kastle. She was one of the officers I trained while I was an FTO and seriously the one officer I was most proud to have had a chance to train. She was a fast learner, you only had to tell her things once, and she had the motivation. She was all cop. We received a report there was some kind of domestic disturbance at a residence that day. When we arrived the female, who was the disturbing party had left the scene already. She was driving a green Chrysler Town and Country van. We sent this information out to all the other units as she would have charges coming for DVO disorderly conduct and DVO battery. The DVO is domestic violence offense and a mandatory arrest for police officers.

Later that night we were again called back to the residence on Nicolet Drive for the same female causing another disturbance with her husband. As I was driving there heading east on University and almost to Sturgeon Bay

Road I saw a green Chrysler van coming toward me and signaling to get up onto Sturgeon Bay Road. I confirmed this was the correct plate on the vehicle and we were off to the races. As soon as the lady saw me she floored it and took off up onto the highway. I activated my emergency lights and siren and the chase was on. I got on the radio and told Officer Kastle, "get up here and call this thing." In a chase the lead officer concentrates on just staying with the bad guy, while the second car is "calling it" meaning going over the radio and transmitting updated locations, speed, traffic, pedestrians in the area and road conditions. Kastle was my hot shot protégé and she joined in behind me calling it. The van got up on the Tower Drive bridge westbound and was going about a hundred miles per hour over the bridge. We stayed right with her. When she exited off at Atkinson Drive I thought she was going to stop for us. Nope, she got right back on Tower Drive going eastbound. Back over the river we went, this time she exited on N. Webster Ave and went north onto N. Webster Ave and then onto East Shore Drive.

I have hated chases from day one. There is too much risk for the gain and most often I would not even engage when someone took off on me, but this instance was back in a day when we still chased people. I wanted this to end in the safest way possible. All officers are trained in what is called a pit maneuver. A pit maneuver is tapping the rear of the suspect vehicle which then spins them out and they stop. I had done this maneuver over and over in practice but never in real life. Well, it was now or never. We had just passed Bay Beach Amusement Park and the roadway was clear with no other cars around and no pedestrians; this was the perfect spot. I pulled up alongside the van which was doing about forty-five miles per hour and tapped my front bumper into the rear quarter panel of her van. The van spun around, went into the ditch and stopped. The woman was taken into custody and neither vehicle had any damage to speak of. It is the one and only time I did this for real, and thankfully no one was injured in the process.

OVER THE CURB

As an FTO, one of the first things I train the new recruits is how to drive a squad car. Not that it is different than driving any other car, but rather, it is learning new driving behaviors. Those behaviors are not something taught in driver's education and many times doesn't seem natural. As a cop, it is the thinking that a curb, an island or lawn is just an obstacle that you need to go over. Realistically, a cop can go anywhere and do anything in a squad that is justified to apprehend the bad guy. Take this call for example.

I was sent on a report of a reckless driver. Several calls had come in from citizens reporting an older green four-door Chevy Impala driving around the area of Taylor and Ninth Streets. There were reports it was running over curbs and driving across the grass near an apartment complex in the area. It was close to shift change and many of the officers were already in the back lot at headquarters waiting to log off for the day. I was not one of them, so I was sent to check the area for the vehicle. Most often by the time the cop gets to the area the suspect vehicle is long gone. All we can do is drive through to make sure and then send out an ATL for the vehicle in the event another officer comes across the vehicle later.

As my luck would have it, that would not be the case today. Upon my arrival, I pulled into the back parking lot of the apartment complex to find the vehicle sitting in the lot loaded with people. I radioed headquarters to send me a backup officer and called out with the license plates on the car. I pulled around back to get behind the car. I was wishing two things; one, that I wasn't alone and two, that my backup wasn't coming from the station. The license plate check came back, the car was stolen. All I could do now was stay put and wait for my cover, who was told I was out with a stolen car and to *pick it up.* In other words, get there now! The longer you wait, the more time the bad guys have time to devise a plan to get away, and that is exactly what happened.

Suddenly the vehicle brake lights came on, and off it went. Over the parking stop, onto the grass, alongside the apartment building, off the curb, and onto S. Taylor Street. So did I. This is the part I am talking about, the mindset of a cop to just *go.* Go over curbs and lawns, it doesn't seem natural to a citizen because that is not how you are trained. To a cop it is the thing to do to catch the bad guy. The vehicle then crossed Ninth Street without stopping at the four-way stop sign and onto the dead-end of S. Taylor Street. There was nowhere to go from here.

The vehicle turned into a driveway, did a cheerio in the parking lot, went back over the lawn, off the curb and was now northbound on S. Taylor Street coming at me. I had to let it pass me and then turned around myself; I did not want to make the stop without backup for obvious reasons. This stop should be a felony stop where the vehicle gets stopped and each occupant is called out of the car, one by one. That would be in the perfect circumstances, but not today. I kept following the vehicle that was now driving over curbs and lawns trying to get away from me. Where was my cover?

The vehicle turned onto Seventh Street and then onto Michaline Drive where it stopped in the middle of the road and all four doors opened. I stopped too. Now what? This is always a quick decision point for an officer. I knew they were going to bailout, and the driver did. He was a tall Native American wearing a white t-shirt and jeans and he took off west toward S. Taylor Street. My first instinct as a cop was to chase after him, but my training and experience says to stay with the car and the occupants. That is what I did. I got out and drew down on the occupants telling them to get their hands up where I could see them. I had already given the description of the driver to the other units responding. Now that this had turned into a chase about a half-dozen cars showed up to help me. A couple cops showed up and stayed with me while we dealt with the occupants of the vehicle while the others searched the area for the runaway driver.

Everyone in the vehicle was intoxicated and one female had a couple minor warrants. After speaking with each of the other four occupants and sorting through a number of lies, the identity of the driver was determined. I ran his name and not only was he the driver of a stolen vehicle, but he was wanted for attempted homicide in Shawano County. Some might wonder why I didn't go after the driver and leave the car and occupants. Chasing a bad guy alone is a huge officer safety issue and leaving a car full of intoxicated people could allow another one of the occupants to get behind the wheel and take off, jeopardizing innocent citizens. I had to be glad to just have recovered a stolen car and take the female to jail on her warrants. The driver wasn't located, at least not that day. Sometime later I ran his name and he had been taken into custody so it all ended well in the end.

OH SNAP!

There is something about the thrill of the chase for cops. We never want the bad guys to get away. Most often with enough resources, man power and a little luck, they don't. This sunny January day would be no exception. It had snowed copious amounts of snow for the past weeks and the town was covered in not inches of snow, but feet of snow. It was 07:00 when I was sent on a call with several other cops to St. Vincent Hospital. Earlier in the day a male had been brought in having major psychological problems. He was being medically cleared, which means a doctor had examined the patient and ensured he was not having any kind of physical problem before going out to the mental health center for treatment. Based on manpower, cops do not stay with the patient at the hospital. Once the doctor gives the all clear we go back, pick up the patient and transport them out to the center. This transport call would be a little bit different.

As I was driving there, the dispatcher reported the male, who most likely heard we were on the way for him, decided he was going to leave the hospital without us. This probably was not the best idea for him since it was a beautiful sunshiny day and a balmy ten degrees outside. He left wearing nothing but a hospital gown. This guy shouldn't be too hard to pick out of a crowd considering his attire. Another one of the officers was also close by and had reported seeing the male running east across S. Webster Avenue and into the neighborhood area near Porlier Street. I circled the block and a couple more cops joined.

There he was running through the yards in knee deep snow, and there I went running after him. Another one of my partners came running up with me and away we went. It is hard work running in snow with thirty pounds of equipment on your body and a heavy winter jacket, which I grabbed just prior to bolting from my squad car. This guy definitely had an advantage since he had hardly anything on and a bit of a head start on us as we trudged through the backyards after him. I had no doubt we would catch him at some point, then we got a little help from Mother Nature and a chain link fence. This guy went over the fence like a hurdler in true form, the only problem was when his one leg came down it sunk deep into the snow bank on the other side of the fence and his momentum kept him going. SNAP!

went his leg and that was the end of that chase. We ended up calling rescue and he was hauled back to St. Vincent with a broken leg.

ADULT HIDE AND SEEK

One of the things I absolutely hated to do was have to go into a house and search for someone. It is sort of like playing adult hide-and-seek. Except the hider could be armed and when located, kill you. As the seeker, it is always our disadvantage going into a home because we don't know all the secret hiding places and the layout of the house. You cannot even imagine the places I have found people. In cabinets, closets, under beds, in piles of dirty clothes. Some of these places are so small, it is hard to believe someone could get in there.

The one call I remember being the most shocked regarding tight spaces was on Shawano Avenue. I was sent with Officer Seroogy to look for a guy with warrants. The guy's name was Ray Perry and I had known him for years. He used to live on Fink Street back in the day and we were constantly at his house for disturbance calls, probation violations, parties, you name it. This guy did not know how to behave. So, I knew him, and he knew me. Seroogy and I went up to the door and his girlfriend answered, she knew me too. I told her we were there to pick up Ray. She told me he wasn't there, but her eyes rolled over her left shoulder indicating to me that he was inside. She just didn't want to be the one to give him up; probably because when he would get out he would beat the shit out of her.

I played along, telling her that we needed to come in and make sure he wasn't there, just so we could document it in our report that we had looked for him. She opened the door and let us in. Officer Seroogy and I went room by room with guns drawn and flashlights lit, looking in closets, under beds, behind doors, just like hide and seek. In each room, we announced, "police, come out with your hands up." Of course, no one ever comes out, but at least they can't say they didn't know it was the police. We had the entire upstairs cleared, now for my least favorite place. The damn basement, cold, dark, and nasty.

This basement was sectioned off into several rooms and we strategically went room to room until we got to the back room of the basement. This room contained the hot water heater and the furnace. As a joke, I grabbed the front panel on the furnace and gave it a yank, it pulled off and my flashlight was now shining on the face of Ray Perry. In the damn furnace. Who looks there?

GRAB THAT GUY

An attempt to locate had been put out on Justin Franks. I knew this kid from working the west side for many years. He was trouble with a capital T. He was never cooperative with officers. He would fight, kick, punch, swear and would always run. Knowing this information about a person's personality can be very helpful when dealing with people like this.

I was driving down Packerland Drive just passing Southwest High School approaching West Point when I glanced over at the bus stop. There he was, sitting in the bus shelter waiting for the bus. Our eyes met for a moment and I looked away pretending I didn't see him. I pulled eastbound onto West Point Road and called over the radio that I had just spotted Justin and needed some units to head my way. I turned around in the roadway and started heading back toward the corner. He saw me coming and took off like a jack rabbit running toward Southwest High School.

In hindsight I should have driven my car over the curb and the school lawn toward the back of the school, but I was still a rookie and figured I could catch him on foot. By the time I got out of my car and kicked in the afterburners, he still had a pretty good head start on me. As he continued to distance himself, I thought to myself, *well that was pretty stupid of you, thinking you could catch up to this guy.* I could hear sirens in the far-off distance, so I knew help would not be here for a couple minutes.

Out of the corner of my eye, I saw another male running at full speed like a receiver going out for the bomb. As he got even with me, he yelled, "Officer, do you need me to catch him?" I told him "yes!" and with that this Good Samaritan took off like lightning. It truly was just like something out of the movies. This guy put a tackle on my suspect from behind that would put many NFL players to shame.

By the time I arrived to where they were, my suspect was all wore out and this citizen had him pinned to the ground. I got out my cuffs and slammed them on the guy and waited for another car. This is the only time in my career that I enacted the Good Samaritan law. Yes, just like in the movies, cops can order you to help, commandeer your car, boat, plane, you name it they have that authority. Most often this law is not enacted because it could put the citizen in danger. Not this guy, I told him he should go try out for the Packers. We both laughed, and I thanked him several times for helping me. He just kept saying he was glad he could help; now he had a really cool story to tell for the rest of his life!

JOHNNY STANDING BEAR

Johnny Standing Bear had been on our department's *most wanted list* for several months. The kid was wanted on about a dozen warrants and was raising havoc on the entire city. He was about twenty-years-old, and had many tattoos, most of which were on his face and neck. This makes it kind of hard for someone to hide since they stand out. I had dealt with him many times in the downtown district, he knew me, and I knew him. On this particular day I was driving down E. Walnut Street and just happened to look off to my left. There he was, standing in a driveway by an old Ford truck. Hesitation is bad, you must react immediately on your first impulse and go with it. I didn't miss a beat. I made a quick left turn into the driveway. Of course, he saw me coming and ran into the side door of the home. I had been on my police radio already and every unit for blocks was already on the way. Within less than a minute we had the place surrounded by cops.

I could have chased him right into the house, this situation is called hot pursuit. This would not have been a good option in this case, I was alone and there were too many safety risks; I didn't know how far away backup was. This guy was dangerous and could have been armed. Once backup was there, we attempted contact at the door, but no one answered.

The next step would be a search warrant. As the initiating officer, I had to write up a summary of all the facts and reasons as to why I felt the police needed to get into the home. This summary had to be reviewed by a supervisor at the department, then go to the district attorney's office for review and then finally a judge or court commissioner could approve it. This process can take hours, and in this case it did. While the search warrant is being processed, the house must remain surrounded. It is time consuming and keeps several cops tied up on the call making it much harder for the road cops to cover the ongoing calls that keep coming in. I bring this up because many times citizens do not realize the reason they are getting delayed police services, there are not enough cops out there; situations like this come up and cops can't just leave.

Once the search warrant is available to be served, a couple more cops are needed as part of the entry team. I was on the entry team because I was the initiating officer of the call. Officer Sandstone and Officer Shaw were both with me. We knocked on the door again. When I say knock, I am not talking about a little sissy knock, I am talking about practically knocking the door down kind of knock. I always called it my night shift knock; you take your boot and really give that door a couple of good knocks. No one answered the door, so the door got kicked in.

This type of entry was always a little hairy. It's almost like a giant game of hide-and-seek. The bad guy has the advantage because they are familiar with the home and the cop isn't, unless of course he has been there before. This was not the case, so we were walking blindly into an unknown situation. Once inside the side door, there was nothing but a set of steps going straight up to another door. In the cop world this is called *the fatal funnel*. A set of steps with nowhere to go but up. In the event the door would open at the top of the steps, there was nowhere for the officer to gain concealment or get out of the way of whatever what might be coming; like gunshots. When officers encounter this fatal funnel, it is always best to get the hell out of that area as soon as possible. We ran up the steps and booted in the top door.

As we made our entry, we announced, "Police!" very loudly. That's when Grandma came out of the living room asking what was going on. Seriously, all the knocking, ringing the doorbell and yelling we had done and she never heard us? I think not. I presented her with the search warrant. She insisted her beloved grandson Johnny was never at the residence and she had no idea where he was. We had Grandma sit back down in the living room and Officer Shaw watched her as Officer Sandstone and I combed the house for Johnny. When I say comb, I mean comb. We looked under every bed, in closets, in cabinets, in dirty laundry, anywhere you could possibly think a little weasel like that could hide.

We did not find him, and I began to doubt myself as to the possibility that maybe he ran inside and exited out a window prior to us getting the place surrounded. Was it possible? Officer Sandstone asked me this very question. No, no it was not possible, he had to be here somewhere. Officer Bolton arrived, and we started the search all over again, retracing areas we had already searched, *where in the hell was he?*

That's when Officer Sandstone who was searching the kitchen made a clever discovery. When he opened the lower kitchen cabinets where all the pots and pans were, he noticed the back of the cabinet appeared to have been pulled away. He called me in by him. He took his nightstick and pushed hard on the back of the cabinet and it fell away into the attic space behind the cabinet. That's when I saw tennis shoes. Both Officer Sandstone and I both grabbed the shoes and gave a forceful yank. Violá, there's Johnny. There is always a sense of satisfaction when you finally find someone who thinks they can outsmart the cops; today was one of those days. Grandma said she had no idea he was hidden in her kitchen cabinets. Johnny went to jail and Grandma got two smashed doors and a nice big fat ticket for obstructing the law.

KYLE BACKUS

It was a beastly hot summer day, I mean a real scorcher. I was working the downtown district when the dispatcher came over the radio stating the Brown County Sheriff's Department had a chase coming into the city. When a jurisdiction has a chase going, it is common courtesy to let other jurisdictions know the chase is coming at them. Green Bay has policies in place relating to chases, and let's just leave it at that. At any rate, the chase was coming in on Hwy 41 southbound at the time it was reported to us. This meant the suspect vehicle could go south onto I-43 or continue south on Hwy 41. I started heading toward I-43 southbound. We hadn't been notified why the vehicle was being chased.

The vehicle was described as a black Dodge Viper convertible. When I heard that, I knew there was no way for a police vehicle to ever catch that car; an 8.0L V10 engine with a top speed of almost two-hundred miles per hour. I continued to drive in the direction of I-43 and University Avenue but honestly, I didn't think that vehicle was still in Brown County; more likely it was in Manitowoc County by now. Even so, I was monitoring our radio and Brown County's radio for updates. That's when Lt. Landers radioed that he was behind the vehicle on University Avenue at Rothe Street.

I floored my squad to get to the area, but I was a little far to give any help and nobody else was in a position to help either. Lt. Landers followed the car to the dead-end of Rothe Street where the driver got out and ran up an embankment and into the brush. There were a few details we didn't know at the time. First of all, the vehicle had been stolen from a cottage on Kelly Lake in Marinette County. It was also involved in a hit and run crash in Marinette County, then was spotted by Brown County traveling over one-hundred miles per hour on Hwy 41. A Brown County Sheriff's Deputy lost control during the chase and was in a head on collision with another motorist. Now the car was here, and the driver was gone. Quite honestly the car was now a smoldering smashed up piece of junk. The entire front end was completely smashed in.

I had arrived on scene with several other officers and details of what had happened were coming in and being reported by radio and cell phone. Had we known then what we knew now, we would have probably handled this situation a little differently; but you are only as smart as your dispatcher and the person calling it in. We had a dog come and search the area for the tall, white, male about twenty-five-years-old with shaggy brown hair, last seen in blue jeans and a white t-shirt running from the car. Most officers would say, "we tried," and leave it for the county to take care of. Well here's the thing, I am not like most officers; if it comes into our city then it's now part of our problem. This guy was last seen running into Baird's Creek, so that put it on us too.

Like I said before, you might get away from me today, but I will hunt you like a dog. And so, the hunt began. I started by checking some of the neighborhoods south of Baird's Creek for anyone who may be walking around who may have seen him, or possibly even the suspect himself walking around. I did not locate anyone who knew anything about this guy. I had called up to Marinette County and talked to the Officer working the crash up there to see if I could gain any kind of useful information from him. He told me the suspect had been seen at Kelly Lake prior to stealing the car and had left a bicycle on the side of the victim's garage which might have fingerprints on it. He also told me the couple who had been victims in the crash in Marinette County were injured, which now raises the stakes. He also told me there was a witness to the crash who lived in Green Bay who he still needed a statement from. I told the Marinette Deputy I would get the statement for him.

I contacted the witness to the Marinette crash. He came to the police department and gave me his eyewitness account of what happened with the Dodge Viper and the young man driving it. The one thing that was very important in this statement was the driver of the Viper had been wearing a baseball cap that flew off when he rear-ended the couple in the pick-up truck. The cap had been picked up by the Marinette Deputy as evidence. This witness saw and described this cap on the suspect's head, so we had DNA evidence if we found the suspect to match to the cap. We just had to figure out who this guy was. I continued to follow every lead that came in and to follow a few of my own. Here is a little information for everyone to consider. If you ever want information about somebody, don't go to the current girlfriend or the family, they are going to cover for that person. Go to the ex-girlfriend. In this case the ex-girlfriend comes to us.

I received a telephone call from an ex-girlfriend of the suspect who told me she didn't want to be identified, she wanted to remain anonymous. She gave me his name and hung up. Kyle Backus, that was all I needed. I started a search in our computer system that lead me to every single person he had ever had contact with. Systematically, I went to every house he had ever been indexed at and talked to dozens of people who knew him. No one knew where he was, and if they did, they weren't talking. Here is another little thing that happens at departments: most often getting a tip like that would be kept under wraps by investigators. They want to be the one to bring the guy in, so instead of dozens of sets of eyes looking for him there would only be one. I don't play like that. I sent the guy's name and photo out as an *all car*, meaning to all cops. Why not have everyone looking for him and not just me? This strategy worked out pretty well for us that day.

Officer Kastle went to a suspicious person call on the west side at a store where a guy was acting suspicious and was believed to have stolen some items. The store owner played the video back; guess who she saw, Kyle

Backus. Officer Kastle called me immediately that she had Buckles on a video from ten minutes prior. The store owner told Officer Kastle the suspect left in a Yellow Cab. I quickly called Yellow Cab and they confirmed they had just picked up a male matching Buckles' description and took him to an address on Viking Drive in Ashwaubenon. The old cop saying, *it is easier to ask for forgiveness than to ask for permission* applied in this situation. I had to act fast and calling a supervisor and explaining the whole thing would have only delayed our response. I asked the dispatcher for a couple more units and away we went to Viking Drive in Ashwaubenon. I called Ashwaubenon Public Safety to let them know where we were going and to ask for a couple of their units as well. This guy was not going to get away from us again! I knew exactly where I was going, my sister used to live in these apartments.

I pulled into a parking lot at the same time as an Ashwaubenon officer. I got out of my car and started jogging toward the apartment building. I met up with the Ashwaubenon officer and was briefing him on what had just happened with the Yellow cab. There he was, I mean seriously there he was-walking right by us, twenty feet away. How gutsy to think he would be able to walk nonchalantly right past us and away from the situation! Not this time buddy boy! The Ashwaubenon officer and I pulled out our tasers and ordered him to the ground. He complied with my order since I yelled it loud enough to be heard in Appleton. All the other cops on the call came running. I cuffed him and put him in the back of my squad. And that was that. Another stellar day for the boys and girls in blue, accomplished only by teamwork!!

Drugs
HEROIN OVERDOSE

I arrived at the station daily at 05:45 and came on duty for 06:15 roll call. Roll call lasted about ten minutes in a room full of tables and chairs. The Lieutenant stands at a podium and recaps the night's events and gives out the orders for the day. It is not like the roll calls you see on TV shows; there's more sarcasm and joking around with the real troops. The day shift was known for being the funniest roll call around probably because there were so many seasoned veterans in that group. It really could be quite entertaining over coffee. Some mornings the shift commander would call down on what I called the "bat phone." When that phone rang during roll call you knew immediately it was going to be something bad otherwise it would have waited.

One day I was ordered out of roll call to go to Aurora Hospital for a heroin overdose. The male who had overdosed had just been brought in by friends who dropped him at the hospital doors and left. The only problem was, the male had been dead since about midnight. I went out to my squad and got logged into my computer on the way out there. As I was driving I couldn't help but think, *who drops off a dead person at a hospital and then leaves? Some friends they must be.* When I arrived at the hospital I entered the emergency room assigned to the victim. Laying on the hospital gurney covered by a sheet was a twenty-four-year-old young man. The attending doctor told me a car had pulled up at the emergency room doors about 06:00. A female got out and came to the emergency desk stating that her friend was not breathing. The doctors and nurses sprang into action and rushed out to the car to get the patient. The emergency staff loaded the male onto the gurney and rushed him into the hospital while the three females in the vehicle drove off. It wasn't until the male had been brought inside that it became apparent he did not just stop breathing but had most likely been dead for six to eight hours prior to being dropped off.

Our Detectives come it at 07:00 and would be responding to my location within the hour. I continued to gather information for the case. I went to security and obtained the video of the car with the three females on tape. The male's parents had been notified by one of the girls in the car that he had been taken to Aurora so now I had the parents to deal with as well. They were in the family room at the hospital. If they ever put you in the family room, that's not good. I called headquarters and had another officer respond to help me with all the statements, paperwork, and the talk we would have with the parents. The medical examiner arrived at the hospital; I assisted her with taking photographs and examining the body. At this point we did not know if this was a homicide or where this male had been when he died. The doctor pointed out the track marks on his arms and his penis. The guy had been shooting up for a long time. After the veins in his arms were destroyed from being used all the time he resorted to the veins in his penis. My next thought was *why didn't these friends of his call 911 when this guy had first overdosed?* If they had, the rescue crew could have Narcan-ed him and he would probably be alive. That is of course if the friends weren't all messed up too.

That is the problem nowadays, usually everyone is high so there is no one there to save them. I have actually heard of a heroin drug user who had a syringe of Narcan in a baggy with a note on it, *In case of emergency shoot this into me.* Unfortunately, his friends were too smoked to do anything. He died with his note still hanging on the bag. For a while we were getting one or two heroin overdoses a week where the subjects died. When Narcan came on the scene, every cop has some in their duty bag, and the save rate completely turned around. It's still pretty sad. I spoke with the parents who were upset but not surprised, which is usually the case as well. The parents often know about their child's drug use, but what can they do about it? Not much. It was later learned after a complete investigation this male was at a heroin party at his own house and everyone was out of it. When the girls went to wake him up and couldn't, they loaded him into a car and drove him to the hospital. The logic of a drug user.

THE BUST

I was still fairly new on the force when I was called over to a drug raid that occurred on N. Oakland Ave. This house had been on the drug hit list for about six months. Every officer in that district was keeping an eye on this residence. Every car that came in and out would have their license plate recorded by one of the neighborhood Crime Stoppers. Crime Stoppers are citizens who help the police in dealing with problem houses in their neighborhood. I cannot count how many times the information provided by these folks has aided in our investigations. When a home gains the reputation of a drug house most officers will sit near the house and stop every car coming and going for a violation when they have extra bits of time. Of course, there has to be justification for the stop. Let's face it, expired tags, improper registration, tail lights and headlights that are out are probably not a priority for a drug addict which makes it pretty easy to make a "courtesy stop." The officer is doing just that, stopping a vehicle to inform the owner that he/she has a defect. It really is a way for the officer to identify the driver and possibly the occupants, check for any warrants, drugs or anything else illegal. I always compared this to fishing. You throw out your line and never really knowing what you're going to pull in; it could be a little minnow or the granddaddy of all granddaddy's. You never know until you put your hook in the water.

Most people think, thanks to TV, the police can get a search warrant in a couple of minutes. Actually, it takes a long time. If a known and wanted felon who an officer recognizes runs into a house, that officer can run right in after him, no warrant needed. This is called fresh pursuit. In this and many drug cases it takes months of documenting criminal activity and compiling evidence. The general public doesn't understand when they call in and report drug activity going on at an address, sending an officer to the door would compromise the investigations. I mean really, what's a road officer going to do or say at the door? Imagine I knock on the front door, a male answers, and I introduce myself, "Hello I am Officer Bennett with the Green Bay Police Department. We have a report you are doing drugs in this home." People on drugs are stupid sometimes, but not that stupid. They are not going to say, "well, yes we are. Come on in."

The process takes a bit of time. The undercover drug agents get the information and set up what they call buys from the dealers. They continue to go through the drug chain in hopes of getting the top dog on that chain's list. All of the gathered evidence from patrol and the drug unit is them typed into a search warrant. This is reviewed by the supervisors then taken to the district attorney for review and finally taken over to a circuit court judge to be reviewed and signed. Obtaining a search warrant can take many hours.

This was the day the entire district and neighborhood had waited for, the drug bust. I couldn't be more thrilled to know we had finally gotten these guys who thought they were getting away with dealing and pulling it over on the cops. When I drove up to the house there were police vehicles everywhere and the SWAT truck was parked in the back. The SWAT team is used on all the major drug cases. The golden rule for cops is: *Where there are drugs, there are guns.* They go hand in hand. The SWAT team are the first ones in the door on a drug call. They have the protective gear and a specially trained team for this type of entry. As I walked up to the front door of the residence I could see the SWAT team had indeed made the entry. The front door was smashed from its hinges and was laying in the front entryway. Once inside I witnessed one of the filthiest houses I have ever seen. There was garbage and dirty dishes everywhere, most of which were molding and stunk unbelievably. There were flies and who knows what else flying around in there. The place was a sty. The occupants of this residence were handcuffed and seated in various chairs around the living and dining rooms under the watchful eye of SWAT team members.

Other members of the team were clearing the house looking for anyone hiding in bedrooms, closets, or attics. Once that part was completed, the team and officers would search the home for more drugs and drug paraphernalia. On the search for persons they found a female hiding in a pile of dirty clothes in one of the bedrooms. Officer Dooley asked me if I could search her for any drugs. He told me to take her into the bathroom and check her rear end because when she was located she had her hand down the back of her pants. I had never really done a search like this before and truthfully wasn't clear on how to do this. There were no other females on the call to ask and I certainly wasn't going to ask one of the SWAT guys and embarrass myself to no end and never live it down for the rest of my career. So, I used my best judgement.

I took this twenty-year-old female into the bathroom and closed the door. This may have been the dirtiest, most disgusting room in the house. The toilet bowl was literally black with scum and the bathtub looked like someone had taken poop and smeared it all over. I am sure the floor was supposed to be white, but was covered by a layer of sticky, black crap. I asked her if she had any drugs or anything else illegal on her person. She told me no. They all tell me no. I warned her if she did I was going to find it. She told me to go ahead. It was summer, and she was wearing a sleeveless summer top and a pair of Daisy Duke shorts; there weren't many places to look. I asked her to drop her shorts and down they went to the floor. She had no panties on and the stench that came from those shorts almost made me hurl right there. I obviously had latex gloves on, doubled. I doubled, even triple gloved on these kinds of calls. I picked up the shorts and checked the pockets and crotch area, no drugs there. I then told the female to face away from me and bend over, she did and there it was. The small corner of a small plastic bag sticking out of her asshole. I told her not to move and that I could clearly see a bag in her anus. I grabbed the corner of the bag and began to ease it out of her butt. The bag was covered in *you know what* and inside were ten small rocks of cocaine. I thought, *My God what kind of person does this?* The answer is a drug addict.

MONEY IN THE WIND

Part of being a good officer is developing friendships with the public, many times those people become informants for you. When I say friendships, I don't mean people you would associate with outside of the job, but rather people on the streets who trust you and would come to you with information. I didn't have a ton of people like this, but the ones I did have were super good to me and in return I helped them by taking care of issues they had.

I received a call from one of my informant friends that there was a guy driving around in a red Pontiac Grand Prix who was displaying a gun to various people in the neighborhood they lived in. The gun was said to be in the glove compartment. The information given also stated this guy was a huge drug dealer in the area. I got on this tip right away and tracked down the vehicle to a house on N. Roosevelt Street. I ran the registered owner through DMV records. He had a suspended driver's license. In addition, he was a convicted felon which means he cannot have possession of a weapon. I got this information out to all units; I did not want one of my fellow officers stopping this guy not knowing he had a weapon in his glove box. I sat down the block from the house and waited but he did not leave the residence before I had to leave go to my next call. When I came back to the area after the call, the car was gone.

So, this dude was driving around now, probably going to pick up or deliver some product. I parked down the block, in a parking lot of a business and watched for the car. In a matter of about ten minutes, there he was driving by. I looked right at him and knew it was the guy. I quickly got on the radio and said I was going to be stopping the car with the guy with the gun and went after him. The problem was there was no one to cover in the immediate area and this guy was now in his driveway when I pulled in behind him. He opened his car door and started to get out when I ordered him back into his car. Good idea, he couldn't run into his house; bad idea because now I knew he was inside his car with a gun and could come out shooting at any given moment, and I was alone. Damn, those minutes of waiting seem like hours when you're waiting for backup. I am not complaining there are departments out there that have so few officers backup can be fifteen minutes away.

Within a few minutes a couple of cops came rushing in and we called the guy out at gunpoint. This was a felony stop, therefore the procedures were a little different. In a felony stop we would call the suspect out and make him come toward us. Then we would have him kneel down or lay down before we approach him to handcuff him. This guy was totally cooperative with us and did as we instructed. I did find a loaded .45 in his glove box with a fully loaded magazine. He could have tried to take me out on my initial contact with him, thankfully he didn't. I also found some weed and seeds in his car. I called his probation agent; she put a hold on him, meaning he was going to jail. When I searched him, he had about two-hundred and sixty dollars in twenty-dollar bills on him. He asked if he could leave the money in his car. Cops leave the money on the person and it goes to jail with them to covers some of the jail fees for the county. I told him it was going with him, put him in the back of my squad and transported him to jail.

When we got to the jail parking lot, this guy was begging me for a cigarette because he knew he was going away for a really long time. I pulled over in the lot and let him out next to the squad car. His cigarettes were in his pants pocket along with his money, and several lighters. I took his cash and set it on top of the squad and set a lighter on top of it, then I pulled out a cigarette and lit it for him. I told him because he was cooperative with me I would let him have a few puffs. He was about three puffs in when a huge gust of wind blew up and the money under the lighter blew off the top of the car and into the wind. Now what?

I pushed the guy into the open squad door, cigarette and all and started chasing cash through the parking lot. I am sure the jailors were having a field day watching this dumb cop running after cash in their parking lot. The bad guy in my backseat was probably getting a pretty good kick out of it as well and enjoying a cigarette in my car! Dang, you try to do something good for someone and it backfires. I was able to locate all the cash, which I am sure was drug money, and get this guy into the jail. Smoking isn't allowed in the squads, so I rolled down all the windows on my way back to headquarters and then sanitized the heck out of my squad. Not one of my best days, but I did get a gun off the streets and that is always a good day!

Drunk Driving
BUT I ONLY HAD TWO

For whatever reason, most drunk people think "I only had two beers," is some kind of standard answer to the question, "how much have you had to drink?" Honestly, that answer is a clue the person is trying to hide the reality they had many more than two drinks. Don't get me wrong, I am sure there are people out there who get stopped and have had only two, but not in these cases.

It was a snowy day in December, just after Christmas and I was working the afternoon shift. About 20:00 I was exiting northbound I-43 onto Atkinson Drive. I saw a red Ford truck on the northbound entry ramp to I-43, the headlights were on and it was running. I observed a male standing next to his vehicle. My initial thought was he was a stranded motorist, until I lit him up with my spotlight and saw he was urinating onto the side of his truck. I swung around and called into headquarters with a suspicious situation. Officer Rivard, (Cowboy) was also in the area and came to cover me. I got behind the vehicle and waited for Rivard who was just pulling up as well. The male had been back inside his truck, got out, and started walking toward our squad cars. This is one thing as a driver you should never do. Always stay inside your vehicle and have the officer come to you. This is mostly out of safety to the driver; being out on the highway is extremely dangerous. Getting out of the car is also one of the things criminals do when they are going to assault or shoot a cop as it gives them a point of advantage.

In this case the male was ordered back in his truck. He did not comply with the order; another sign that this may not go well. Who doesn't follow a police order? I would come to find out over many years, that a lot of people would not obey orders. I call these "no" people; this person is going to be a problem. Officer Rivard was able to get this guy to at least stop in his tracks and patted him down. A pat down is when an officer does a quick patting of the clothing to make sure a person is not armed. I started talking to the guy. I asked him what he was doing outside of his truck, even though I had already witnessed him writing in the snow. He told me in slurred speech, "I was taking a leak." I could smell the odor of intoxicating beverage on him. I asked him if he had been drinking, and to this he replied, "I had two beers." There it was, the universal response. The guy's eyes were bloodshot and watery and he was wobbling in his shoes. Then he said, "give me the breath test."

We certainly would be doing that, but first we'd be doing other tests. As officers we are trained in Standard Field Sobriety Test (SFST). The walk and turn, the one leg stand, and horizontal gaze nystagmus. In these tests, officers look for clues, like not being able to follow instructions, not able to walk the straight line in the demonstrated fashion, unable to balance or count, but the most incriminating clue is the Nystagmus test. This is a check of the person's eyes. If intoxicated, the eyeball moves in an uncontrolled manner, it is an involuntary response, the person has no control over the reaction of their eyes. The person cannot tell their eye is doing it, but the officer can. He failed the first two tests miserably. I checked his eyes for the clues, the first thing I noticed is that he was staring at me and not the end of my pen. Officers hold a pen and ask the person to follow it with their eyes as the officer moves it. As I was moving the pen, he was still staring right at me. I explained the test to him again, but he was unable to follow my instructions.

He was swaying back and forth when Officer Rivard had him blow on the Preliminary Breathe Test (PBT). After he blew, and we were waiting for the results, he said to me, "well, maybe I had more than two, maybe three or four," and then he laughed. His PBT was .169. He was arrested for OWI. I took him to the hospital for the blood draw.

It always floors me how a drunk thinks. This guy for example, he was clearly driving drunk and he tells me "Maybe you should be arresting the real drunk drivers that are leaving Lambeau Field after the Packer games, instead of a guy who is just out having a few beers." Well, I guess there's logic.

It was January and I was working the afternoon shift. At 15:30 I was dispatched to a traffic crash in the 1200 block of Velp Avenue. The caller reported a vehicle up on the sidewalk and stuck in a snowbank while several citizens were trying to push the car back onto the roadway. When I arrived, all of the above was true. There were about a half-dozen guys trying to push this Chevy Cavalier back out onto the roadway. A female was sitting in the driver's seat, gunning the gas and spinning her tires. I walked up to the car and the males who were assisting this female scattered. I asked the female what happened.

She began telling me she almost hit the back of a slow-moving vehicle and ran up the snowbank to avoid crashing into it. I could smell the odor of intoxicating beverage on her person. I asked her how much she had to drink. She told me, "I am not going to lie to you, I had four or five or six beers." Now that's an answer, a truthful one anyway. I ran her through all of the SFST and she failed miserably. She was arrested for second offense operating while intoxicated. Her PBT was .34. Here's the kicker, she told me she knew she was intoxicated and shouldn't be driving but she had to pick her kids up from school. Yowza.

It was another January day on the afternoon shift. I came upon a two-vehicle crash that had just occurred on Newberry and Main Street. A female was out of her car and flagging me down. As I pulled up behind the two vehicles, the woman ran to my window and said, "hurry, this guy is drunk." I called for a cover officer and got out. The male driver of the Red Pontiac was leaning up against his car. I noticed he had a wet area between his legs. As I walked up to him he said, "what the fuck did I do?" I could smell the odor of intoxicating beverage on his person. I asked him how many drinks he had, and he replied, "I didn't do nothing."

He started walking away from me, but he couldn't really walk and fell into the side of his car. I grabbed his arm and tried to escort him out of the roadway, so he wouldn't get hit by a passing car. He pulled away from me and then took a swing at me. Several other officers arrived to assist with this guy. He kept saying, "this is bullshit!" and in my mind I was thinking, *yes, it is!* He fought with both of my back up officers and was taken into custody for disorderly conduct and OWI.

Once I had him in my car and was driving him to the hospital he told me, "my wife is going to kill me," and he began banging his head into the metal cage that separates the front seat from the back seat. I always hated the metal cages primarily because the arrested person in the back could spit at you through the cage. These metal cages were replaced years later for that very reason. Anyway, this guy was bouncing his head off the cage over and over again, and I thought to myself, *your wife isn't going to kill you, you are going to accomplish that all on your own.* I stopped the car and opened the back door. I asked him if he would please stop hitting his head or I would have to get out the hobble. A hobble is a nylon cord with a clip that is used to tie the person's feet and hands which makes it impossible for the person to move. I never liked the hobbles; there have been problems with them in other departments where the person's ability to breath was compromised by the positing of the person and hobble. I didn't want to do it. I always tried reasoning with a person and tried to calm them down. In this case it worked, he calmed right down.

Once we arrived at the hospital, we needed a wheelchair to get him inside, and for a moment I thought it was going to be smooth sailing. When we got into the OWI room and he was helped into a chair, he started yelling loudly for all the emergency room to hear. He called me a "fucker" and said, "this is mother fucking bullshit." Imagine being in an emergency room and hearing that from down the hall. I am sure that would be terrifying to a sick person.

I tried to calm him, but this guy had been through the drill a couple of times before and he knew how to play the game. Hospital security arrived with leg and arm restraints and everyone took an arm and a leg and secured this guy to a gurney. The entire time the guy is screaming, "this is bullshit, this is bullshit." And again, in my mind, I was thinking, *I couldn't agree more.* After his blood draw, he was transported to jail for his fourth OWI charge. We never did get a PBT on this guy, but it would have been a bell ringer.

At 17:30 on a Thursday night in June, I was on patrol on the city's west side when I observed a red, four-door Oldsmobile traveling on Western Avenue at Oak Street. The department had received complaints that people were not stopping for this stop sign, nor the one at the railroad tracks on Oak Street just north of this intersection. I was monitoring the area for ten minutes when this vehicle came flying up to the intersection, rolled through the stop sign at Oak Street, drove north on Oak, and never even slowed down for the stop sign at the railroad crossing. I activated my emergency lights and siren and the vehicle pulled over, running over the curb as he did so. That is another clue this person could be impaired, usually people don't run over curbs, or at least not up onto them.

When I approached the vehicle, the driver was clinging to the steering wheel with both hands and looking straight ahead. I introduced myself and the guy still just stared straight ahead. I told him I stopped him for running the stop signs and asked him for identification. He told me he did not have any. I could smell that he had been drinking so I asked him, "how much have you had to drink?" His answer, "a lot." Once my cover arrived, I got him out of the car and began instructing him in the SFST. That is when he told me, in slurred speech, that he had a fake leg and would not be able to perform the tests. I attempted the eye check on him, but he refused to cooperate. He told me, "you got me, just take me to jail." With that, he was cuffed and placed in my squad car. When I told him that I would be taking him to the hospital he said to me, "I was drinking big time, you know I was drinking, so why do you have to take me to the hospital?" I attempted to explain but it's pretty hard to explain or reason with drunk people, he got upset with me and said, "fuck you." I closed the back door and drove him to the hospital. He was cooperative with the nursing staff during the blood draw. And by the way, he didn't have a fake leg, but that was a nice try. His PBT at the jail was .37.

It was a Sunday in December when I was on patrol in the Broadway district. At 18:30 I saw a brown Buick LeSabre driving north on S. Broadway in the 900 block. The speed limit in this area is twenty-five miles per hour and it appeared to me this vehicle was traveling well over the speed limit. I saw the vehicle pass another vehicle just south of the Canadian National Railroad Crossing. This is a no passing zone and really, passing someone in a twenty-five mile per hour area, what's up with that anyway? I pulled the vehicle over and went up to the driver's window.

The male juvenile driver opened his car door to speak to me because his window wouldn't roll down. As soon as he opened the car door I could immediately smell the odor of intoxicating beverage coming from the vehicle. I told the driver I stopped him for speeding and passing in a no passing zone, his response was, "so." Honestly, that is the answer he gave me, "so." Who says that to a cop? When I did a license check on him, he came back as revoked. Officer Barker had just arrived as my cover.

I asked this seventeen-year-old young man how much he had been drinking. Of course, he said, "two beers." Under the law, he cannot have a drop and he knew that. I asked him to step out of the car and escorted him back to my squad car. I opened the rear squad door to place him inside and as I did, he hocked up a big greenie and spit it in my face. It landed on my lips and nose. He then tried to pull away from me, but I held on tight and alerted Officer Barker that I needed help with this guy. We attempted to take this guy to the ground, but he resisted and in doing so he knocked me to the ground and landed on top of me along with Officer Barker.

Officer Stowe arrived, and we were able to get this guy in cuffs. I told the male he was going to jail for battery to a police officer. His response was, "what? All I did was spit at you and knock you to the ground." What Mr. Smarty Pants didn't realize is that in the eyes of the law at seventeen you are considered an adult, so off to jail we went with him. I issued him a couple tickets for speeding, illegal passing, fourth offense underage drinking and he was charged with battery to a police officer. He was uncooperative with the jail staff, which is never a good thing. This kind of behavior lands you in a padded room with no clothes on. This entire call would have been so much easier if this kid would have just been civil and took his tickets like a man instead of acting like some animal. His PBT was only .03 but because he was a minor it's supposed to be .00.

I was working the afternoon shift on a cold day in November when I was dispatched to a call at Chappell Elementary School on N. Fisk Street. The notes of the call indicated the principal was reporting an intoxicated female in the school office with her three-year-old child. According to the principal this female was supposed to be at the Head Start office at 200 S. Broadway to register the small child, but instead the mother came to Chappell School. Rather than send her driving away, she told the drunk woman she could help her and then called the police. Smart move on the principal's part.

When I arrived at Chappell it was 15:25 and children were leaving; school had just dismissed. There were kids everywhere and just the thought of a drunk driver in the area made me cringe. I entered the school and met the principal outside her office. Officer Palmer arrived as well. When the principal told me the drunk lady's name, I immediately recognized her as a woman I had dealt with several nights ago on a check the welfare call, on W. Mason Street. On that particular call, it was for checking the welfare of several small children living in deplorable living conditions. That fact was confirmed. I knew there had been dozens of prior calls to her residence, most of which related to child neglect and her intoxication.

As soon as I walked into the principal's office I could smell the odor of intoxicating beverage. The female looked at me and in slurred speech said, "hey, I know you" to which I said the same back to her. She was having trouble keeping her head up and she kept resting it on her shoulder. She told me, "I just want to go home." I told her it was my belief that she had been drinking today. She told me she had two beers. She told me again, "I just want to go home." I asked her how she got to Chappell School today. She told me she drove and then fumbled into her purse and pulled out her keys. Having prior contact with her, I asked her where her one-year-old child was at this time. She told me she left him at home with the child's father who was sleeping. I thought to myself, *yikes this is getting worse by the minute.*

Not wanting to have a huge scene at the school, I told her I would take her and her three-year-old home, so the child could be with the father. This way I could make sure her story was correct before running her through a SFST. Officer Palmer took the car seat out of her vehicle and locked it up, she had parked right in front of the school. I transported the drunk mom and child the few blocks to their home. We made contact at the apartment door, the child's father answered after several minutes of hard knocking. He admitted he had been sleeping and the one-year-old was also sleeping. The three-year-old was left with him.

We ran the intoxicated female through SFST outside her apartment door in the hallway. She pleaded with me saying she was not intoxicated. She said, "honest to God, I only had two beers at Farlin Park." Well the real honest to God story was she couldn't even do any of the field sobriety tests and she blew .41 on the PBT. She had been driving in that condition with her three-year-old through a school zone. Thank God, we stopped her, or this could have been a lot worse.

It was a nice summer Saturday afternoon in June and it wasn't very busy on the road, not in the way of calls anyway. I always used this time to run traffic or radar on speeding vehicles. I was parked by the Titletown Brewing Company and running radar gun on the Ray Nitschke Bridge eastbound. I saw a vehicle that was obviously traveling faster than the posted twenty-five miles per hour limit on the bridge. It was the only vehicle on the bridge at the time. I locked my radar on the vehicle. I pulled out and activated my lights and siren.

I caught up to the vehicle in the 300 block of Main Street. When I walked up to the vehicle I could clearly see a twelve-pack of Bud Light Beer on the rear seat; it was open with several cans missing from it. I called for a cover car. I then spoke to the driver. I informed him that I was stopping him for speeding. He said he was following the flow of traffic. Hmmm, there was no traffic! I could smell the odor of intoxicating beverage on his person. I asked him for the keys and he gave them to me. I asked him for a driver's license and he told me he did not have one. I then asked him how much he had to drink today, he told me, "three beers." Well, at least it wasn't the standard *two beers*. But I could tell by the way this guy was acting and talking, it had been a lot more than three.

Officer York arrived, and we got the guy out of the car. He had to use the side of the car to steady himself and I had to grab him by his arm, so he wouldn't fall. Once up on the curb it became obvious this guy wasn't going to be able to perform any field sobriety tests, he couldn't even stand up for God's sake. He did blow a .33 on the PBT. I would have thought he was going to be higher than that. Everyone has a different tolerance to alcohol and there are several factors that affect a person, like not eating before drinking. He was taken into custody for OWI.

Once I had him in my squad car he told me, "I'm drunk, I will admit it, just take me to jail." I told him I had to take him to the hospital to do a blood draw on him first. He didn't like the sound of that and he started yelling at me about suing me if I took his blood. I continued talking to him on the way to the hospital and got him to calm down. Once we got into the OWI room he was confessing to me that he was an alcoholic and told me he "had honestly, drank nine beers." I told him I appreciated his honesty. The nurse took his blood and off to jail we went. I gave him his tickets for speeding, operating without a license and OWI. He thanked me and apologized for being drunk. I told him my standard line. Drink as much as you want, just don't drive. That's a hard one for some people to grasp.

Sometimes people think they are cleverer than the police. Like the man on this call. It was 21:00 in December. I was dispatched to a report of a reckless driver complaint on S. Taylor Street. The notes indicated that a blue Buick was traveling in the oncoming lane on Larsen Road and passed three vehicles at a high rate of speed. It had also run the red light at S. Taylor Street. The license plate was given by the complainant and when I ran it, it came back to an address in the 1700 block of Badger, which was close by. Luckily, I was close by as well. The complainant said she was able to follow the car and saw a white male with long brown hair, about thirty-five-years-old, wearing blue jeans and a three-quarter length tan Carhartt jacket get out of the driver's seat and go behind the vehicle. I pulled into the parking lot at the apartments, hit my spot light on the vehicle and there standing by the trunk was the male matching the description. He tried to stagger away, but I told him over my PA to stop and he did. He then leaned up against the trunk. Officer Barker was just pulling in. I got out and approached the male in the Carhartt jacket.

When I got near the trunk I saw solid ice cubes and a brown liquid on the trunk lid, this indicated to me someone had just been finishing up his cocktail. I saw another male standing outside who turned out to be the vehicle owner. He told me that he and the driver had gotten back from drinking at the Rendezvous Tavern. The vehicle owner just threw his friend under the bus for driving him home drunk. I looked over at the guy in Carhartt Jacket and he looked at me. He said, "I was driving but you didn't see me driving, so you can't catch me." Hmmm another world scholar. Oh yes, I can, and oh yes, I did. Based on the description given by the witness, the owner telling me he had been driving and the guy actually telling me he was driving, that was enough for me.

I told him I was going to run him through some tests. He told me he wasn't doing them because I didn't see him driving. He actually told me, "you can't arrest me." Oh yes, I can, and oh yes, I did. The guy was not cooperative as you might have already guessed. It took four officers to get him into handcuffs and at the hospital he told every person he saw to, "suck my dick" including his nurse. He was yelling at me and the other officers calling us, "pussy ass mother fuckers," and trying to kick us. He was yelling as loud as possible throughout the emergency room "suck my dick." The poor sick people in there were probably petrified at the sound of this commotion. We never did get a PBT on this guy, but he was definitely intoxicated no doubt. He had to be express booked at the jail, which means no clothes and into a padded room. In addition to his OWI arrest, we added a disorderly conduct charge for his disruptive behavior at the hospital. Some guys just don't know when to keep their mouth shut and this was one of them.

If there is such a thing as a favorite OWI story, this would be it, just for the pure logic of the drunk. It was a Wednesday afternoon in November when I was dispatched to Speedway Gas Station on W. Mason Street. The store clerk was calling to report a suspicious vehicle at the gas station. The clerk said there was a white Pontiac Grand Am pulled up to pump five right in front of the windows. When the male got out he could not reach the gas door which was on the passenger side of the vehicle. The clerk said the male then drove around in a circle and stopped again but the gas door was still away from the pump because all the guy did was a circle. The clerk reported that the male did this four times. The clerk said she called because she thought the male may be impaired since he could not figure out how to get turned around to get the gas door on the side of the pumps.

As I was driving there, I had this mental picture of this guy pulling up, getting out, getting back in, pulling around to the other side of the pumps, getting out, getting back in, and pulling around to the other side of the pumps; pretty comical when you think about it. By the time I arrived, the driver had actually pulled closer to the pumps and stretched the hose around the back of the car to reach the passenger side. I guess that's one way of doing it.

He was now in the store paying for the gas. I pulled up behind his vehicle and as he came out of the store I approached him. I asked him if this was his car. He told me it was his friend John's. I asked him if he was the driver. He said yes. I asked him for his keys and he pulled them out of his front pocket. He asked, "what is the meaning of this?" I told him the police received a call from a concerned citizen that was reporting a suspicious vehicle driving around and around the gas pumps. The driver told me that he couldn't figure out what side of the car the gas door was on, and that he drove around a few times to get it on the right side.

I could smell the odor of intoxicating beverage on his person. I asked him how many drinks he had today. He told me, "four or five." Now that's an honest answer. This driver failed every field sobriety test. He kept saying over and over again, "this is unbelievable," if he said that once he said it fifty times, he just couldn't believe it. At the hospital after the nurse took his blood he shouted out, "ladies and gentlemen, I am sure I am legally drunk, but I am not a problem." He was actually pretty good compared to many of the drunk drivers we deal with.

This was his first offense, so he was allowed to call his sober brother to come and get him. I went back to Speedway and collected the evidence from the clerk. The entire episode was video recorded on their surveillance cameras, from him driving into the parking lot from W. Mason Street to his version of Ring- a-Round-the-Rosies and his arrest; all on video for the court to see. That is pretty tough to beat.

It was mid-October and I was working on the afternoon shift. It was around 16:30 on a Tuesday, when I was dispatched to a report of a vehicle disturbing in the area of Phoebe Street and Lincoln Street. The caller reported a gray Ford Thunderbird driving erratically on Phoebe Street. The caller said the vehicle drove up on some front lawns and then back down. The car was now parked in front of a gray house on Phoebe Street and the male went inside.

While I was driving to the area, some updated notes came through stating the male had now staggered back into the vehicle and was leaving. I came up N. Ashland Avenue and when I turned onto Lincoln Street I saw a gray Ford Thunderbird coming right at me. The plates matched those given by the caller. I turned on my lights and siren, turned around and went after him. He did not stop immediately. He instead went down the alley and drove about eight houses before he finally stopped. His vehicle was smoking from the front end and had several smashed quarter panels that appeared to be fresh damage. I walked up to the car and the first thing the male says to me was "what the fuck are you stopping me for?" Really? Is that any way to introduce yourself to an officer when you are driving without a license and intoxicated?

I could immediately smell the odor of intoxicating beverage on his person. My back up, Officer Klein arrived just as this driver went into *psyco-mode*. I tried explaining that we received call about a reckless driver in the area. The driver's response was "that's fucking bullshit, you're stopping me because I am Mexican." Wow, that's a new one. I informed him the police received several calls about his reckless driving. I then asked him how much he had to drink. He said, "fuck" really loud and then said, "a six pack." I could tell this guy was just getting started, he was in wind up mode. I wanted him in cuffs as soon as possible, it became very clear he was a "no" person and could get violent.

Officer Lane arrived and said the male had violent tendencies and gang ties. Officer Lane also said he talked to two separate witnesses who had seen this guy driving up on lawns at a high rate of speed, an estimated fifty-sixty miles per hour in a twenty-five miles per hour residential neighborhood. Our driver was now yelling, "fuck" over and over again. I wasn't going to wait for him to assault one of us.

I told him to exit the vehicle and when he did, he got out in a defensive stance, like a boxer who is preparing to take a swing. Officer Klein grabbed him and pushed him up against the car. I grabbed the guy by the right arm and tried to get the cuffs on him, he was resisting the whole time, but I was able to get him cuffed. I got him in the back seat of my squad car. That is when he said, "I want your names, all your names." This is something that people say when they want to try to intimidate the officer. This never intimidated me at all, I would actually give people my business card when they asked for my name. I was never afraid or worried that my actions were out of line, never. You do what you have to do to take the bad guy off the street for the safety of the community and to get yourself home safe at the end of the day; *that* is the main goal here.

The guy gave me a fake name, when he found out that I had found out who he really was, he continued saying, "fuck" over and over again. He had seven Green Bay warrants and two Brown County warrants, this was his second OWI and he was driving while revoked, and one open can of beer in the car made for an open-intoxicants in vehicle as well. I transported him to the hospital where he caused a disturbance in the OWI room. He continued yelling his favorite word over and over again and he told me his lawyer would get him off the charges. I thought, *yes, I am sure he will.* I transported him to jail where his PBT was .17 I was just glad we got this guy off the streets before he ran someone over.

I was dispatched to the 800 block of Cora Street for a report of a suspicious situation. I arrived at the residence and spoke to the complainant. She said her boyfriend took her two small children ages three and five to get some beer at 11:00 and they had never come back. It was now 19:30. She said she called all of his friends and they had not heard from him that day. She said she was worried for her children's safety because her boyfriend does cocaine. Let me get this straight, you know your boyfriend uses cocaine, but you let him take your children anyway? Okay, I will help you. I asked her for the description of the vehicle. She told me it was a blue Ford Van and she gave me the plates.

As I was speaking to the complainant about the situation, headlights pulled into the driveway. I walked outside with the complainant. The vehicle was the blue Ford Van and her boyfriend was driving. Based on what she had just told me about him being a drug user, I called for backup right away. I was standing on the porch and saw the two children sitting in the front passenger seat without seat belts or car seats. I walked toward the vehicle. The boyfriend had his window rolled down and said to me, "what the fuck are you doing here?" That is not the way to start off a conversation with a police officer.

The first thing I said to him was, "do not swear in front of the children." That is one of my pet peeves. Then I calmly told him I had been called by his girlfriend because she was concerned that they had been missing all day. I could smell the odor of intoxicating beverage on his person. I asked him how much he had to drink today. He said, "Honestly, seven beers." Officer Londo arrived to help me with the field sobriety tests. The mother of the children took them out of the van and into the house. I started with the horizontal gaze nystagmus and he presented all the clues. I also did what is called a vertical nystagmus which is an indicator for possible drugs. I got jerkiness in both eyes, so this guy was probably on drugs as well. I asked him if he had taken any drugs and he told me no, but the eyes don't lie.

I continued with the field sobriety tests, but this guy couldn't even walk a straight line, he was staggering all over the place. For his safety we had him stop to avoid injury. He told me, "I am too drunk to do this." He blew .17 on the PBT which I thought should be higher considering he couldn't hardly walk. Once I had him at the hospital, he finally admitted to me that in addition to having seven beers he also had used cocaine all day. That explains a few things! And with kids in the car, what is wrong with some people? You want to mess up your own life that's one thing, but you don't take kids with you on your party bus.

Last, but not least, in my series of drunk driving tales comes one from August of 2003 at 18:30pm. I was dispatched to a traffic crash behind Sass Bar in the 800 block of S. Broadway. The notes of the call said a male in a black Ford F150 pickup truck with some kind of business logo for plastering on the side of it had just struck the fence behind the bar. The notes went on to say the driver was now parked behind the bar and was sleeping in his truck.

When I pulled into the parking lot I saw that two four-by-four posts had been snapped off and the eight-foot section of fence was laying on the ground. This damage would be consistent with a vehicle backing into it. I saw the black Ford F150 with the plastering logo and the same plates given by the complainant. The crash was also on video from the rear camera at the bar.

Lt. Bailey arrived to assist me on this call. I walked up to the driver's side window of the truck and he walked up to the passenger side. The driver's window was all the way down. I looked in and saw a can of Miller High Life standing upright near the driver's right foot. I then shook his left arm and said loudly, "Hey, are you alright?" He lifted his head and opened his eyes. He was having trouble keeping his eyes open, and I again asked if he was alright. He slurred out, "yes." I could smell the odor of intoxicating beverage on his person. I reached in and shut off the truck and took the keys, there was no way this guy was going to drive away on me.

I asked the guy what he was doing. He turned his head and was trying to focus on me and he told me, "I'm resting." I asked the male how much he had to drink. You guessed it, he told me, "two beers." All I could think was, *they had to be really big beers to get you that wasted.* We got the driver out of his vehicle and he refused to do any field sobriety tests. His PBT was .21. He asked me if I could just call him a cab or someone to come and pick him up. I told him no I could not. That might have been something that was done in days gone by, but those days are over. People always tell me stories about the cop that let 'em off years ago; just let them park their car and gave them a ride home. That may have happened in the old days but not today. I mean think about it, who would do that? Take a guy home and then later on, he comes back and drives and crashes and kills someone. That would be on the cop, who would take on that? Certainly not me. I loved my job too much and would never do something that could potentially hurt an innocent person. No way!

I transported him to the hospital where his blood draw was completed. He refused to answer any questions. I was contacted by teletype and informed this would be this driver's ninth OWI; nine. Holy cow! When I took him to jail he told me that he was not a bad guy he just had a drinking problem. I told him that his problem really wasn't so much the drinking as the driving. He agreed and then said "I am going to prison for five years. Damn, I fucked up." I told him, "yes, but at least you didn't kill anybody; yet."

I know that you may have enjoyed the preceding stories about drunk drivers and maybe got a bit of a chuckle about them. But the truth of the matter is, there is nothing funny about people who go out and get shit faced drunk and then drive their cars. If these were people who really just had "two beers" I wouldn't be writing about them. These are people who have had many drinks and been caught many times for drinking and driving. I urge you, if you are one of those people, please stop before it is too late. Call a cab or designated driver. There must be someone you know who is sober that can come and get you. Better yet, stay home and drink, it's cheaper and there is no temptation to get behind the wheel. Detroit makes new cars every day and those can be replaced, but there is no replacement for a human life.

I SAW THIS ONE COMING

I was dispatched to a call on S. Fisk Street with Officer Matthews. It was a report of an intoxicated male who was making telephone threats to his ex-wife. She also reported the male was constantly driving while intoxicated and she feared he was going to hurt someone. I arrived at the residence; a two-family dwelling with the male occupying the upper rear apartment. The residence had one of those steep, rickety, exposed outer wooden staircases going straight up the back of the house. I always gave these staircases a good shake to make sure they were going to hold up before walking up them. I got to the door and gave a good knock. After several minutes a male came staggering to the door, clearly intoxicated. It was 10:00.

He allowed us to come in; we went and sat in his living room together. I looked around, there were empty beer cans everywhere: kitchen counter tops, kitchen table, coffee table, end tables, floors, I mean everywhere. I had a conversation with the male about making threats toward his ex. Our usual protocol is to first verbally warn a person to stop, a verbal police order. If the behavior doesn't stop, a written warning is next. If the behavior continues, we issue a citation, and then if it doesn't stop, jail. I explained to him that he needed to stop with the harassment or he could be put in jail, which was the truth; I just didn't tell him the in-between steps.

Explaining something to an intoxicated person is always a bit tricky. I often wonder if they really get the meaning of my words. He was able to care for himself and was not unable to function, so there really was nothing we could do about his intoxication level. It is a free country, you can drink as much as you want to. I also spoke to him about his drinking and driving. He had not driven that day so there wasn't much that could be done other than give him a good talking to about the consequences of hurting someone with his vehicle and going to prison for a very long time. I could tell my warnings were going in one ear and out the other, but I tried my best to warn him. I also left a crisis center business card with him and told him he should call and get some help. When we left the residence, my partner Officer Matthews, told me she knew this guy for many years. He was a horrible drunk. I recall the last thing she said to me about him was, "someday this guy is going to kill someone."

It was a beautiful Sunday morning; the sun was shining, and all was nice and quiet. All the drunks from the night before were sleeping it off and the good church going people were off to church to pray for the world. I was sent to a crash scene on Dousman Street at Gray Street with Officer

Matthews. I was coming from the east side and by the time I arrived there, Officer Matthews had already assessed the crash scene. A lady on her way to church had been killed by a drunk driver leftover from the night before. The drunk had blown through a solid red light going about thirty-five miles per hour. The unsuspecting victim never had a chance. The drunk was already in the rescue squad and going to be transported to the hospital.

When I opened the door to the rescue squad and looked in, there he was, the drunk guy I had warned not two months earlier about this day. It made me physically sick to my stomach to think he had taken an innocent life due to his irresponsible behavior. I had to follow the rescue squad to the hospital and stay with the male until he was medically cleared. Then I would be taking him to jail. I had to sit in a hospital emergency room with him for several hours, all pissed up with no remorse. I had to stay with him as they took him to x-ray and took care of his minor bumps and bruises. He was slurring his words and talking a bunch of gibberish, asking about the condition of his vehicle. I wanted to strangle this guy, but as you know, cops must treat everyone equally.

Never once did he ask about the lady he hit, he had no idea she had been killed. I wanted to tell him at the hospital, but I did not want a disturbance in the emergency area, so I held it in. I was boiling inside. After several hours of babysitting this guy, he was finally medically cleared. Officer Brady had arrived to assist me in getting him into my squad car. Once he was inside my car, I activated my tape recorder and told him he was under arrest for homicide by intoxicated use of a motor vehicle. He asked, "does this mean I am going to jail?" Really dude, you just killed someone and that is what you say? I read him his Miranda rights and he said he wanted a lawyer. I transported him to jail without another word to be said. I booked him into the jail and left.

This is one of those calls where inside you just want to beat the living shit out of the guy, but you know you can't. What good would it do anyway? But the emotion is there, believe me. My heart was very heavy that day because I had seen this one coming. There was nothing I could have done to change it, but he could have.

About six months after her death, I was sent on a call to the victim's residence where her husband still resided on the west side. The call was a check the welfare call. A relative had called asking us to check on the male because he was struggling hard in dealing with the death of his wife. I responded to the residence and made contact with the male. He invited me inside the home. The home was a bit unkempt and slightly messy, which is understandable considering he had lost his wife in the last six months.

This was one of those opportunities neither a dispatcher nor an officer usually get; to see a call full circle. As a dispatcher you take the call but never get the follow through, as a cop you get the call and remedy the situation but rarely see the aftermath. I was seeing the aftermath, a frail, broken-hearted man who was struggling hard with life. I sat down with him in his living room and we talked. I let him talk as he told me about the crash that had claimed his wife's life. I told him that I had been at the scene.

He asked me some questions about the crash, his main concern was whether or not she had suffered at all. I couldn't be absolutely sure, but based on what I had seen, I was pretty sure she had perished instantly, I told him so. He kept asking me why this had to happen to her. All I could say was "it was God's will." I spent about an hour talking with him and I felt like I left him in a better state of mind than when I had arrived.

Sometimes people just need to talk and being with someone who was there at the time of the event seems to give them some peace. I hated being at this horrific call, but I loved the fact that I could comfort someone who was in so much grief. I often wonder if the drunk driver who had killed this beautiful soul and destroyed this man's life, has ever yet grieved what happened; if he even realizes what he did. I said it before, but I will say it again, drink as much as you want, but don't get behind the wheel.

HAPPY NEW YEAR

It was New Year's Day, a fresh start filled with resolutions and do overs, new beginnings. For me it was the start of my shift at 06:00. New Year's Day morning is usually very quiet because all the hell-raisers are already tucked in from a night of whooping it up. Since it's a holiday, most people are sleeping in and enjoying the day off. I have to say *most* because not *all* are sleeping in, there always has to be that one exception and today would be no different.

I had just gotten into my squad car after roll call. I usually had all my stuff in my squad prior to the start of my shift so I could pick out a good car and have it warmed up and ready to go. This also meant while other officers were picking out their cars and getting their gear into them and inspecting the equipment, I was already done and ready to go on calls. That was just how I had always done it and today my reward for being early and ready was a dispatch to a car/tree crash with unknown injuries on the west side. I activated my emergency lights and away I went.

I was kind of hoping this was going to be some minor fender bender where someone slipped on the icy roads and bumped a tree on the terrace. As I was coming down 11th Avenue where the crash was reported, my hopes of a minor crash faded immediately upon seeing the crash site. There was a debris field for two full front yards, a snapped off tree and a red Mitsubishi Eclipse with both sides caved in laying on someone's front lawn.

I remember getting out of my car. There was no sound, nothing. There was no one outside, no people, no dogs barking, nothing. It was a totally peaceful, quiet New Year's morning. I ran up to the car and looked inside. The driver, a male, was still in the driver's seat, unconscious and bleeding everywhere. The front seat passenger was a female, but she was no longer in the front seat; the front seat had been pushed into the back seat and so had she. She was also unconscious and bleeding everywhere. I called on the radio that rescue should pick it up as both patients were unconscious.

Officer Knapp arrived and got under the smoking hood to disconnect the battery; if it caught fire this situation would only get worse. Both occupants were trapped in the vehicle. Fire and rescue arrived and used the jaws of life to remove both people from the car. They were transported to the hospital, and I went with.

The driver smelled of intoxicants and even though unconscious, I read him the Informing the Accused paperwork, so they could do a blood draw on him. This is a very odd situation, reading to an unconscious man while doctors and nurses are working on him to save his life. There had to be at least a dozen people in the room and I was reading off of a piece of paper into a tape recorder. None of this would matter in the end because the male passed away right there in front of me. A twenty-five-year-old kid gone due to drunk driving. I said a prayer standing at his bedside.

I left the room and went to the female's room. She was now conscious but intoxicated. I did not tell her that her boyfriend was gone, I just couldn't. Officer Knapp was working the accident report as well as accident recon. My part was the OWI which didn't matter anymore, so my job was done here. It was now 08:00 New Year's Day. What a new beginning.

BEER PARTIES

Things were different for me growing up in the 1970's. The drinking age was eighteen. Sixteen and seventeen-year-old kids had fake ID cards. Back then they were paper with no photo so if you had an older sibling you just borrowed theirs to go buy whatever you wanted. It was pretty easy to do. This was back in the day when if you did get caught by the cops with alcohol, they took it away. I found out the cops would drink whatever they confiscated for the night after work. I don't know exactly how I feel about underage drinking, to me it's almost a rite of passage into adulthood. Maybe I think that way because that is how I grew up. As a cop it took a bit to get this mindset changed. I recall my first traffic stop with some young teenagers who had beer in the car. They were not drinking but were on their way to a party with a cold case of beer in the back seat. I confiscated the beer and let them go, no tickets no nothing. They must have thought Christmas had come early for them that year. I just didn't have it in me to write them tickets for having a few beers. That ideology would change in a quick hurry on my first call to a big underage beer party; when underage meant anyone under twenty-one-years-old. Throughout my career I went on a lot of underage party calls but there are two that stand out to me, my first and my last.

It was around 21:00 on a Saturday night when the call came in reporting there was a large underage party going on out on Nicolet Drive near the UWGB campus. Don't you often wonder how most of these parties get called in? Most times it is someone who was at the party, possibly even took part in the partying, and then had some falling out with someone. After leaving, they call it in. I am sure that was the case with this one.

I drove out to the area and parked about a half block away. Cops are trained never to park in front of the address where the call is and never to pull into the driveway. It is a safety thing as well as offering some element of surprise to our arrival on calls. This was an understatement on this particular call. As all the cops arrived on this call we had a row of squads parked out on the road, all blacked out. The house we had been called to was actually a small cottage down by the water. We had about six cops there surrounding the house. I looked in the window and could not believe my eyes. The place was basically a one room cabin, maybe twenty feet by twenty feet in size packed wall to wall with kids. All of them were drinking out of plastic cups with a keg in the middle of it all. We knocked on the door and someone let us in. It was mass confusion there for a little bit. Initially my thought was to break up the party and send them on their way. I think that was the thought for several other officers on the call, but the boss arrived and gave strict orders to issue every single kid, so we did.

The one good thing about this party was these kids were all over the age of eighteen which made them adults. We did not have to contact any parents about their drinking, just issue them a ticket, take their beer away, and send them on their way. We issued seventy-three tickets that night to some very unhappy, intoxicated, college kids. Not that we wanted to, but we had to, it was our job.

The last underage party call I ever went on was at a house on Gray Street. This party was also most likely called in by some unhappy kid who had already had his fill of alcohol and wanted to get his friends in trouble. This house was located near Velp Avenue with a Sure Way store nearby so as the squads arrived we all parked in the Sure Way Parking lot and walked up on the house. There were kids standing outside smoking in the garage and driveway. Were they surprised when they saw us coming out of the bushes alongside the house! A couple of the kids yelled, "cops!" loudly to warn the kids in the house we were there, but it was too late. Officer Alberts was already in the back of the house with a couple other cops and came in the patio door. We had a house full of kids again.

This call would be very different from any underage call I had ever been on. We had to sort these kids out. There were the eighteen-year-olds who would get issued a ticket and released. The seventeen-year-olds and under who would get issued a ticket and each parent would have to be contacted to come and pick up their child or would have to be given a ride home. Another thing that made this party in particular a little hard for me was that I knew one of the boys in attendance. I had sort of taken Andrew under my wing for a couple of years. He had been involved in a hit and run crash at West High a few years earlier and I had cut him a break on the crash. I knew his mother from previous calls, she was having a tough time raising this kid without a father.

Through our investigation we learned the boy hosting the party was left home by his parents for the weekend for the very first time. The parents went up north (a common weekend getaway destination in Wisconsin) and entrusted the older son who was seventeen-years-old to watch over his younger brother who was fifteen. The party was supposed to be a small get together that quickly got out of control. News was passed around West High that there was going to be a party at the house; the word travelled around to many kids who weren't on the guest list as well. This is pretty common when it comes to underage parties. The house was trashed, and there were beer cans everywhere. We were at the house for several hours because we had to wait for many of the parents to come and get their kids. I recall the seventeen-year-old host being very quiet. His words to me were "my parents are going to kill me." I could tell he had deep regret for letting his parents down.

Once things were under control and most of the kids had been picked up, I contacted Andrew's mom and told her I had Andrew. She did not have a car to come and get him, so I offered to bring him home to her, she agreed and gave me consent. He was intoxicated and not happy we had busted the party.

I dropped him off and was heading to headquarters when the dispatcher came over the air asking if any cops were still on scene at the party house. The 911 center had just received a call from the home that "shots had been fired". I turned my squad around and headed for the house. A couple of the other cops from the call were also on the way back there. When we arrived, we found the boy who had hosted the party had shot his head off with a shotgun in his parents' bedroom and the fifteen-year-old was inconsolable. I was shocked and dismayed that a child could think that getting busted for having a beer party was so bad that he would end his life. I also replayed that kid telling me that his "parents were going to kill him" over and over in my mind, wishing I would have been able to read his mind as to what he was thinking. Most of all wishing we had never snuck up on that house, but that is our job.

THE LADY IN THE ATTIC

I was dispatched to a report of a deceased forty-three-year-old lady found in the attic on S. Irwin Avenue, at 09:00 on a Saturday morning. Officer York was sent with me on this call. Even though the notes of the call said the lady was dead, rescue is always sent, just to make sure. This might sound odd, but what if the caller was incorrect and the person had just passed out or lost consciousness and needed medical help. Sending just a cop there and having the cop find out the person was still alive and then sending rescue would waste precious time in the event it really was a medical emergency. I responded red lights and siren and was the first responder on scene. I ran up to the house and found a male crying on the front porch. He told me she was dead upstairs in the attic bedroom. I ran up the stairs and into the room. He was correct she was dead. Rescue arrived a minute after me and officially confirmed she was dead. We called for the ME. Officer York arrived and we began our death scene investigation. Anytime a person is found dead, we do a death scene investigation. When it is a younger person there seems to be more suspicions of foul play.

I used to think an older person was sixty until I turned fifty. Now old seems more like eighty, so pretty much every scene I would go to was suspicious to me. As we started talking to the people this lady was living with about the events leading up to this morning it became clear something had gone awry here. She lived with three male friends she had known and been friends with for many years.

The previous evening, Friday night, they had been partying a bit and playing cards. "Partying a bit" to some people would mean something totally different to others, so when the friends said, "a bit," I needed a little clarification. As it turns out they had all been drinking with other friends at the home from 15:00 until around 22:00; seven hours of good, hard drinking and no dinner I might add. At around 22:00 she told one of the males she lived with that she wasn't feeling right, like she had a very bad headache. It was so bad they called a sober driver, (I give them credit for that) and brought her to the hospital. She said that her brain felt like it was going to explode.

She was seen at the ER and given some medication and sent home with instructions to call her primary physician on Monday if her headache hadn't gone away. I found the discharge instructions and that was exactly accurate. After arriving back home, she took the medication and laid down in the attic bedroom, the quietest place in the home. Her friends continued to party on into the wee hours of the morning and then finally passed out.

When the first one awoke at 09:00, he went up to check on her and she was deceased. I thought to myself, who knows what really happened that night since everyone there was intoxicated. We did locate the sober driver who took them to the hospital. He said she was in real bad pain and kept saying her head was hurting badly. The driver said he only picked them up, took them to the hospital, took them back home and then left. The ME arrived, and I assisted in taking photographs. One of the things cops never do is move the body until the ME arrives; then we are witnesses to what might turn up once he moves the body. She could have fallen on a knife that was still sticking into her which would only be seen after the body was rolled over. That was not the case here, when she was rolled over, she just looked dead.

I told the ME this call really bothered me because of her medical complaint the night before; certainly, this had something to do with her death. He told me he would let me know. The funeral home employees arrived and zipped her into a body bag and hauled her out. I went on to the next call. I didn't know until about a week later when I received a call from the ME that her cause of death was a brain aneurysm. I guess the hospital staff missed this one. The moral of this story is if you truly believe something is wrong, it probably is.

TOWER DRIVE BRIDGE –
THE LEO FRIGO

The Tower Drive Bridge has been the scene of many events over the years. In 1991, prior to the time I started with the department, there was a horrific crash involving thirty cars and trucks which killed several people and injured many more. Back then I could never understand how something that terrible could have happened. I understand it now. There are things about that bridge the general citizen doesn't know. Most people do not have the opportunity to be out of their car and standing on the concrete of the bridge; I have done it many times. By design the bridge is constantly swinging back and forth, as well as moving up and down. Both are ever so slightly, you would not realize this as a motorist driving over it at sixty-five miles per hour. As an officer I can tell you it is very noticeable and to be honest a little bit freakish. The idea of standing on solid concrete and having it moving in all directions can be a little unnerving. I can only compare it to vertigo or seasickness, that awkward feeling of having nothing stable and a constant feeling of motion.

The other thing I have seen firsthand is that the bridge freezes very quickly. One minute it can be wet and the next it just appears wet but is actually a sheet of ice. I can recall being up there on a winter day when the conditions changed over to ice. I was traveling northbound and had just gotten onto the bridge from Webster Avenue. I immediately turned on my flashers and emergency lights and reduced my speed to a crawl to warn those behind me to slow down. I moved into the middle of the bridge to take up both lanes. If only the people behind me would have been paying attention, but they weren't.

In my rearview mirror, I saw one vehicle rear-end another vehicle and two more vehicles smash into the center wall to avoid hitting the first crash. I called out to headquarters to get some help up to me, but once on the bridge you have to get to the other side before getting off and getting back on at Atkinson Drive. I again traveled slowly with my emergency lights on as I already knew the concrete was a solid sheet of ice. By the time I was back over there were two more crashes in the northbound lanes. I had already called for salt trucks but when the conditions are windy, salt doesn't really do much to improve conditions before getting blown off the roadway. Other units were on the way as I made my way to the turnaround just south of Webster Avenue. I had to get the northbound lanes closed off before more crashes occurred.

I had just pulled into the turn around when someone was exiting from northbound I-43 onto the Webster Avenue exit and struck the guard rail spinning in circles onto the ramp. Now every available means of diverting traffic was closed. I had to call for units to shut down northbound I-43 up at Sturgeon Bay Road and divert all traffic to get onto University Avenue. I left my car on I-43 at N. Webster Avenue, put on my traffic vest, and began to walk to the closest vehicle. When I stepped onto the concrete, I was barely able to stand; it literally was a solid sheet of ice. That is how bad that bridge gets, looks can be very deceiving. Needless to say, the bridge was closed in both directions for several hours while rescue crews worked on the injured, tow trucks worked on the smashed vehicles and road crews worked on getting the ice off the highway.

This bridge is also known as a means for people to end of their lives. People have been jumping off the top of this bridge for years. It didn't get famous for its suicidal deaths until Trooper Bolt was chasing a lady in a vehicle who had threatened suicide. The chase ended at the top of the bridge when the lady got out of her car to jump. He sprinted from his cruiser and caught her by her wrist just as she took the plunge over the side. She literally disappeared from sight and then Trooper Bolt pulled her back over. The whole thing was caught on his dash cam in his squad car. The story made national news and Trooper Bolt ended up on several high-profile talk shows. He received many awards and medals for his bravery. The other thing this did was glorify the jumping off the bridge as a way to end life. Trooper Bolt killed himself this year which came as a total shock to Wisconsin law enforcement. You never know what is going on inside a person's mind.

The crisis center has put signs with their telephone number on both crests of the bridge in an attempt to get people standing on the edge to call them on their cellphones. I highly doubt that someone who is ready to kill them self is going to see a sign and think, *wait, I can call this number from here and get counseling.* I applaud their efforts, but if someone is really at that point, they are going over. I often thought placing a large net like you see at the circus to catch the man they shoot out of a cannon would have done something to help. Most of the jumpers jump from the peak areas, so it's a very specific area. I am not sure how the person would then be retrieved from the net, but at least they would be alive. The number of people jumping from that bridge has increased yearly and the end result is almost assured death.

Sometimes the bodies would not be recovered immediately due to the currents and weather conditions.

I was dispatched to The Green Bay Yacht Club one beautiful sunny day for a report that a fisherman had snagged what he thought was a large black garbage bag. Once he pulled it closer to him he realized it was actually a bloated body. When I arrived, he had the body pulled up against the rocks, where I took over with a stick and held the body there until the firemen and coroner arrived to pull the body out. She was later identified as a person who had been missing for several months.

I also worked a call where a male had driven his pickup truck onto the bridge and the witness behind him said the male just got out of his truck and did a superman jump, arms out in front like he was going to just fly away. He didn't of course, and I had to locate him with other officers under the bridge. He did not make it to the water and had died landing on one of the concrete footings. The sight was pretty graphic.

Not all those who jump succeed in their endeavor. One day as we were coming on duty, it was reported to me and the other east side units that around 03:00 a male's vehicle had been found on the top of the bridge with a suicide note inside. He was not located during a search of the water and area below. It was possible that someone had picked him up or he called someone to come and get him, but probably not. At about 08:00 the 911 center got a call reporting that a male in his underwear was walking on N. Quincy St. I responded to that location and there he was, the male who jumped off the bridge and lived. His clothes had been torn off on impact and he then swam to shore where he laid on the riverbank and passed out. When he regained consciousness, he walked to the roadway where I picked him up. Aside from a few bruises, physically this guy was alright. I took him to The Brown County Community Treatment Center where I hope he received the help he needed. Most people who make that jump don't get a second chance.

The bridge has also had its share of animal calls from little baby ducks and goslings walking into traffic to dogs and deer running on the bridge. All of these sound so cute and harmless but they are actually very dangerous situations. The driver's natural reaction is to swerve to avoid hitting any kind of animal but doing this could have serious effects on the driver's ability to control his car. It also causes many traffic crashes and at the speed limit of sixty-five miles per hour these harmless little animals can cause some pretty serious wrecks. I recall working at the time Officer Knapp and Animal Control Officer Henry chased a dog back and forth on the bridge and the surrounding areas for about an hour. In the end Officer Knapp shot the dog which caused a huge media blow up. I guess sometimes you're damned if you do and damned if you don't. In this case Officer Knapp weighed out the greater danger and shot the dog. Many people questioned this decision. But from a safety standpoint, if that dog would have caused a multi-car crash and killed a family of five, people would have questioned, "why didn't the officer just shoot the dog before it caused this crash?" It's easy to be an armchair quarterback.

  I made my own blunder one time while working in this area. I was dispatched to a report of a car-deer crash in the area between University Ave and N. Webster Ave. It was about 21:00 and the highway is pitch black out there. When I arrived on scene I spoke with the driver of the vehicle who told me the deer had come from the north, jumped right in front of his car, and then flipped into the median. I imagine this was one of the deer that had gotten out of the sanctuary area. I walked into the median and there it was, a large deer with an enormous rack; he had snapped off a rear leg and his eyes were glazed over. I went back to the driver of the vehicle and completed the crash report. The driver asked if he could saw off the deer horns to bring home to his son. I thought, *sure why not, it's only going to lay there and rot anyway.* I told the guy to do it quickly and I stood by with my emergency lights on. He sawed off the rack and left the area. I had already called in to have the deer picked up. The next day they would load it up and take it away, or so I thought. I got off the highway and went down to a parking lot to complete my paperwork and report. It was nearing the end of my shift and it was always nice to be caught up before the end of the day. I slowly made my way back to headquarters when I heard a call go out to the late shifters of a report of a deer on the Tower Drive Bridge that was limping around on three legs and had its rack cut off. I never ever let a deer lay in the ditch again without giving it a bullet to the head.

THE HOMELESS

Somehow Green Bay turned into a melting pot for the homeless. I think because it is located just a few hundred miles north of two major cities, Milwaukee and Chicago. The cost of living is cheap and the services available to the less fortunate are many. Working the downtown district and inner city gave me much exposure to the homeless. Our homeless community started out years ago in very small numbers. Several shelters were available to those who were less fortunate. Over time word got out and homeless people from around the county flocked to Green Bay for the easy life. Originally the homeless shelter on N. Broadway housed most of the population. This particular shelter took in everyone except the drunks. One of their rules was that you could not enter the shelter if you were intoxicated. This meant the habitual drunks slept in the streets, bushes, garages, vacant houses, wherever they could find a place to lay their heads down for the night and not be discovered by the police.

The first homeless person I dealt with was a male nicknamed "Rooster." He was a veteran with a serious drinking problem. He had nowhere to live and carried his belongings around in the pockets of his Army jacket. He could be seen walking the streets day and night, hanging out in parks or sitting on a street bench. He is one of the only people I can recall who could blow a .50 on a PBT and still be walking and talking. I never had a problem with him. I knew that somewhere behind that weathered face, stringy hair and crystal blue eyes was a man who had fought for our freedom and payed a heavy price, even becoming an alcoholic to deal with what those eyes had seen. Although Green Bay offered much to the less fortunate, it did not treat or deal with alcoholics at all. In years past we had a thing called an alcohol hold. This was similar to what some people call the drunk tank. When the drunks were located and incapacitated, we would scoop them up and transport them to the old Brown County Mental Health facility. It was a pit of a place built in the 1960's and had not ever been updated. At least it offered a roof over their heads and a hot meal. A drunk would be brought out there and held until their alcohol level came down, then they were released, and the process started all over again; they would get drunk and we would find them laying somewhere and take them back out to Brown County. Many times, I would deal with the same person over and over again, sometimes three times in one week. It was a vicious circle then and still is.

I grew up with a girl, Kerri Smits, who lived a few blocks down from me as a kid. We rode the same bus to school and I knew her entire family. Kerri's problems started in high school when she got into drugs and not the recreational marijuana that was prevalent in the 1970's. Kerri got into the heavy stuff like LSD. I lost touch with her once she dropped out of school in her freshman year and had a child. I didn't have contact with her again until I became a police officer. She was so fried that she did not even remember me. I saw her almost daily walking the streets; she was homeless. I learned that she had five kids, all of whom had been taken away from her. Kerri was a really bad drunk and had brain damage as a result of all the drugs. She was a handful to deal with, belligerent and out of control. Most often she had either wet her or shit her pants and had sat in it for days. I recall one time at the 4th of July fireworks celebration with thousands of people and children around, she pulled down her pants and urinated in the grassy area near the museum with hundreds of onlookers. She was the same age I was but looked about twenty years older than me. Life on the streets had definitely taken its toll on what was once a very pretty woman.

My favorite homeless person was Tom Larock. He was also someone I had known from high school. He was a friend of my sister who I had gotten to know in the 1970's. He was not a druggy, he was a drinker. He was a hard-core drinker from the time he was a young person. When I made contact with him as an officer he remembered me. He was usually good with me unless he was really intoxicated, then he would give me trouble just like the rest of them. I knew it was the alcohol and always tried to help him when I could. Whenever he saw me driving around the beat, he would flag me down and talk to me. I would always make sure he had something to eat and many times would take him into a gas station to pick up some coffee and some snacks to put in his pockets for later. I couldn't give him money because he would use it to buy more alcohol. I did what I could for him.

I could not have been prouder of him when he gave up drinking and got a job. He had cleaned up his act, cut his hair and it appeared he was going to make it out of this crazy life of homelessness. It was short lived, about a year. I got the call of a male passed out in front of the court house. When I arrived, there was a male face down on the concrete. When I rolled him over, I found Tom Larock, drunker than Cooter Brown. I won't say I wasn't a bit disappointed, because I was. I actually thought he had it licked. He didn't and the last I saw him he was at Whitney Park sitting at a picnic table, living on the streets.

Chet Zanders was another of our *frequent flyers*. This was what we called those we had frequent contact with. His story was very interesting. He was another drunk. He came from a wealthy family who lived in Ashwaubenon. Chet was younger than most, good looking and smart. The only thing he didn't have was the word *stop* in his vocabulary when it came to alcohol. It was not uncommon for him to drink an entire bottle of vodka, and not the little bottle, the liter bottle. Most of these guys could and did drink on a daily basis. Not long ago, Chet was intoxicated and walked out in front of a vehicle that was traveling twenty-five miles per hour on Walnut Street and was seriously injured. The crash was worked as a fatality, but as all good drunks do, he pulled though. That is sort of an interesting paradox for cops, the drunk ones survive, and the sober ones die.

As the years went on, Brown County built a new psychiatric facility and did away with alcohol holds so the chronic alcoholics could not go there anymore. The New Community Shelter built a brand-new three-story building but did not allow anyone in who had been drinking, so they couldn't go there either. Things got really rough for the drinkers. They were sleeping wherever they could and the number of calls for them being in places they didn't belong rose tremendously. Many times, we had nowhere to go with them. If they offered the criteria for disorderly conduct, most of them *were* disorderly because they were so drunk, we would take them to jail for the charge. This became quite common and they called it "three hots and a cot."

Finally, the Catholic Diocese stepped up and opened St. John's Homeless Shelter. It was a converted gymnasium that offered a place for intoxicated people to go. The only way the city would approve this facility was if it was temporary, so it had restrictions. It opened on November first and closed on March thirty-first with limited nighttime hours from 17:00 to 07:00 daily. Intoxicated homeless people could go there anytime throughout the night and would not be turned away. One would think this type of open door policy would create many police calls for belligerent drunks, but it was actually quite the opposite. I think they knew this was the only place they had to go to avoid freezing to death and survive the nights the temperatures fell below zero. When the homeless people would get sent out every morning they would start their pilgrimage to the Brown County Library.

The library was about seven blocks away and didn't open until 09:00. A Marathon gas station was on the way and the Monroe Shell station was nearby. This was a good stop off for coffee or to stay warm until the library opened. Once the library opened, they had free reign for the entire day; it was a public library and could not discriminate who was there. The library offered warmth, toilet facilities, comfortable chairs, reading materials and computers with internet access. Those who smoked could go outside and have a cigarette and then come back inside. I did get reports of homeless people in the restrooms washing their hair in the sinks and once I found hypodermic needles in one of the stalls. This had definitely turned into a place where you would not allow your children alone.

One of my most interesting calls at the library dealing with the homeless was the report of missing bottles of hand sanitizer. Dozens of quart sized bottles of sanitizer that had been placed around the library had gone missing. As the days went on and contacts were made with homeless subjects, guess what was located. The hand sanitizer. It wasn't being used for their hands and cleanliness. They were drinking it because of the alcohol content. That's desperation.

OFC. SUSAN BICKETT

YES MA'AM

COWBOY

There are certain people in your career who you just connect with and that are like you in many ways. It is a special connection that is made without saying a word; the knowing what that person is going to say or how they will react, because it is the same way you would. I started in the communication center with Tim Rivard. We were both dispatchers and we both made it out on the road as cops. The only difference between Rivard and me is that he is a guy about twice my size. We both shared the same kind of cop mentality, to take care of people. He wasn't that macho cop that comes in the door and tries to flex his muscles and belittle the less fortunate or the less intelligent. We had the same motto, *treat people how you would want to be treated.* And as cops we spoke the same, say what you mean and mean what you say. In other words when you tell someone if they don't stop what they are doing they are going to jail, if they don't stop then you take them to jail. If you tell someone they are going to get a ticket, then you give them a ticket. The thing about Rivard and me is that we shared a bond that went way back, and we were both true to our word. Rivard and I had the same kind of humor, an odd sort of twisted kind of humor that most people wouldn't understand, but we did and that always made working with him a little easier.

Back in the Radio Room and then out on the road we had a code word for when someone was feeding us a line of bullshit, *banana.* It was short for "I'm not going to fall for the banana in the tail pipe." A movie one-liner from *Beverly Hills Cop* with Eddie Murphy. Anytime we were on a call together and were getting the story from those involved, if it got to the point where we knew we were being lied to, one of us would slip in the word banana, our own special code for bullshit. This actually did help in dealing with people obstructing us. Once the banana came out, we would stop them from talking and question their lies or have them start the story over. A liar can't tell the story the same way twice because it is a lie, if it were the truth it would be the same. It was a good tactic and always put a little smirk on my face, and his too.

Rivard and I earned our nicknames for each other on a call on James Street early on in our career. We responded to a highly intoxicated male lying in an alley behind the homes. When we arrived, we found the male. He was definitely drunk, but a funny drunk. Most drunks you deal with are ornery and can be real jerks but believe it or not there are some happy drunks out there and this guy was one of them. I am not saying he was easy to deal with, because he wasn't, but at least he found humor in the situation he had gotten himself into. He had peed his pants and could not stand up. He did try standing by himself several times, but we had to finally stop him before he hurt himself. Rivard and I were deciding what we were going to do with this guy.

The first option was calling a friend or relative to come and get him, so we didn't have to put him in one of our cars, that is always option one. We were trying to identify him, but he could not get his wallet out of his pocket so Rivard put gloves on, rolled him over, and took out his urine soaked, brown leather wallet and found his ID card. Once we knew he wasn't wanted on any warrants we tried to get a name or phone number from him of someone we could call to come and get him.

The guy sat there on the ground and looked to be trying to think of someone, so we let him for a minute. He finally looked at Rivard and blurted out, "you know what? You're a cowboy and she is a big mama." What? We cracked up and our nicknames stuck with us for the rest of our careers. The guy ended up going to Brown County on an alcohol hold, but he sure gave us some cute names. Thanks, drunk, funny guy.

Rivard and I were working the northeast side district over by Harvey Street when we got a call that a child had just been taken from a residence. This usually means one of the parents took the child without permission or in violation of the court order. I responded to the call and Rivard showed up within minutes. I met with the hysterical mother who reported her crazy ex-boyfriend, who was not the child's father, had just taken her child and was taking him to Milwaukee. The mother was frantic because she said the male was unstable and could possibly hurt the child. I quickly conferred with Rivard and our gut instinct was to call the shift commander and put out an Amber Alert. This was something new for law enforcement and definitely a first for out department. I just had that Spidey feeling about this call and I didn't want to find out later that our failure to act caused harm to a two-year-old child.

We put out the Amber Alert. I took a long statement from the woman about how her relationship with the male had been abusive and when she broke it off he began to stalk her. When she reported the situation, he continually got worse mentally about the broken relationship. After taking her statement I was glad we did what we did, this guy was bonkers. The State Patrol stopped the vehicle and the baby was recovered without injury. The bad guy went to jail on child abduction charges and Rivard and I received a commendation from the Wisconsin Attorney General for our quick thinking and the safe return of the child. That was a good day!

Rivard and I had some bad days too. One in particular that comes to mind happened in the alley by Job Corp downtown off of Pine Street. We responded to a call of a male who appeared homeless acting strange. He had previously been at Whitney Park and the caller observed him talking to himself and what was described as "scaring the children" in the park. We located him just north of the park in the alley. He was carrying a large brown paper bag and did in fact appear to be a homeless person.

I got out of my car and Rivard got out of his. We started questioning the guy who seemed a bit out of it, but that is the norm for many homeless people because they have usually been drinking. There was something a little bit off about this guy, but I couldn't put my finger on it right away and neither could Rivard. I had the guy put his bag down by his feet and Rivard asked him for his identification. The guy started rooting around in his bag for his ID, or so we thought. He finally pulled out an ID and handed it to Rivard. Rivard went back to his car to run the name. I tried talking to the guy about what he was doing in the park, but he wasn't very forthcoming with any answers, another clue this guy wasn't right. Rivard got out of his car and gave me the crossed arms sign which meant to handcuff him.

When we both moved in to cuff him he started going into his bag for something. We took him down to the ground in one swift move. He resisted us, continuing to try to get something from his bag. We got him cuffed and put him in the back of Rivard's car. We went back to the bag, that's when we found he had two taser guns in his bag, one for each of us. This call could have ended a whole lot differently than it did; we were both thankful that it didn't. Complacency kills, and this was a good reminder, Cowboy.

No summer was complete without the infamous Fourth of July inverse. It really didn't matter how much seniority you acquired, if you were not fortunate enough to get this day off as a vacation pick it was inevitable that you would be forced to work Independence Day. It was dreaded by most, except for those who thought money was more important than family, those cops loved it. Rivard and I did not fall into the latter of the two categorizes. It was a horrible time of the summer for us. Our day would start out at 04:30 when you rolled out of bed and reported for your shift at 06:15. July fourth is a hot time of the summer and the uniform and equipment made for a long, hot day.

We would put in our entire shift of chasing calls all day long until our shift ended at 14:45. We would get a one-hour unpaid break that most of us used to change out of our sweat soaked uniform and into a clean one and grab a quick bite to eat. Then we had to report to the police garage at 16:00 for the Special Event roll call. This is where we would get our updated assignments although most of us already knew we would be on a walking team in a crowd of thousands of people, most of who were intoxicated. I was teamed up with Rivard which was the only good thing about the whole stinking day.

At least we could commiserate together while our families were having their cookouts and social events without us. The afternoon and evening were spent breaking up fights, dealing with highly intoxicated people and making arrests right up till the end of the evening. It would be fair to say this was worse than working a Packer game because of the fact that people attending the fireworks display didn't pay hundreds of dollars to be there and didn't have anything to lose; Packer fans would lose their tickets for misbehaving. This was definitely the worst of the worst when it came to the unruly crowds. The later the evening went on the worse the crowd would get due to the amount of alcohol. It was definitely my most hated holiday ever. The worst part of the whole thing was knowing that when you finished your shift at midnight, you had to be up again at 04:30 and put in another shift, dog tired, but with the expectation of being at the top of your game.

Who can do that?

COVER

I have had many people ask throughout my career if I am alone in my squad. The answer is yes, Green Bay has one-man squads. Our policy, however is that two cops are dispatched on each call where there is a possibility of danger or confrontation, which nowadays is every call. It's called cover, this is where one cop runs the call and the other looks out for the cop running the call and assists with anything that needs to be done on the call. If the call needs more cops, then you call for more cops. Sometimes you call off your cover, even though you're not supposed to. I will admit to doing this a couple of times, not because of staffing concerns but because the guys were assholes. There are certain guys you knew if you went on calls with them you would end up in Internal Affairs. I learned early in my career, not all cops are looking out for their partners. Some have their own agenda that is not for the betterment of the department.

    I went on a runaway call with Officer Howell during my first couple of months on the job. The girl had returned home after being gone from home for several days. The mother was calling to report the girl was acting up and wouldn't listen to her mother. When I arrived at the call, Officer Howell was already there. He was one of those cops who had what we called the *little man's disease*. This is a cop with a small stature who thinks he has to be a tough guy to prove he can keep up with the macho cops. On most of his calls, he was a jerk to people to prove he is the big tough cop.

I walked into the home and he was already giving this girl a tongue lashing about disrespecting her mother and how she was a spoiled brat; which I am sure was probably true, but it is the way he went about things that was wrong. When the girl rolled her eyes at him, he shocked me and the girl, by pinning her up against the wall by the neck. I honestly could not believe this. He told her, "don't you ever roll your eyes at me, little girl, or you'll go to jail." All I could think was, *dang this is going to go to Internal Affairs. Have some control!* I got off that call as soon as possible. He was one of the guys I would always cancel as my cover.

I was sent up on Sturgeon Bay Road, also known as Highway 57 on the far east side for a report of a male hitchhiker on the highway. Hitchhiking is illegal. I was sent alone for some reason. Looking back, I probably should have asked for a cover right away, but I didn't and thought, *I will go talk to the guy and get him on his way.* I pulled up by him and instantly sensed some apprehension in talking with him. He had a large backpack and when I asked him for his identification, he told me he didn't have any.

This is one of the biggest clues ever that this person will be a problem. In this day and age, who doesn't have identification? You can't do anything without it, everyone has an ID. He gave me a name that did not come back on file. I wasn't surprised. I asked for a cover car right away. I continued to make small talk with the guy, waiting for my cover car before questioning his identity any further, he was obviously hiding something from me. My cover was Officer Lewinski and was coming from the station. Maybe ten minutes in traffic at the most. Ten minutes turned into fifteen and I was still waiting.

I had a very uncomfortable feeling about this guy and now our conversation was almost awkward as I continued to stall. I asked over the radio if Lewinski was on the way and he said he was a few minutes out. I decided to start with my line of questioning about this guy's identification, certain that Lewinski would be pulling up any minute. I told the guy his name did not come back through our system and that I needed to recheck the information he had given me. He gave it back to me again, except this time with a different date of birth. I did not let on that he had changed his date of birth and re-ran him again. This time, something hit on the teletype end and I was told there was a near hit on the name. A near hit is when the information given is close to information given on a warrant, like an alias name or alias date of birth. Still, no Lewinski.

The warrant was for felony escape from out of state. When I heard this the hair on the back of my neck stood up and I thought *damn it, Lewinski! Where the fuck are you?* I had to keep pushing on with this guy. I finally told him that I knew he was wanted and to my surprise he admitted he gave me a false name for that reason. I'm standing on the side of the highway way out in the boonies with this felony bad guy; I know he is wanted and so does he. Taking someone into custody alone is never a good idea, there are too many things that can happen. A sudden assault, a hidden weapon, who knows with a person who knows he is going back to prison. He has nothing to lose and everything to gain by trying to hurt me and get away. I had no choice. I stood a short distance from him and told him to kneel down, he did. I told him to place his hands behind his back and he did. I took him into custody alone and brought him to my squad car. Luckily this guy was cooperative with me, but what if he hadn't been? I confirmed the warrant and transported him to jail.

Lewinski never did show up on this call. From that day on, I always cancelled him as my cover and would send a message to another unit nearby to cover me. I never looked at either Officer Howell or Officer Lewinski in the same way after these events. They were both the same, assholes.

PUT YOUR GUNS AWAY

Our department is a seniority-based department. It always has been. I'm not sure that is the best way to run an organization, but that is just the way it is. It doesn't really offer any advancement by merit, or who is most qualified for the position, but by who puts in the most time. Seniority plays a role on patrol as well. If there is not a supervisor on the call, the most senior officer is in charge, no matter what. This usually doesn't come into play very often, but if and when it does, this is the department policy and the rules we must follow. I only had this happen once in my career and once was enough.

I was sent on a call with Officer York; both of us were seasoned veterans in the department. The call was a report of a male who had felony warrants and an active restraining order; he was outside the home of a female victim. The male's name was given and a brief clothing description. While I was en route to the call, I looked up a mugshot of the male. I pulled up toward the address and saw a male matching the description given, a white male wearing a dark jacket, trying to enter a back door of the residence the female was calling from.

I got out of my car and pulled out my gun. I pointed it at him and told him to get his hands in the air. Officer York had arrived, and he too had his gun on the male. The male was now stuffing something down his pants. I don't know what it was; it could have been a gun, drugs, we will never know. As I called the male off the porch and toward us, I could see it was not the male in the mugshot. What was he doing in the area? Why was he trying to get into the home? What did he stuff down his pants? I wasn't taking any chances with this guy, he seemed shifty and my six senses were high.

That is when Officer Edmund came storming up on the call. This guy was a seasoned veteran as well and was far more senior than either of us on the call. He had spent the last number of years in detectives. He had come back to be a dog handler and was now the most senior cop on day shift patrol. He yelled at both Officer York and me to put our guns away. Sadly, we did because of a direct order from a senior officer, stupid! Officer Edmund took over the call. He asked this guy for an ID, took down the information, and let him go. I will never forget watching this guy leave the call at a full run. He jumped over a fence and was gone.

I later learned the guy Edmund let go was wanted on a couple of serious felony warrants. What really pissed me off is that he made us look like dumb ass cops and he jeopardized our safety by exercising his authority of being a senior at our expense. I did report this to Internal Affairs; he got a slap on the hand for it. I would never look at this guy the same way again. Don't come on my call and take over when you don't know what the hell is going on, jack donkey.

TRAFFIC STOPS

I always described traffic stops to a new officer as going fishing. You throw out your line and you never know what you're going to pull in. A traffic stop could start as a headlight out, a taillight out, expired registration, and it could turn into an axe murderer from Louisiana with a pound of weed in the back seat and bodies in the trunk. Or, it could just be a soccer mom. You really do not know who the person driving that car is, or what they are hiding from you until you make that stop. Traffic stops are probably the most dangerous thing a cop can do because of all of the unknowns. The driver is in their car and knows what is in that car, but the officer doesn't.

Early in my career, I loved these fishing expeditions. You never know what kind of fish you're going to pull in, so I did a lot of them. When I say a lot, I mean everyday as many as I could when I wasn't on calls. I tried to get my zone partners to play the game with me. If it was a slow night, we would see how many stops we could make and who could get the biggest bust. We did not have quotas as some people thought we did. I always looked at it as the public is paying our salary. If we are not on calls, then we should be doing something besides sitting at a gas station waiting for the next call. My zone partner for many years on the west side was Officer Seroogy. We started on patrol within a year of each other, she was senior to me, but always treated me as an equal. We spent many nights competing to see who could get that big stop.

One night, she called out with a traffic stop and I could tell just by her voice on the radio, she thought this one was something big. That is something that you get to know about your fellow cops, their tone on the radio. Most people listening on a scanner would not catch this change in a voice, but the dispatchers and fellow cops do all the time. This night, I caught it and I hurried over to cover her as fast I possibly could drive within the legal speed limits. Sometimes even though cops can't really exceed the speed limits unless it is a true emergency, they do put a little pepper on it to cover. I guess you could call it cop's intuition.

I picked up the pace and got there as quickly as I could. This would be one of those calls where you throw out your line and pull in the record bass. It was 20:00 on a Friday night. Officer Seroogy had a car pulled over for a headlight out, always such an easy stop. I have no idea why criminals continue to do this and think they are not going to get stopped for it, it's just too easy. This was a black four-door Chevy Impala sedan. When an officer does a traffic stop, they pick the spot they want to pull you over to avoid danger to themselves and the public. When a cop puts his reds on and hits his siren, that is where he wants you to pull over; not down the block and onto a dimly lit side road out of sight. That is what this guy did, hence the reason when Officer Seroogy called with it, her voice was elevated.

When I arrived Officer Seroogy was already up at the passenger window, this is another indicator to me that she thought something was suspicious about this stop; most often cops do a driver's side approach. I pulled up and went up to the car immediately. Since she was on the passenger side, I came up on the driver's. I did not have my flash light lit as I was walking up to the car. If the occupants wanted to shoot me, there I would be lit up like a target. When I got to the driver's side rear door, I hit my flashlight on the rear passenger. Imagine my surprise to see he had a gun between his legs, with his right hand on it. I pulled out my gun and pointed it directly at the guy and yelled, "don't you fucking move" and yelled, "gun" to Officer Seroogy, who already had her gun out.

I called for more units since there were four of them and two of us. We got the gun toting guy out of the back seat with the loaded .45. I am pretty sure his intentions were to shoot Officer Seroogy because she was about to locate their stash of drugs. After it was all said and done, she pulled two guns out of that car, one guy with a felony warrant, and a couple pounds of marijuana. That's a pretty nice haul for a headlight out. It was nice fishing with you partner.

GONE TOO SOON

One of my favorite lieutenants was Lieutenant Johnny Taylor. This guy was full military and could be very intimidating looking but deep down this guy was butter to the core. He was not a man of many words but when he did say something, you stood up and took note of it. He was most noted for standing at the podium to give roll call and tugging at his ear, a nervous habit. He would be giving the briefings and if someone in the back or the roll call room was talking when he was, he would stop and give the evil eye to the guy until he shut up. Rivard and I often joked around about this, it was as if he was saying, "shut the fuck up or I will shoot your kneecaps off."

One night, Lt. Taylor was working as the radio room lieutenant. He got up to go to the bathroom and Rivard thought it would be funny to send out an all car message from the Lt.'s computer that read, *bring me a black coffee*. After he did this, every squad on the road brought in a coffee. I am not too sure Lt. Taylor thought it was funny, but we thought it was hilarious. This guy would go to bat for you and stand behind you on your calls, just an all-around good old boy. There sure are not many men like that man. He retired from the department and died of lung cancer a few years after his retirement. He did not even get to enjoy his retirement.

But the real kicker regarding guys retiring and not getting to enjoy it was Captain Hull. I have to be honest, the guy was not the Captain I liked most. But, I respected him because of his rank and I obeyed him for the same reason. He was one of those guys who really didn't care what you thought, I call that a *my way or the highway kind of guy*. It really didn't matter what your opinion was on any given topic, Captain already has his mind made up on his way and that was that, no room for discussion. This was a common management style in our department for many years before and for many years to follow. I was never a big fan of it because it is a true moral killer. For any managers reading this book, when you kill the moral, you lose the troops. That would happen to me later in my career.

Captain Hull put in over thirty years. He worked all the Packer games and took all kinds of extra overtime to beef up his pension. Our pension for the department is calculated on the three highest years of service, so getting big dollar years is always a goal for officers. Not all officers, but many. There are some things money can't buy, like time with your family and friends, you can never get that back, ever. The Captain retired and died of a massive heart attack within the first month of retirement. I heard he didn't even get his first retirement check. Now that is sad.

I remember standing at attention at his funeral all dressed up in my dress uniform and white gloves with tears rolling down my cheeks. That was the only time I cried in my uniform. It was just so incredibly sad to think the man worked his whole life to finally be able to enjoy his family and do things other than police work; and it was cut short just like that. I bring this up as some good advice to those who think working all kinds of overtime is the answer to your life. Think about this story, you certainly can't take it with you.

CHILI

One of my all-time favorite Officers was Officer Shelly. He was a mountain of a man and a jolly old fellow. In an ass kicking contest you definitely wanted him on your side. When the stakes were high, and things were getting out of hand at a disturbance or on a belligerent drunk call, this was the guy you wanted to come and back you up. Just his mere presence dictated respect and compliance. But there was another side to him; he was so damn funny.

He had a sense of humor and would say something straight faced, when you finally realized he was jerking your chain, he would bust up laughing. I had the pleasure of working with him on a special assignment dealing with some cold cases. As tedious and boring as the work was, I swear I never laughed so much as I did in those three months. It would only be fitting that I share what I think is one of the most humorous jokes he ever gave me. Thanks for the laughter Shelly!

Texas Chili Cook Off
(Notes from an inexperienced Chili Taster from the East Coast named Frank)
   Recently I was honored to be selected as a celebrity judge at a Chili Cook-off in Texas because no one else wanted to do it. The original person called in sick at the last minute and I happened to be standing at the judge's table asking for directions to the beer wagon when the call came. I was assured by the other judges (native Texans) that the chili wouldn't be all that spicy, and besides, they told me I could have free beer during the tasting. So, I accepted.

Here are the scorecards from the event:

Chili #1 Mike's Manic Monster Chili
Judge One: A little too heavy on the tomato. Amusing kick.
Judge Two: Nice, smooth tomato flavor. Very mild.
Frank: Holy Shit, what the hell is this stuff? You could remove dried paint from your driveway with this stuff. I needed two beers to put the flames out. Hope that's the worst one. Those Texans are crazy.

Chili #2 Arthur's Afterburner Chili
Judge One: Smokey, with a hint of pork. Slight jalapeno tang.
Judge Two: Exciting BBQ flavor. Need more peppers to be taken seriously.
Frank: Keep this out of reach of children! I'm not sure what I as supposed to taste besides pain. I had to wave off two people who wanted to give me the Heimlich maneuver. They had to walkie-talkie in three extra beers when they saw the look on my face.

YES MA'AM

Chili #3 Fred's Famous Burn Down the Barn Chili
Judge One: Excellent firehouse chili. Great kick. Needs more beans.
Judge Two: A beanless chili. A bit salty. Good use of peppers.
Frank: Call the EPA, I've located a uranium spill. My nose feels like I have been snorting Drano. Everyone knows the routine by now. Barmaid pounded me on the back, now my backbone is in the front part of my chest. I'm getting shit faced.

Chili #4 Bubba's Black Magic Chili
Judge One: Black Bean chili with almost no spice. Disappointing
Judge Two: Hint of lime in black beans. Good side dish for fish or other mild foods. Not much of a chili.
Frank: I felt something scraping across my tongue but was unable to taste it. Sally, the barmaid, was standing behind me with fresh refills, that three-hundred-pound bitch is starting to look *hot,* just like this nuclear-waste I'm eating.

Chili #5 Vera's Very Vegetarian Variety
Judge One: Thin yet bold vegetarian variety chili. Good balance of spice and peppers.
Judge Two: Aggressive use of peppers, onion and garlic.
Frank: My intestines are now a straight pipe filled with gaseous, sulphuric flames. No one seems inclined to stand behind me except that slut Sally. I need to wipe my ass with a snowcone.

Chili #6 Susan's Screaming Sensation Chili
Judge One: A mediocre chili with too much reliance on canned peppers.
Judge Two: Ho Hum. Tastes as if the chef literally threw in a can of chili peppers at the last moment. I should note that I am worried about Judge #3
Frank: You could put a f#$@#*&! grenade in my mouth, pull the f#$@#*&! pin, and I wouldn't feel a damn thing. I've lost sight in one eye, and the world sounds like it's made of rushing water. My shirt is covered with chili, which slid unnoticed out of my f#$@#*&! mouth. My pants are full of lava-like shit, to match my f#$@#*&! shirt. At least during the autopsy, they will know what killed me. I've decided to stop breathing, it's

too painful. I'm not getting oxygen anyway. If I need air, I'll just suck it in through the four-inch hole in my stomach.

Chili #7 Helen's Mount Saint Chili
Judge One: A perfect ending. This is a nice blend of chili, safe for all, not too bold, but spicy enough to declare its existence.
Judge Two: This final entry is a well-balanced chili, neither mild nor hot. Sorry to see that most of it was lost when Judge #3 passed out, fell and pulled the chili pot on top of himself. Not sure if he's going to make it. Poor Yank.
Frank: ...Mama? (Editor's note: Judge #3 was unable to report).

DOG CATCHERS

Our animal control officer was Henry, or as we called her, Red. A brassy outspoken redhead that would tame an alligator if she had to. This lady was all business when it came to animals and she knew her stuff. More than once she helped me when I had to deal with gang members. She had a great rapport with them because she had dealt with most of their dogs. If you ever want to really piss off an animal control officer, just call them "the dog catcher." That is an insult to what they truly do out there. They deal with every kind of animal, not just dogs. More than once I have seen Red take snakes, lizards, turtles, and even a cougar out of a house. It is not a career for the faint that's for sure. But what many did not know about Red is she was part of a dog rescue up in Keshena and the surrounding area. She would donate her time on a weekend to help dogs that needed veterinarians or needed to be surrendered. You know the dogs I am talking about, chained to a tree, no food or water and no one around that cares about the poor animal. Well Red cared, and for that I always felt honored to work by her side.

My other good friend was Animal Control Officer Keifer. Many of the new officers would not recall her. There isn't anything at the station showing that she had ever existed, which is a shame. She was great at her job even though back in the day, she truly was pretty much a dog catcher. Well, cats too. Keifer's greatest asset was her sense of humor. This was a lady who always had a joke ready and a smile on her face. You could be having the crappiest day ever and just seeing her would make you smile. You don't meet many people like that. Keifer died in a single vehicle rollover crash on I-43 at Hwy 41. She lost control of her vehicle and was ejected and then crushed when the vehicle rolled over her. She was not wearing a seatbelt, please buckle up. I said it before and I will say it again, I have never unbuckled a dead person.

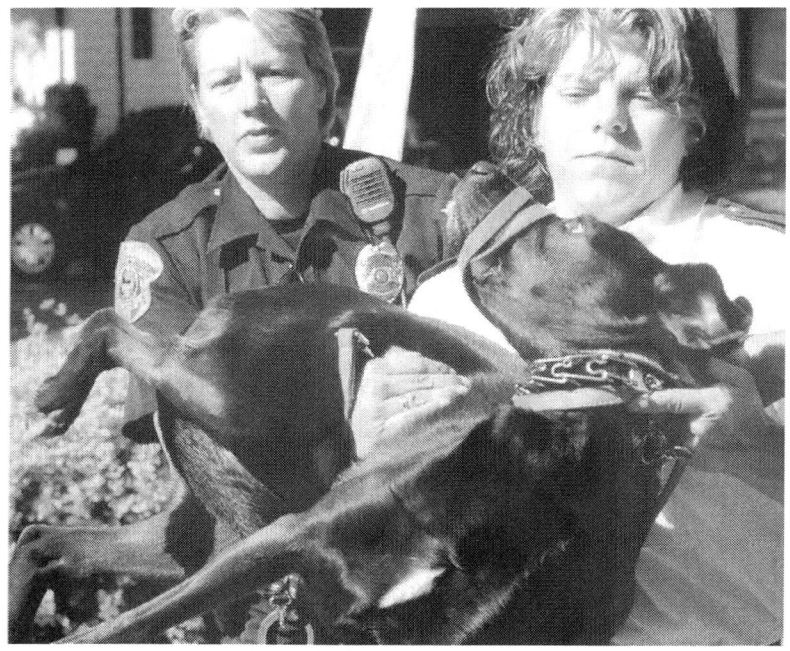

NINE LIVES

This is one of those stories that I don't like to talk about. I wasn't even sure I would include it in this book because of how badly I felt about it, but it is part of my career and everyone makes a mistake or two. I was called out to the north end of N. Military Avenue to dispatch a cat. The word *dispatch* is used over the radio as a means of telling an officer they are going to have to shoot an animal and to let other officers know if they hear shots fired, it is an officer shooting an animal.

I was sent to meet Humane Officer Massart. She had a cat that was sick beyond help and needed to be dispatched. She had the cat in a small cage, except it wasn't a cat, it was a small little kitten. I have shot deer, skunks, rabbits, opossums, and never had a second thought about it, ever. The idea was for Massart to open the cage, let the kitten out and I'd shoot it with my .45 before it could run off.

In theory, I guess that would've worked. I stood back a bit the truth of it is, I didn't want to see it up close. When it came out of the cage, I took a shot at it and missed. I took a couple more, all misses. Maybe this was intentional, or I was just having a bad day, but after six shots the little thing was still suffering. I went to my trunk, got out my shovel and beat it to death. I know that sounds cruel and inhumane and looking back it probably was, but it was dead just the same. I know what you're going say, *a cop who can't even shoot a kitten, but is required to shoot a person if need be?* I will say this about that idea: someone pointing a gun at somebody or at me with the intention to kill is a hell of a lot different than killing some defenseless animal.

The rest of this story is that police officers are accountable for every single bullet that comes out of their gun when they are issued. I had to go in and see my shift commander to get six replacement bullets assigned. He asked me why it took six bullets to kill a cat. I told him my aim was a little off, which was the truth. The next day the captain ordered me to report to the shooting range. I spent the next couple hours with the rangemaster shooting the shit out of targets and got a perfect score. I know it was part of my captain's job to make sure my shooting skills were on target, however that was not what the problem was. The problem was my soft heart for an animal that meant no harm to me. I never talked of this day again until now. It was not one of my more shining moments. I wish I could have do-overs on this one, but I can't.

FTO

I worked as an FTO when I was in the radio room and as an officer. It is probably one of the hardest jobs in the world to train someone in the field. It can be rewarding to see a new recruit succeed and know that you had a hand in their success but on the flip-side is seeing a new recruit come into the program and just not "get it" and flunk out. You would be surprised at the number of people who make it through the interview and hiring process only to get washed out in the FTO program. I trained many officers, some still work with the department and some don't. Officer Kastle was my easiest probationary officer to train. I would tell her something once and it stuck, there was no need to say things over and over again. She turned out to be one of the best officers at our department. I was always proud to have a part in her early development as an officer. And then there is always that one on the other side of the spectrum. Officer Smith, this guy literally almost killed me.

Part of becoming a cop is the ability to operate a squad car and using something called due regard. Many people think a cop just turns his emergency lights and siren on and away they go. That is not true. Even though cops are screaming to a call, they still have to yield the right of way to traffic, be prepared for that person who is not paying attention or pedestrians in the roadway. You can't just flip on your lights and go like hell and expect citizens to get out of your way. Well, in the movies you can because that's what Hollywood shows. But in real life, you better have that car under control. Running someone over or crashing into someone on the way to a call is going to make for a bad day, a real bad day.

Officer Smith was not one of my probation officers. He was being trained by another FTO for about three weeks when his FTO had a week of vacation. I got to be the fill in FTO, which made it even harder because I didn't really know the guy or what he had already been trained on. But after three weeks, one would think the elementary elements of being a cop would be there, like driving a squad car. I never believed in having the FTO drive, primarily because they already know how to drive so I would always have a probationary officer drive, from day one. After all, they are the ones who need the practice in multitasking. There are a lot of things to consider in squad car operation, you have to be able to multitask. In layman's terms it means walk and chew gum. For a cop it means listen to the police radio, operate the emergency vehicle, watch your surroundings and be ready for anything.

I was working the afternoon shift and training Smith. He was at the wheel most of the afternoon with no issues. It was now 18:00, traffic was heavy downtown at this time in the evening. We had just left headquarters and were traveling northbound on N. Monroe Avenue when a call came in of a disturbance with a weapon out on University Avenue, way out by N. Danz Avenue. As a training car you try to get the probationary officer exposed to as many "hot calls" as possible and weapon calls are about the hottest. This was a report of a man with a gun inside a residence. There were several officers dispatched on this call.

Smith radioed headquarters that we were responding to the call and away we went, red and blue lights flashing and siren blaring. By time we hit Main Street he was doing about sixty miles per hour and coming up to a solid red light. I was waiting for Smith to get out in the center lane and hit the brakes, but he never did. We went flying out into the intersection on a solid red light. Out of the corner of my eye I saw a car heading westbound on Main Street. I actually yelled, "STOP!" at the top of my lungs. Smith hit the brakes and so did the westbound car. When everything had stopped, that car was about a foot from me at the passenger door.

I radioed headquarters that we were not responding to the call. I told Smith to pull up to the curb and get out of the car and get in the passenger seat. I got in the driver's seat and drove to headquarters. I went into the FTO commander and told him, "this guy is going to kill someone, and it isn't going to be me!" I am sorry but operating a squad car is Cop 101. If you can't do that, then you don't belong here. I drove the rest of the night. The next day Smith was gone.

LET ME SEE YOUR HANDS

I had mentioned the one most valuable lesson I had learned as a cop was from one of my FTO's, JT. He taught me, *the hands kill, always know where the hands are. Always see the hands, being complacent about it will get you killed!* It stuck with me through my entire career and thankfully so. I was working the afternoon shift on the west side in the S. Ashland Avenue area when a call came out in the 800 block of S. Chestnut Avenue. A report of a male causing a disturbance at a residence. It seemed a pretty average type call as it was being dispatched, no big alarming flags, just your normal, everyday type call where people can't get along, so they call the police. As units were being dispatched, a description was given out of the male who was causing the ruckus. I was not dispatched on the call, but I also wasn't on another call at the time, so I hung out in the area in the event I was needed. This is something most cops do, if extra cars are called for then you're close by.

I was coming from Ninth Street and S. Ashland Avenue very near the area. I had heard the units that were dispatched call 10-23, which indicated they were on scene. Ten codes are codes given to the dispatcher over the radio to keep air time at a minimum and freed up. Our department didn't use many, just a few specific ones, this was one of the most frequently used coded. As I drove north on the S. Ashland bridge I saw a male matching the description of the male in the disturbance on S. Chestnut Avenue. I had not heard anything from the units on scene, so I quickly asked over the air if they had all the people involved accounted for. There was no response. I called out to dispatch that I had a male matching the description on the Ashland viaduct and got out of my car.

I walked up to the guy and asked him to stop, he did. The guy seemed really nervous. I understand most people are nervous around police officers, but this guy was over the top. I recognized that Spidey feeling, the sense that something wasn't right. I called for a cover but had no idea how far that unit was. The dispatcher was trying to reach the units on the call over the radio. I had to do something to ease this awkward uncomfortable feeling I had. The guy had already made two attempts to put his hands in his pockets, which I instructed him not to do. Sometimes it's a natural reaction to want to put your hands in your pockets and I get that, but that would not be happening until I had patted him down for weapons. This pat down is usually done with another officer present in the event the subject tries to arm himself or is already armed; it's always a good idea to have your cover officer there. I was not going to wait for that.

I told the guy to turn around and place his hands at the center of his back, he did. I grabbed both his hands tightly. I asked him if he had any weapons on him. I always ask this and up until now, no one had ever said yes. Well, this guy said yes. I tightened my grip on his hands. He said, "I have a loaded .357 down the front of my pants." That's what you call pucker factor times ten for a cop. I stood there almost shocked as to what he just told me; but in the cop business, the longer you stall or fail to act the more time you are giving the bad guy to figure out how he is going to assault or kill you. I told him if he made one move toward the gun I was going to shoot him, which I would have done if I could have gotten my gun out quickly enough while I was holding his hands. I held both of his hands real tight with my left hand and quickly grabbed my handcuffs with my right hand. I slapped those cuffs on very quickly. I told him to kneel down real slow, so he couldn't break free and run away, even in handcuffs. I reached around the front of his pants at his belly line, lifted his shirt, and there it was, a chrome plated .357.

Luckily, he was cooperative and didn't give me any problems. He could have easily shot me as I approached him. My cover arrived just in time to take the loaded gun from me which allowed me to get this guy into my patrol car. It turns out he was a convicted felon and had a warrant. This made me even more thankful, felons can't have firearms and this guy knew he was going to be arrested. He could have made this a much different situation. You never know what someone will say to you, but you have to ask.

Of all the foreign languages I could have taken in high school, I took German. I came from a German family and it was always interesting to me that my great grandparents and grandparents spoke German around the house. In looking back, I am sure they did this so they could converse with each other without the grandkids knowing what was being said. Whatever the case, that language class was twenty years ago. The one language I wish I had taken was Spanish. The department offered a four-hour class called Law Enforcement Spanish. This class taught us a few lines to use and gave us a small pocket-size translation guide. We had translators available who could be called in for translation on cases. We also used Language Line, a translator you could call on your cell phone and pass the phone back and forth between you and the Spanish speaking person. Both of these translation services worked great for controlled situations, but what about the active calls? That is where the danger lied.

Because of my obsession with the hands, I learned a couple quick lines that would help me in an emergency. Alto, manos arriba! and Arroja tus pistolas al piso! Stop, hands up! and Throw you guns on the floor! I would often joke around about seriously having to say any of this to anyone, until one night.

I was working the afternoon shift on the west side in the N. Ashland Avenue area. There had just been a large disturbance involving several Hispanic males on the east side. The call went out these males had just pulled knives on several other males and then fled the scene in a gray Cadillac. Someone had gotten the plate. The plate came back to a house on the corner of Kellogg Street and N. Ashland Avenue. I started heading in that direction. I rounded the corner to see if the car was there, at that very moment all the doors opened and everyone inside got out.

I pulled up, hit them with my spot lights and yelled, "Alto, manos arriba!" To my surprise the four Hispanic males stopped and put their hands up. Excellent! I guess that worked. Now what? I am alone with four possibly armed subjects and I have no possible way to communicate with them. There was a long uncomfortable pause; they started talking in Spanish to each other. I have to say that made me a bit nervous. I yelled, "Alto!" again, and they stopped talking. In my mind, *someone hurry up and get here to help me!* No sooner did I think it, and two squads came squealing in on two wheels. When I saw one of the guys was one of our bilingual officers, I let out a huge sigh of relief. The males were taken into custody without incident. It was the one and only time I ever used that line. I can laugh about it now but at the time, it was an *oh shit!* moment for me.

Protecting the children and the elderly
JUST A BABY

Some of the east side cars were sent to a residence on the far east side for a report of a non-breathing baby. This type of call was always the worst to go on, for obvious reasons. I recall as a 911 operator getting these types of calls and going to the emergency medical cards in hopes that any second I would hear a crying baby in the background, and often times I would. Sometimes an officer would arrive on scene and take over where the phone call left off, now I was that officer.

I wasn't sent on this actual call, Officer Pride was. When he arrived, the baby was in fact not breathing and he quickly started CPR and used his defibrillator until rescue arrived minutes later. The baby had been found by the mother floating in a pool in the backyard. Rescue took the baby and did a load and go to Aurora Hospital. Officer Pride stayed with the distraught mother and was going to complete the investigation at the home.

I was sent to be with the baby at Aurora Hospital. It is policy for an officer to stay with the child since we still did not know if the child really drowned in the pool, if someone had drowned the baby in the pool, or if this was a cover up for some other way the child had become unresponsive. It is the sad truth that even when parents tell us what happened, it is our job to make sure they are telling the truth and not covering up some crime. My assignment was to stay with this child and document what the medical professionals said about what happened.

I was in the trauma room watching a dozen nurses and doctors, hooking up monitors, doing CPR, inserting breathing tubes, IV's and doing everything possible to save this child's life. I was also doing everything I could possibly do, I was praying like crazy. After about an hour of efforts, the doctor finally "called it" which means the team stopped their efforts.

The child was dead, he was thirteen months old. All the medical staff left the room, I am sure for a well needed mental break, leaving me and one nurse in the room with this lifeless child. I stood over him. He looked like a sleeping angel, which is what he was now. This situation makes you feel so helpless. In my mind I was asking God, *why?* Even though I know this is part of life, seeing it is really, *really* hard; especially the babies, who have not even had a chance to live.

I would not be human if I wasn't asking myself, *where the hell was the supervision for this helpless child?* It is a natural reaction and natural question to ask, but that wasn't up to me to answer, that would be up to Officer Pride to find the answer to. My job now was to stay with the baby and be present for the ME's preliminary examination of the body. I sat in that room with the deceased child for over an hour waiting for the ME and then spent another half hour taking notes and photographs of the child. Then the ME zipped him into a little blue body bag and he would be taken to the morgue for the baby autopsy. All I can say about this call is, keep a very close eye on your children. Very close.

YOU THINK YOUR HOUSE IS DIRTY

I was sent on a call with Officer York to the area of the Wendy's restaurant on Radisson Street for a report of a naked child wandering around the area. The child was described as a white female with long, blonde hair and approximately two-years-old. Yowza, this requires an emergency response! Many thoughts started swirling through my head. First of all, who would call in this type of call and not grab the child for safekeeping until we arrive? Second, where are the child's parents? Probably napping and the child got out of the house. And third, I must get there immediately before the child gets hit by a car or picked up by some psycho child molester!

As I was driving there, red lights and siren, additional notes came in that the child had just walked south on N. Clay Street, and again I am asking myself, *what person watches and reports but does nothing to act?* I arrived in the described area and could see clear down to Wendy's, not a child in sight. I pulled off to the side of the road and called the complainant who told me the child had gone into an apartment building right where I was currently parked. I thanked the caller even though I wanted to say something about not acting. This was a two-year-old child! I didn't, at least he had called.

I waited for Officer York to arrive and we went up to the building. It was a small eight-plex of apartments with four on the lower level and four on the upper. We entered the building. It was approximately 13:00 on a Sunday afternoon, the Packers were scheduled to play that day at 15:00. Officer York wanted to get this call done so he could go to the stadium to work the game. I told him no matter what happened, I would handle the call. I wasn't expecting this.

We walked up the stairs and listened for the sound of children. Apartment number six was the winner, I could hear what sounded like three kids inside. I knocked on the door. No answer. I knocked on the door. No answer. I did the night shift knock on the door, a little voice from behind the door said, "who is it?" I said, "it's the police, open up." There was a pause and then the little voice said, "I am not supposed to open the door for strangers." I almost laughed out loud, but he was correct. I told him it was okay because we were the police. A minute went by and I heard the lock being turned and the door opened.

The best immediate description I could give you is the place looked like a tornado had occurred inside the apartment. I have never, ever seen an apartment that looked like this. Ever. There were pans of rotting food on the stove, what looked like last week's macaroni and cheese and some kind of meat soaked in animal fat. There was food all over the counters and the floors. The floors had juice and liquids spilled all over them, mixed in with cereal, bread crusts, dirty diapers filled with poop, and articles of clothing all over. There was not a spot on that floor that wasn't garbage.

The living room had a small TV turned on with one sofa, minus it's cushions. There were several blankets laying amongst the rubble. This is just my first observations, there's more to come. The boy who answered the door told me his name was Jason, he was ten-years-old, and he was babysitting his two little sisters ages four and two. In itself this wouldn't have been a bad thing except the more I talked to Jason, the more I realized Jason had some cognitive issues. He told me the little two-year-old snuck out of the house without him knowing and had returned on her own.

I located her in a bedroom laying on a pile of dirty clothes, nude. The bedroom she was in smelled of urine and again there were dirtied diapers laying all over. Jason told me he ran out of diapers, so he was letting her go without. The four-year-old was also in the room playing with some kind of Barbie doll and seemed unphased that a police officer was in her bedroom. There were only two bedrooms in this apartment, the kids' and the mother's. Her door was locked.

I asked Jason where his mother was. He told me she went out last night for her birthday and hadn't come home yet. In my mind I was thinking, *wow, that must have been some party,* but what I asked was, "do you know how to get ahold of her?" He told me he had her number in his phone. He pulled out the phone and showed me the mom's number. I called the number from his phone, it went to voicemail. This lady clearly was not going to be Mother of the Year this year.

Officer York made contact with one of the neighbors across the hall who said the kids were left home alone all the time. He also said last week he found the little two-year-old naked in the laundry room trying to get inside the dryer.

I walked into the very small bathroom, complete with dark black molding rings around the toilet and a matching one in the bathtub. It smelled of urine and there was no toilet paper, so I assumed the dirty clothes in that room were getting used for wiping. I made my way back through the jungle of garbage and into the kitchen. I opened the refrigerator door and almost got blown back by the smell of rotting food, it looked like a bad biology experiment. I closed the door as quickly as I could, but in reality, that odor could not have done any harm to this place. That was my last straw, I didn't care if the Packers were playing in two hours, I was calling Child Protective Services.

Officer York left for the game and I stayed in the apartment with the children. Child protection workers arrived about the same time the mother did. Apparently one of the neighbors, a friend of hers, had called her and told her the cops were at her house. I had the opportunity to assist child protection with the interview. The mother had in fact gone to Appleton overnight for her birthday and left her autistic ten-year-old to babysit her other two children. She thought nothing of it, big deal.

I knew this apartment could not have possibly gotten this messed up and dirty since yesterday. I called her out on it and she told me the place was clean when she left. If Rivard was here I would have said "Banana." The child protection worker had previous reports of neglect and did not fall for the story the mother was attempting to feed us. The kids were removed from the home and the mother got a nice birthday present, three counts of child neglect.

WRITING ON THE WALL

I was working the downtown beat when I was called to Whitney Park for a report of graffiti. One of the park workers had been in the men's bathroom and noticed someone had written on the bathroom stall walls. As most of you know this is a pretty common thing people do to post their little messages. Many times, this is a heart with a couple's names in it or a message calling someone a derogatory name. There is even a song about this, who wouldn't recognize the phone number *867-5309?*

I met with the park worker who told me he felt this writing was something more than just a post on the wall. I entered the stall with camera in hand. On the back of the door was the writing, *call me if you wood like to cum in my mouth,* followed by a phone number. I agreed with the park worker, this was totally inappropriate, especially since children use this restroom many times when visiting the park. I photographed the writing and the park worker covered it with paint. Most cops probably wouldn't have given this a second look, but I was disturbed at the brazen comment and the fact that someone would leave their telephone number, really? Another odd thing about this note is the fact the person spelled would "wood"...very odd.

I went to headquarters and began an investigation to try to identify who this person was. I began with the telephone number and was able to trace it to a seventy-year-old man who lived on the far west side. My initial thoughts were, *certainly someone had used this old guy's number.* I wanted to be sure before I closed out the case as unfounded. I could have called the guy and asked him if he wrote his number on the wall but really, even if it was him, would he say yes? I think not. So, I did some more digging. I looked him up in our files. He hadn't had any entries with our department in twenty years.

The entry from twenty years ago was for suspicious writings but because these files were so old they could not be accessed by computer, they had to be searched on microfilm. This would take some time and efforts from the department records girls. I needed to know, so I ordered the report be located and printed out for me. About a week later, I received the report and to my dismay the suspicious writing was a note left on a bathroom wall at Prange Way on the west side of Green Bay that said, *I wood like to suck you off, call me* followed by the same phone number. I could hardly believe it, this was my guy!

I could have easily called him in for an interview and presented him with the evidence but that would have only resulted in a graffiti charge. I wanted to see if he in fact would actually go through with his advertisement on the wall. I got with a couple of detectives and our plan was put into action. The male detective hooked up his telephone, so the conversation would be recorded.

He made the call to the telephone number and claimed to be a fifteen-year-old East High student who saw the message and was interested in some action. The old guy agreed to meet the "student" at Whitney Park and they could have a secret meeting in the bathroom to perform the act. The plan was in place. The old guy said he would be arriving in a blue Chevy S10 pickup truck and our "student" (detective) said he would wait on the bench outside the bathroom door. He said he would be wearing an East High jacket. The meeting was scheduled for the next day around 11:00 when the student had lunch.

That day several detectives in unmarked vehicles and in plain clothes were posted around the area. Our "student "detective was dropped off in advance to the actual meeting time. I was down the block but could see everything clearly with my binoculars. I honestly did not think this guy was going to show, but sure enough at 10:55 a blue Chevy S10 pickup truck rolled into the parking lot.

I watched as this old man walked toward the bench where our detective decoy was sitting with his face down waiting for the proposition to begin. The old guy walked up to our detective and placed his hand on his shoulder. That is when our detective sprang into action and so did the other detectives who were circling the area. The old guy was arrested for soliciting sex with a minor. When I went to his pickup truck, there sitting on the front seat were dozens of male on male porn magazines open to men doing it in every imaginable position. I think I just took a child sex predator off the streets of our fine city and it all started with the writing on the wall.

THE BLACK MONTE CARLO

I was working the downtown district when a call came out that an elderly male had just been beaten and robbed in the alley on N. Maple Avenue. The description of the males was given out and several cars were sent on this call. I was close to the location just over the bridge. The first few minutes of a call are very important; this is the time when you either catch the bad guy or he is making his getaway. The information the caller is giving the call taker, the questions the call taker asks, and the information given by the dispatcher are all crucial to catching the bad guys. The preliminary information given on this call was that an elderly male had just been severely beaten in the alley near St. Pat's church and was unconscious. The suspects were described as two black males, one was wearing a white t-shirt. The suspects last direction of travel was north down the alley toward the Express Gas Station. That was it. I was just over the river by the KI Center.

I activated my lights and siren and away I went. Green Bay PD started a new in-car camera system called COBAN. The system starts recording anytime you activate your emergency equipment and also captures the 30 seconds prior to activation. I really liked having the camera in my car because

I could replay it later to write details; it also recorded everything that was said. A lot of guys didn't like it for the same reason, it recorded everything you said.

This day it was activated as I drove over the Main Street bridge and into the Express Gas Station within minutes from the call going out. As I pulled in I saw a black Monte Carlo parked on the east side of the building but did not give it much attention at the time because we were looking for two males on foot. I saw a male walking away from the Express and was just going to stop and ask him if he had seen two black males running in the area; that was until I got out of my car and he took off running. I took off after him, he ran back and forth across Dousman Street several times. I did not know it at the time, but he was trying to get back to the black Monte Carlo, it was the getaway car.

Several other cops joined in the foot chase and the suspect was apprehended in the parking lot at St. Pat's church. He fought with us until he was decentralized to the ground. This means he was forced to the ground by officers and handcuffed. Because of his actions and fighting with us, he did clunk his head on the concrete. That's the thing about fighting with the police, we will fight back and although we are not trying to injure you, injuries do happen when you are swinging at us and resisting and sometimes you are not going to get a soft cushy landing. We try, but most of it is on the resistive person. The male was taken to the hospital and then to jail. He refused to talk to police and asked for a lawyer.

The male who had been beaten was approached outside his garage and the two males demanded he give them all his money. The elderly male was a combat Marine from WWII and told the thugs to take a hike. They beat him to the ground, stomping on his head over and over again until he was unconscious. The male I caught was the one who had done the stomping. The black Monte Carlo was the getaway car, the other suspect was already inside the car. The male I caught had gone inside for something and when he came out he saw me there and took off, otherwise he too would have been in that car and gone. Luckily, I was in the right place at the right time.

My in-car camera captured the Illinois license plate on the black Monte Carlo and it was traced to a person in Milwaukee. Coincidentally, the registered owner and the guy we captured had done this same thing, beat an elderly couple down in Milwaukee for their money and were facing charges down there for the same thing. The elderly veteran had permanent brain damage and later died of complications relating to his injuries. The two thugs were convicted and sentenced to prison for thirty years. Thank you COBAN for being such an alert partner.

CAT EYE GLASSES

Every cop goes on dead people calls, some more, some less, but we all see dead people. I don't know if I can say you get used to it, but you kind of do after a while. I was sent on a call to check the welfare at a lady's house on S. Roosevelt Street. The notes of the call said a neighbor was calling in that a lady hadn't been seen in a couple of days and her mail and newspaper had not been taken in. This was a pretty common type call, many times the elderly person was in the hospital or was at relatives and hadn't told the neighbors.

I arrived at the home. A nice well-kept little brick Grandma house with white awnings over the front windows. I went up to the door and saw the mail and papers had been sitting for a few days. I walked to the side of the residence where there was another entrance door, that's when the neighbor who had called walked up and introduced herself. The neighbor told me she had a key but was scared to go inside for fear of finding the woman dead. The neighbor explained the woman did not have any children and lived there alone for many years. I took the key from her and told her to wait outside and went in. The house was as neat as a pin, cozy and well kept. I was hoping this lady was not going to be lying on her bedroom floor face down, but she was. She was stiff and cold and had probably laid there for a couple of days.

I called headquarters to send the medical examiner and went outside to tell her neighbor friend. It usually takes about a half hour for the ME to arrive. The officer has to stay for the initial examination to determine if there are any signs of foul play. As I waited, I walked around the residence completing the death scene checklist. This is a document the responding officer fills out recording observations of the residence and body. Things like, were all the doors and windows locked upon arrival, were lights on, what was the heat set at, an overall assessment of the environment.

As I walked around the residence completing the form I couldn't help but notice pictures hanging on the wall of what I assume was her family. One appeared to be a group of sisters, I of course was only guessing based on the fact they all looked alike. The sister in the middle was wearing cat eye glasses and the biggest smile of them all. There was also a photo of a man in a military uniform. My mind wondered, *could that have been an early picture of her husband or possibly her son who was killed in the war?* There were other pictures on the walls, most of them old-fashioned looking paintings, most of the décor in this home was old-fashioned. Very simple. It is an odd feeling to be standing in someone's house looking at all their personal things. I am not going to say that death calls did not bother me because they did, but it was part of the job and someone had to do it.

This particular call bothered me more than the others. I sensed such a lonely feeling in that house. After I completed my form and was still waiting for the ME, my mind began to wonder about this woman's life and how she ended up here in this house on S. Roosevelt with no one. I always said I want to die in my sleep when I am ninety, but I want someone to find me right away. When the ME arrived, and he turned the body over, I had to do some more paperwork and record my observations. When he did this, there was the lady in the photo with the big smile and the cat eye glasses, except her glasses were all smashed, and she wasn't smiling. I guess I included this story in my book to let people know they matter. Check in with people and take care of them. Contact the people you care about and make sure they are alright. If it hadn't been for that one neighbor that lady would still be lying there.

Crashes
SUN GLASSES

Cops and sunglasses seem to go hand-in-hand. From the days when the dark-lens aviator frames were popular, like on the television series Chips, it seems anytime an officer is shown in a movie or TV show he or she always has those sunglasses on. At our department we had one guy that I swear slept with his sunglasses on, I don't think I ever saw his eyes. He would wear them to training, to seminars, even to work out. They were the dark wrap around frames; he looked like Mr. Incredible from the Disney movie *The Incredibles*. Our department had a pretty strict rule about the type of glasses you could wear, no bling, no flashy mirror lenses, pretty much your basic black frames with dark lenses.

I wore prescription sunglasses all the time in my squad. They were a small framed pair with a green accent. The lenses were clear on the top and prescription readers on the bottom, they had a lineless lens, so no one knew I had readers on, they just looked like normal glasses. There was nothing normal about the price though, they cost me a couple hundred bucks. They made reading the computers in the squad and driver's license info out in the field a lot easier. When I would get out of the squad and talk to people I always took my sunglasses off. I guess you could call me old-fashioned, I think it's always nice to look someone in the eye when you're talking to them. I would always hook my glasses on the top button of my shirt, so they wouldn't get misplaced.

I was dispatched to a traffic crash with injuries at the corner of Washington Street and E. Walnut Street. I was just leaving the station, so I was pretty close to the scene. I took off red lights and siren and was there in thirty seconds. I ran to the vehicle the bystanders were pointing to. Inside the vehicle was an injured lady in the driver's seat, she was very scared. I talked to her to calm her down; she reminded me of my mother and I was sure she was someone's mother. I told her the rescue squad was on the way and I would stay with her as I held her hand and told her it was going to be alright. She was shaking and asked me if I could call her husband. I said certainly and pulled out my flip phone to dial the number, I reached down for my glasses, but they were not hooked on my shirt. Dang, I knew I had them when I left the station. That's when I looked over toward the middle of the intersection and saw them laying on the roadway.

They were in perfect condition. I was just about to run over and grab them, but before I could react the rescue squad came screaming in and ran them over, flat as a pancake. Well, at least I kept my promise and stayed with the lady until the rescue squad arrived. After the paramedics came over to help the injured lady, I walked over and picked up my smashed frames with the lenses crushed into little tiny pieces of glass. The guys on the rescue squad realized what had happened and I got a few chuckles out of them. I ended up getting them replaced with the same frames. That's kind of how cops are, well this one anyway.

ROAD RAGE

An attempt to locate reported a male driving a red Ford Mustang convertible coming into the city from Brown County on S. Webster Avenue driving recklessly, cutting people off, and the driver was flipping people off. These attempt to locates, or ATL's for short, are sent out when a complainant calls in and reports a reckless driver but there are no cops available to respond or the cops who are available are not in a position to get to the reported area to catch the driver. An ATL gets sent out countywide to all units in an attempt for any cop to try to get into a position to observe or catch the driver. There is always that chance a cop is coming back from another call and can get into the proper location and possibly locate the offender.

That day I was really close. When the ATL came out I was out of my squad car in the 600 block of N. Webster Ave working a traffic crash with injuries. I had just completed my investigation of the crash and the injured had been transported to the hospital. My partner was standing by to wait for the wreckers to clear the smashed cars from the roadway. I got into my squad car, pulled away from the scene, and put my window down since it was a warm sunny day. I was in the 800 block of Pine Street, just two blocks from N. Webster Avenue. I had pulled off to the side of the road to type some notes into my call and read any updates from headquarters. That is when I saw the reckless driver ATL. I looked at the time of the ATL it was about 4 minutes old.

I was just about to move to the corner of Pine Street and N. Webster Avenue when I heard a large crash. I looked up from my computer screen to see a red Ford Mustang convertible smashed into a large tree in the 1000 block of Pine Street. I activated my red lights and siren and headed toward the crash. I radioed headquarters that I believed I just located the Mustang from the ATL. My partner who was at the previous crash scene said he was on his way to help me. When I pulled up to the crash, a young male was out of the car, stomping his feet, swearing and dancing around on the sidewalk.

I approached him and asked him if he was the driver of this Mustang. He swore a little more as he told me he was, and it was his vehicle. I asked him if he was injured, and he said he was not. I then asked him what happened. He told me he had been driving from E. DePere on S. Webster Avenue when some guy in a white Chevy Camaro had cut him off. This started a road rage. He and the other vehicle kept swerving in and out of traffic, sort of playing chicken with each other. He told me this went on all the way down Webster Avenue until they started to approach Main Street. He realized they would both have to stop for a red light behind traffic and he feared the guy in the white Camaro was going to get out and beat him up. He waited until the very last minute before quickly turning onto Pine Street in an attempt to lose the Camaro. He was going a little too fast and couldn't complete the turn on the pavement. He jumped the curb, went onto the terrace, and struck the tree. Luckily, he wasn't going any faster or he would have struck a brick building about ten feet from where his car was now resting.

To recap, the guy totaled his own car because he couldn't control his ego and he let the guy driving the Camaro get the best of him. He could have disengaged from this incident at any time prior to this, but he chose to stay involved. He now had a totaled vehicle and received three traffic citations. Boys and their toys!

WEDDING CAKE

It was just after lunch on a beautiful September Sunday afternoon when I got the call for a single vehicle rollover on northbound Sturgeon Bay Road at Algoma Road. The caller said that the driver of the vehicle had been ejected and was laying out on the highway. I was coming from downtown and was the closest unit to the crash. I activated my lights and siren and went screaming out there. Fire and rescue had also been dispatched and were on their way.

When I arrived, there were many cars pulled off to the side of the roadway and traffic had stopped. Rescue rolled up and made its way up to the crash scene by weaving in and out of stopped cars. By the time I actually got up to where the ejected male was, rescue was loading him on a gurney and getting ready to leave. This is called a load and go, which means the injured person is in grave condition. When I stuck my head into the rescue squad, one of the rescue guys told me this guy was probably not going to make it. That's when I saw the cake. The patient was covered in cake, wedding cake.

I closed the door and rescue pulled away to head to the hospital. As several other units arrived, we were able to get traffic diverted at Huron Road. As I walked into the ditch, the blue Chevy S10 pickup was laying on its side about a couple hundred feet off the roadway. The ditch had wrapped presents, wedding cards, wedding paper and bows strewn about. I asked myself what all this meant, but I knew it was not going to be good. When I got down to the vehicle I saw the interior was covered in wedding cake. The box the cake had been in was smashed up against the headliner of the vehicle. There were also wedding items in the cab of the truck.

There was a larger pickup truck pulling a big trailer full of wood pulled off to the side of the road. This driver witnessed the crash and was most likely why the little pickup was passing him, he had been moving slowly. The little S10 tire tracks showed that at the last minute he made a quick and abrupt turn to try to get onto the Algoma Road exit. The vehicle went sideways and started to roll. The driver was ejected on the first roll. Several witnesses said he flew about one hundred feet straight into the air before landing on the highway. A female witness told me she could not believe she had seen what she had seen. It is very difficult to see something happen right before your very eyes.

I continued to speak with witnesses and wait for the accident reconstruction team to arrive. This is a team of highly trained officers who are called to scenes where a fatality has occurred. They do the accident report and figure out the speed of the vehicles based on skid marks and drag marks. They take measurements of everything, take photographs, collect evidence and once the scene is cleaned up, they have the vehicles taken by flatbed to the police station. At the station a thorough inspection of the vehicle is done by the mechanics and the team to determine if the cause of the crash was some type of mechanical malfunction. In most cases, the mechanics of a vehicle have nothing to do with the crash; it is usually operator error.

I had already been working on figuring out who this male and the girl on the wedding cards was. I located a cell phone lying in the grass, this proved to be very helpful. I called the last number called on the phone, a shot in the dark. A male answered the phone and told me the phone belonged to his sister's fiancé. He told me they had all just left the wedding shower and were heading to their parents' house for more family celebration. I wouldn't usually do this, but I knew time was of the essence. I told the brother to gather up his family and get to the hospital as quickly as possible, there had been a horrible accident. The brother seemed stunned and with good reason. One minute they were having a wedding shower with all of their family, a joyous occasion full of fun and laughter, to this. My insides were in knots when he asked me, "is it serious, do we have to go right now?" I told the brother things did not look good for his future brother-in-law.

After I hung up the phone, I received a call from the officer at the hospital. The male had passed away. My heart dropped, and I remember saying, "God dammit." I believe in God and that everything happens for a reason, but holy smokes. I was relieved by the accident reconstruction team and went to the hospital where I met the family in a private room. They had already been told the groom did not survive, but they had all kinds of questions about what had happened. I didn't have a lot of answers for them. I did the best I could and was as diplomatic and as courteous as I could be, but I wanted to ask, "why didn't the groom have a seatbelt on?" There is no doubt in my mind that man would be here today if he had. I have said it before and I will say it again, I have never unbuckled a dead person.

WINTER DRIVING

The closest I ever came to getting killed was on I-43. It was winter, and the road conditions were hazardous. There were vehicles going in the ditch everywhere and a snow emergency had been declared. After about fifty cars went into the median and ditch it was decided that we would block off I-43 between the Sturgeon Bay Road exit and the E. Mason Street exit until a couple of plows could at least scrape off the highway. I was assigned to divert traffic from I-43 southbound onto the Sturgeon Bay Road exit ramp.

I had flares out in the roadway making a gradual marked lane in red flares to move traffic over and onto the ramp. I also had my squad car positioned sideways across the lanes. People were going slow enough that they would slow up prior to arriving at my location and then realize the highway was closed and get off on the ramp. Well, not all the people. I had just gotten out of my car to replace a couple of flares that were starting to burn out. As I walked on the highway my feet were slipping and sliding around. I replaced one flare and was heading to the second when I saw a vehicle that appeared to be coming up on me pretty quickly. I waved my light flair in front of me as to make some kind of motion that I was there, but the vehicle did not seem to be slowing. I thought to myself, *surely any second this vehicle will see the highway dotted in flares and my squad. Certainly, this will warn them of the impending danger.*

I had one of two choices, either jump into the ditch head first like I was diving off a diving board or become a hood ornament. I took the ditch and made it out of the line of fire just in time to see the vehicle slide over where I had just stood, crash through all my flares, do a spin in the middle of the highway nearly striking my squad and land in the ditch. I ran down into the ditch to check on injuries. I found a teenage driver behind the wheel and her teenage friend in the passenger seat, both very shaken up but uninjured. Obviously, my adrenaline was pumping, and the girls got a little taste of my inattentive driving speech.

MOTORCYCLES

As a young person, I always thought motorcycles were pretty cool. I rode a few back in my younger days, and I loved riding trail bikes around the railroad tracks where I grew up. But out on the roads, it is a totally different situation. It's not generally the cycler who is not attentive, but rather the drivers of vehicles around them. I have heard and seen so many horror stories involving motorcycles it is unreal. I could not imagine anything worse than sliding down the highway and your flesh being scraped off like cheese on a cheese grater.

Even one of our own officers had a brush with death on his cycle. He was coming home from working the night shift and heading out Sturgeon Bay Road at 07:00. He was traveling fifty-five miles per hour when a deer decided to hitch a ride on the front of his cycle, literally. This of course caused the officer to fall backwards off his bike, but not before breaking his ankles on his pegs. He then hit the concrete backwards and slid down the highway and into the ditch on his face. He was completely off the roadway. Luckily a citizen witnessed the crash and called it in right away. Had it not been for that one citizen, our officer would have easily bled out in the ditch due to his injuries. The good Lord was with him that day.

Sometimes people can survive the crash but not the aftermath. A couple was driving in the slow lane over the Tower Drive Bridge at about 23:00. The motorcycle they were on was rear-ended by a speeding drunk who didn't see them. The woman on the back of the cycle got her hair caught in the bike and her scalp was torn off as she slid down the highway and into the concrete side of the bridge. The driver of the cycle was thrown from the bike and landed in the passing lane, he had two broken legs. Before emergency crews could get up on the bridge a semi-truck pulling a full load saw the vehicles had crashed and moved into the passing lane to avoid striking the car and ran the driver of the cycle over, killing him instantly.

The cycle story I want to share isn't that gory, there wasn't even a drop of blood involved. It was April and one of those sunny spring Sundays when people are getting the itch for warm weather. People were out washing their cars and shining up their bikes. Even though it was still only fifty degrees out, I did see people out riding their cycles that day. I was dispatched to a report of a motorcycle crash on S. Baird Street. It came in as a one vehicle crash, meaning the cycle with unknown injuries. I was right down the block at Joannes Park and was at the scene in less than a minute.

I located a male laying in the roadway with his cycle on top of him. Several citizens had stopped to help me, and we lifted the bike off the top of the driver. Rescue was already on the way. This guy was swearing up a storm and was asking me to leave him alone. I noticed he had urinated in his pants. When I looked at his eyes, I saw his pupils were dilated to pin points. I kept him on the ground and told him to stop moving around, rescue was on the way. He continued to try to fight me but with the help of citizens we were able to subdue him until the paramedics arrived. He was placed in a collar and loaded onto the gurney and away they went with him.

I spoke to a witness who said the guy lived two houses from where the crash happened. The witness said the guy was only going about fifteen miles per hour, when he hit a large pothole in the roadway and went over the handlebars and the bike landed on top of him. I went into the roadway and there was in fact a large pothole that had not yet been patched from the winter weather. The cycle was wheeled into his driveway and I went to the door.

I knocked on the door and a female answered. She said she had been taking a nap and didn't know what had happened yet. She asked me why her boyfriend's cycle was in the driveway. I told her there had been an accident, she needed to get her shoes on and I would take her to the hospital. I drove her to the hospital and that is where I learned the male had suffered a traumatic brain injury. Just something to keep in mind, this guy was doing fifteen miles per hour without a helmet, imagine what it is like at seventy miles per hour.

The other cycle story that stands out in my mind involves an Iraq war veteran and some alcohol. I was dispatched to a one vehicle crash involving a motorcycle on Huron Road on the far east side of the city. The dispatcher said a passerby was calling in a motorcycle that had crashed into a curb and the male driver of the cycle had been ejected into the woods. I activated my emergency lights and siren and headed toward the scene. I was waiting for any updates from the witness or units who were closer to the scene on the status of the driver, but none were given.

I was the second car there; Officer York was speaking with the witness. I saw the Honda CBR up on the terrace with the front end smashed but I did not see the driver. Fire and rescue were still on the way. I walked up to Officer York and he told me that he couldn't find the driver. I started walking in the wooded area, sort of estimating where the guy would have landed based on where the bike hit the curb. Additional units arrived, and we combed the area well but still didn't come up with him. Now what?

Well, Lt. Heller arrived on scene and I briefed him on what we had so far, which was a bike, an ejected male and no body. Here is the question: is it our duty to find this male, since he is most likely injured, he may have suffered some type of head injury and is wandering around the woods? Lt. Heller said yes and that is all I needed to hunt this guy down. We set up a perimeter for the area with several units. I got to go on the hunting for him part of the call. I ran the license plate on the motorcycle and it came back to a thirty-year-old male who lived off of Huron Road and Finger Road. I went to the residence. There was no answer, but I did notice another name on the mailbox and when I looked her up. She had a bartender's license for Highland Howie's.

I drove to Highland Howie's and April was working. I asked her about the male on the motorcycle. She told me it was Jeremy, her boyfriend, but claimed she had not seen him at all that day. *Banana*, but I didn't let on that I knew she was lying through her teeth to me. She told me Jeremy was an Iraq Veteran and a Navy Seal. When she told me this, I knew this was going to be interesting because those guys can survive eating ants and dirt in the wilderness for days. I told her if she heard from him at all she needed to call me right away. She said she would. Before I pulled out of the parking lot, I ran the plates on two cars that were parked in the lot. A green Buick Century came back to April.

Officers were still searching the woods and others were holding their perimeter positions. I was driving around all the roadways back in the area. About thirty minutes had gone by and still no sign of Jeremy. We were getting close to calling this one off. I was parked on Humboldt Road a good six blocks from Highland Howie's when I saw April in her green Buick driving on Humboldt Road. She apparently didn't think I knew her car. As she drove past me, I looked down at my computer like I was doing something. I watched her car pull into a driveway and a male come from the garage area and get in her car. She then backed out and came back toward me. I waited until she passed me, and I pulled the car over. Guess who was sitting in the front seat. There was Jeremy, with a broken arm, a bloody face, black eye, busted lip and intoxicated.

Once we had him out of the car and he knew he was caught, he was nothing but respectful to me. He admitted he had been drinking all day at Highland Howie's where his girlfriend works and had lost control of his motorcycle at the curve. He told me he left the scene because he was drunk, and he didn't think we were going to look for him like we had. He had obviously never met me. Rescue was called, and he was taken to the hospital for his injuries. Because it was his first OWI he was issued a citation and released to a sober adult person, April. And April, she got a nice fat citation for obstructing.

Theft
ARMED ROBBERY

I have been sent to many armed robberies throughout my career, all of which had already occurred and were being called in afterward. Many times, these robberies occurred at banks, cash stores or convenience stores. I have never arrived to one that was actually in progress. As the responding officers arrive, it is their responsibility to tape off the area and hold witnesses there until the detectives arrive and take over the scene. If the robbery had just occurred, responding officers would set up a perimeter and try to locate the suspect. Sometimes we get them and sometimes we don't. In the end, the detectives usually get the bad guy. If a detective gets information on who the suspect is, or the vehicle involved, most of the time patrol never hears about it. The mentality is that they want to make the arrest and they don't want patrol screwing up their investigation. For you TV crime show watchers, it is nothing like what is shown on the crime shows where everyone is working together, even though it should be.

I happened to be back in detectives talking to one of the guys about a case I was working on when I overheard another detective talking about an armed robbery suspect he was looking for who drove a white Chevy Nova. I have always been a bit of a car buff. A Nova? They hadn't made those since 1988 and it was now 2000. That twelve-year-old obsolete car would stick out like a sore thumb. I also overheard they were looking for a black male with dreads in his hair. I kept this information tucked in my mind; since I obtained it through eavesdropping I did not tell anyone else. My thought was I would wait until that detective put out the attempt to locate before really looking hard for that car. That didn't happen either.

It was around 21:30 on a Sunday night and I was patrolling the west side area near West High School. I was driving on Shawano Ave when I spotted the white Nova; he spotted me as well. The vehicle was packed with people and the driver was in fact black with dreads. I immediately called the detective that I had heard talking about this vehicle earlier in the week. I was told to get the license plate and let it go. The vehicle made an abrupt turn south onto Oak Street, then onto Lake Street and then Sixteenth Street where I was able to get the license plate. I then backed off and let the vehicle pull westbound onto W. Mason Street and take off. I am sure the driver and occupants were already devising their plan on how to get away from me, and I had just let them go.

I gave the license plate information to the detective working the case and as it turns out, it was the armed robber and his vehicle. I guess he wanted the *collar* as they would say in the detective world. I looked at it as maybe not stopping that white Nova that night saved my life. I could have easily done it and gotten the armed robber.

BIG MONEY

I was a patrol officer for most of my career. I did spend about a half of a year in the detective division, which was about a half of a year too long. I am not knocking this division. Most would see it as a promotion. Obtaining a coveted spot with the elite group of guys that really dig in and solve crimes. TV makes this out to be a glorified position where every day you are going out solving murders and shootings or on stake-outs taking down drug lords. New flash, it is about the most boring job in the world. I don't say this to knock the detectives, but rather to say it is very sedentary and requires a lot of sitting at a desk doing computer work. I knew after my first two weeks working in this division that it was not for me. but I made a promise to Captain Timms that I would give it six months. It was the longest six months of my life.

On my first week in detectives I was given all the current counterfeit cases, all one hundred of them. It appears the detective who had previously been assigned to these wasn't really doing much with them other than letting them pile up on his desk prior to his retirement. I started the task of sorting each case down by the serial numbers on the twenty-dollar counterfeit bills. Most of the counterfeits were twenties that were being passed all over town, at gas stations, fast food joints, taverns, rummage sales and farmer's market; places where most people taking them would not check them out closely. To be honest, these bills were pretty darn good, even the feel of the paper they were printed on was top quality.

It took me a couple of weeks to sort down the stack of cases on my desk and get them organized into a spreadsheet using the serial numbers. Most of the bills were passed at places without any video surveillance cameras, but there were a few so I started there. I obtained the videos out of evidence and printed out still photos of the few suspects that had been identified as the bill passers, but not their actual identity. The hard part about counterfeit cases is you can have someone with a counterfeit bill, but proving they knew it was counterfeit is a whole different animal. Imagine you as a random citizen going to a gas station and getting a twenty back from the clerk that had been taken in earlier. Neither of you knew it was counterfeit. Then you go to a fast food joint and give that same bill to the girl at the counter. She checks it, says it's counterfeit and calls the cops. You would have no idea it was counterfeit. The trouble is, that is what everyone says, including the counterfeiters. So how do you prove it?

You go after the top dog, and that is exactly what I did. I passed around the photos I had printed from the videos to try to identify who the people were, men and women alike were passing the bills. I would later learn the guys would give them to their girlfriends because a woman is less suspicious than a male, which is pretty smart thinking on the criminals' end. Sometimes it isn't what you know, it's who you know, and my biggest asset was having made a lot of *friends* on the road, most people call them informants.

I got a call from one of my friends who said she had some information for me about the counterfeiters. I went to her house with the photos. She not only identified most of the people in the photos, but she gave me the name of the guy who was printing them, "Big Money." Of course, this was his street name and after doing a bunch of research I found his real identity. He was a counterfeiter from Milwaukee who was on probation and came to Green Bay for a better life, or more likely to get away with more crimes. I had identified about eight guys who were working under him, and we picked out the guy who had the most to lose by getting caught and I brought him in. The dude had a wife, a couple of kids and was also on probation. I played *Let's Make a Deal* with him. The guy agreed to set-up Big Money.

This all sounds so easy and as I am writing about it, almost simple, but honestly there is nothing simple about this case. It was not a one-hour detective show. This entire case took months to sort, watch video, identify, interview witnesses, victims and suspects, and then to orchestrate the grand finale. We brought in a couple of Big Money's boys and grilled them pretty good but didn't arrest them. We made sure to tell them we knew the top dog was Big Money, then we let them go. As planned, they ran back to him and told him the cops knew he was printing. This motivated Big Money to try to get rid of the printer and all the evidence, or at least move it to another location. This is where my *Let's Make a Deal* dude comes in.

He called Big Money and said he would take him to go destroy the evidence and he agreed. The trap was set. When my *Deal* guy went to Big Money's house and Big Money brought the stuff out to his car and left with him to go destroy it, we had patrol do a traffic stop on the car, and violá we had Big Money and the evidence in one nice little package. My *Deal* guy was also taken into custody on the stop to make it look good but was later released after Big Money was hauled away. Once we got him off the streets and back in jail where he belonged, the counterfeiting stopped. You just have to get to the source of the problem.

LIPS

As a cop, I guess you notice things that most people wouldn't even give a second look to. This is part of the culture. Like always sitting in a restaurant with your back to the wall and facing the door, always be aware of your surroundings. It is ingrained into you and it is what makes a good cop. In this case, that is exactly what happened.

I was off duty and had just parked my car in a parking lot at a local grocery store. In the back seat of my car on the floor was a portable DVD player and some movies that had to be returned to a friend. It was probably bad that they were in plain view, but someone would have to actually look into the rear window and down on the floor to see them. They should have been in the trunk and out of sight.

As I got out of my car, I noticed a male and female getting out of a car across from me. I'm always aware of my surroundings. I gave them both a good look as I walked into the store, maybe that cop sixth sense had a little something to do with it. The one thing I noticed about the male is that he had a set of red lips tattooed on the left side of his neck. I thought to myself, *what a unique tattoo.* I went into the store and picked up a few things. When I returned to my car and placed my grocery bags in the back seat, I immediately noticed the DVD player and movies were gone and so was Red Lips guy's car.

I went back into the store to check if they had video surveillance of the parking lot but unfortunately, they did not. The next day I completed a report for the theft and started my own investigation on Red Lips guy. I didn't actually see him take my things, but I was certain he was the suspect. I did a search of his tattoo and sure enough our records system had him identified as Andrew Sherwood. When I looked up his prior contacts, and photo, there he was staring at me. Then I did a search on his prior contacts, he seemed to spend a lot of time with a blonde girl named Kayla. I looked up her photo, it was the same girl from the grocery store parking lot.

Sherwood was under investigation for a bunch of crimes and I saw that one of the detectives was working on several cases involving him. Usually I would just go after a guy myself, but since this detective had a bunch of cases going with this guy, I did not want to mess things up for the detective. I went to Detective Lewinski and he told me he did not want me contacting Sherwood. He said he would add my case to the ones he was already working on. This Detective Lewinski was the same guy who as a patrol officer had left me on the side of the road without cover and never showed up on the call. I thought, *okay, maybe he has changed since becoming a detective.* Not so.

I checked on the status of my case a few weeks after that with Detective Lewinski and he told me he was still "working on it," but could provide me no updates. I then checked on it a few weeks after that and he had closed it out without even talking to Sherwood. If that is how Detective

Lewinski treats one of his own cops, imagine the stellar work he is doing for the community. Whatever, that is not my concern, it is for his supervisor to worry about. But it still pisses me off that Sherwood "Lips" got away with it and left me as the victim. I think of my old saying about lazy cops, "If you don't want to do the job then get the hell out of the way and let someone through who wants to do it." Or the famous Lee Iacocca saying, "Lead, follow or get the hell out of the way." My lesson learned the hard way, don't leave anything in plain sight for bad guys to break into your car!

One of those days
OH, MY ACHING BACK

As I had previously mentioned an officer carries around about thirty pounds of equipment. That isn't a lot for a two-hundred-pound officer. But for the one-hundred-thirty-pound officer, it's like carrying around a quarter of your body weight, all day long. Imagine sitting in your car, driving around with handcuffs digging into your back because there isn't any more room on the front of your belt for equipment. Carrying around all this equipment can be very hard on your back, but not as hard as these calls.

I was dispatched to an apartment on Amy Street at Bellevue Street for a warrant pick up. This guy had felony warrants for drugs. Officer Seroogy was dispatched on the call with me. The call came in from an anonymous caller stating the male was currently in his apartment. The caller was most likely someone who had just been there and wanted this guy busted for revenge or possibly a deal gone bad; who turns in their dealer? It was a bitter cold day with temperatures with the wind-chill in the minus twenties. The sidewalks were a sheet of ice.

I met Officer Seroogy down the road and we talked car-to-car for a few minutes discussing the fact this guy probably wasn't going to open the door. We still had to get out and make the effort, but really, what guy with felony warrants is going to answer his door? We got out of our cars and had to walk through the yard and the snow because we couldn't even stand up on the frozen sidewalks. The apartment building was a two-story with eight units. Our subject's apartment was on the second floor at the top of the stairs. We quietly made our way tip-toeing up the steps. I leaned my ear to the door. I could hear a TV on in the apartment, but I could not hear anything else. I looked at Officer Seroogy as if to say, *oh well, here goes nothing*. I knocked on the door and a voice from inside called out, "come in." What? We just got invited inside to make the arrest, easy-peasy.

I am positive this guy was expecting one of his friends or maybe a girlfriend, instead he got two cops standing in his living room. He was wearing nothing but a pair of boxer shorts. We would have to at least let him get some clothing on to dress for the weather. This is always a tough spot to be in. We are in the bad guy's house and he knows where all his weapons are hidden. I typically don't let anyone walk around their place. I would rather grab some clothing off the floor or closet and dress them myself. Officer Seroogy took this guy into his bedroom to get some clothing and I stood just outside the door.

He put on a pair of jeans and a cotton button-up shirt. When he bent down to pick up some socks, he charged Officer Seroogy like he was a middle linebacker making a block. He smashed her into the wall, bounced off of her and came charging toward me. I attempted to grab him, but he was in a full sprint toward the living room. I grabbed his shirt and held on tight. There was no way I was letting go of this guy's shirt. Officer Seroogy had already got on the radio and yelled for help.

In the meantime, there was a sofa positioned in the room and the male hurdled the back of it, up and over, and I went over with him still hanging onto his shirt. He opened the apartment door and started his way down the steps with me in tow by his shirt tails. He was moving a little faster than I was as I went down on my stomach, bump, bump, bump on each step, with him dragging me. By the time we reached the bottom and were in the entrance hallway, the buttons on his shirt had all popped off. At this point the shirt tore off of him, and out the front door he went; into the freezing cold wearing nothing but a pair of jeans, that's it. I ran out the front door holding his ripped shirt. When my feet hit the icy sidewalk, one second, I was standing up and the next I was looking up at the sky, flat on my back. Damn it!

I got up just in time to see this male run into the East River Trail area and disappear from sight into the brush. Other officers were just arriving, and we quickly set up a perimeter around the area. My back was killing me but that did not stop me from going after this guy. After all, how long could he hide in the brush before he would get cold and surrender? I was thinking five minutes and he would come out with his hands up. After thirty minutes went by, it was pretty clear this guy would rather freeze to death than go back to prison. This meant we had to go in after him. We walked into the brushy area and about one-hundred feet in, there he was curled up in a little ball, freezing to death. A rescue squad was called; he was suffering from hypothermia and frostbite. All I kept thinking was, *this could have been so much easier on all of us. My aching back!*

It was a hot summer day in the downtown district, the dog days of summer. The temps were in the high 80's with lots of sunshine and humidity. I love the warm weather but not in a bullet proof vest and polyester uniform. On these days, when I got done from my shift, I could literally wring the sweat out of my t-shirt and underwear.

As I drove down the alley in the 900 block of Day Street, I noticed a vehicle parked oddly. In running the plate, it came back as a stolen vehicle. I continued down the alley and turned around at the end. I called for backup and sat watching the vehicle. I sat there about a minute when I saw two males come out of the backdoor of a residence and start walking toward the stolen vehicle. I did not want them to get into the vehicle and take off because then the car chase would be on, and that was too much risk to innocent people.

This is one of those, *oh shit* moments as a cop. Do you get out and stop them from getting in and hope your backup is very close or do you let them get into the car and follow them until other units arrive? For my own safety it would be better to wait, but for the safety of the community and the neighborhood full of children, it would be better to get out. I pulled up and got out. This sent both males running in separate directions. I ran after one male and called out the description of the other male and his last direction of travel to the arriving units. Anytime a chase is going on, all available units usually head in that direction to help even if they are not dispatched directly. Thankfully that was what happened in this case.

The male I wasn't chasing was snagged up by one of the cops who was trolling the area. The one I chased decided that he was going to try to enter someone's house via the front door. I chased him up a set of steps to the door, but the door was locked, thankfully for the homeowner's sake. But now I was on the landing to the front door with him in a very tight spot. I was struggling with him, when out of nowhere came my back up, a big guy named Officer Goral. He grabbed onto the bad guy who was being resistive at this point and we both attempted to get the guy cuffed. He did not want to comply with our orders and continued to fight us. Officer Goral attempted to put the guy onto the ground however in doing so the momentum of his pushing the guy sent all of us off the top step and down we went five steps onto the concrete. This would have been okay had the bad guy been on the bottom of the pile, but he wasn't, I was. Four hundred pounds of men slammed me into the concrete. We ended up getting the guy into handcuffs and charging him with a variety of charges. I kept thinking, *this could have been much easier on all of us. My aching back!*

One of the officers on the west side was looking for a hit-and-run driver who happened to live in my district. I was sent to cover him as he went to the residence. The house was on Harvey Street, a two-story old-fashioned house with a big porch and white pillars on the front. This was a probably a one-family at one time but was now converted into a two-family home. The guy we wanted to speak with was supposed to live in the upper unit. It was a Sunday afternoon and was raining pretty hard. Based on my observations, all the neighborhood kids were huddled up on this porch because it was covered. There were also several mothers sitting on the top step to the porch, visiting and smoking cigarettes. One of the mothers had a one-year-old little boy sitting next to her. When we arrived the ladies on the porch were not all that thrilled to see us. Let's face it, not everyone likes the police, that was the case here.

I asked a couple of the ladies if they knew the guy we were looking for, and I got the standard answer, "never heard of him before in my life." We made our way past the blockade of mothers and children to the front door. This house had a common front door that was wide open, this too is pretty common. Once inside it had a lower door to the left and a set of stairs going up to the upper unit. These steps were the really steep kind and were shorter than a normal step. My partner and I were both soaked to the skin and dripping all over the place as we made our way up the stairs to knock on the door.

The male did not answer the door, so my partner left his business card on the upper door. We started our way back down the steps that were now wet and slippery from our dripping clothes and wet shoes. I was leading the way. I got to about midway down the steps when my feet slipped out from under me and I slid down the last six steps feet first. I slid out that front door onto the wet porch. The mama had set that one-year-old right in my path. My boots kicked that baby in the back and he was launched off the porch. I was now laying where he had been sitting, next to his mother. Mama was not happy with the police before, but now she really wasn't happy with us.

The child was crying hysterically, and the mama was demanding to see my supervisor, who my partner had already called for on the radio. The mama seemed to calm down when she realized her child was not injured and that I was. If the guy would have just stuck around from the accident we would have never been on those slippery steps. I was thinking, *this could have been so much easier on all of us. My aching back!*

I was working the afternoon shift in the Broadway district with Officer Gleason. It was mid-March and the snow had been melting gradually. It was raining pretty hard, which would speed up the melting process. We were called to a house on S. Broadway for a medical assist for the fire department. Usually officers go on these calls for several reasons. Many times, the cop is the first one on scene and can get immediate updates to the responding fire units. In the event the person was injured in some type of altercation the response time is important and we can begin the necessary action. We also help out if there are children and pets that need tending to after the person is hauled away to the hospital.

Gleason and I arrived and got out of our cars to head to the house to assess the situation. The driveway had about two inches of water collected on it, or at least it appeared to be just water. Underneath this illusion was a solid layer of ice. One minute I was walking along with Gleason and the next minute I was feet straight out and flat on my back laying in two inches of water. I was able to get my arm down to break the fall a little bit otherwise I would have hit the back of my head on the ice, that would have been really bad. The rescue squad guys were just coming up the walk when this happened, and they were able to pick me up out of the water and get me back up on my feet. I continued on the call with Gleason just in case she needed a cover officer and then I went to the hospital. *Oh, my aching back!*

I was working the afternoon shift in the west side district near West High School. I was sent with Officer Webb to a check the welfare call out on Chantel Street. There was a report of a male acting oddly and believed to be off his psychiatric medications. The caller was reporting the guy was "freaking out." The term *freaking out* can be interpreted in many ways. To one person it could be as little as yelling and screaming, to another person it could be all out smashing the place apart. While I was driving to the call I asked the dispatcher if she could ask the call taker to ask the complainant what "freaking out" meant.

I arrived at the residence about the same time Officer Webb did. We approached the residence and the front door was open, I took a quick peek inside. I notified dispatch they could disregard my request for additional information because the place was trashed. Officer Webb pushed the door open further and announced, "police!" A voice from the back of the house said, "go away." We stepped inside the door into the living room. There was furniture tipped over, broken lamps, pictures, and papers thrown all over. As we further entered the room, I saw the male sitting in a chair in the kitchen rocking back and forth and mumbling to himself.

Officer Webb started to talk to him in a calm manner trying to make small talk and find out what happened. After about two minutes of Officer Webb doing all the talking and this guy just rocking on the chair with a far-off stare, I knew this was not going to be good for us. This guy had what they call the *thousand-yard stare.* To cops that means you need to get your best game on because here it comes and come it did. When this guy realized we were the cops and were going to take him to Brown County, he went absolutely berserk. He started throwing things off the kitchen table and yelling about who knows what, all I kept thinking was, *let's get this guy in some cuffs.*

Officer Webb had his attention and I came up behind him and grabbed his right arm and slammed a cuff on it. Officer Webb didn't get the memo and did not move in and grab his left arm, so I had one cuff on this guy and he was swinging it around like a weapon. I called for more squads ASAP. He bonked the loose handcuff off the top of Officer Webb's head and turned toward me. All I could think was, *this is going to be bad!* He picked me up off my feet and threw me backwards into a wooden kitchen chair. It crumbled like one of those stunt chairs in the movies, but this was no stunt chair and I ended up on the floor on top of the broken chair.

This would have been a really good time to tase him but the taser hadn't been invented yet. Officer Webb had the OC spray out as reinforcements came through the door. The male was overpowered by the additional arriving officers and taken into custody. I got up off the floor and headed to my squad car to get my camera for pictures. All I could think was, *oh my aching back!*

HOT AND COLD

Dressing for the weather is always an issue when you are on patrol. You are in a car some of the time which is temperature controlled but when you get out of the car you have no way of controlling what happens. In the summer, you dress as light as possible but there isn't much you can take off to lighten the load. You are still wearing the thirty pounds of equipment, a ballistic vest, t-shirt, polyester short-sleeve shirt and pants, black socks and either boots or tennis shoes. That is the minimum. On a ninety-degree day with high humidity levels, you spend as much time in your air-conditioned squad as possible. But when the calls come in you leave the comfort of your seventy-degree squad and go where you must.

It was one of those hot sunny ninety-degree days; you could fry an egg on the sidewalk. I was sent with Officer Londo to a house on S. Broadway in the Broadway district. The call was from a mother who wanted to talk to us about her daughter. She had been giving the mother problems and not coming home at night. Officer Londo and I arrived on the call and walked the several houses from our squad to the call location. By the time we reached the front porch I could already feel the sweat running down my chest under my vest. It's weird because although you can feel it, you can't get to it to wipe it away; the ballistic plate that protects you from getting stabbed is in the way.

I knocked on the door and the mother invited us inside. The mom was wearing some cotton shorts and a tank top. We entered the living room area and began to speak to her about her troubled daughter. The house had no air conditioning, the air inside the living room was stagnant and there was not a fan in the place. We were standing in a rather large living room with a half-dozen windows wide open. As I stood listening to this mother go on about the history of problems she has been having with her daughter, I began to feel the effects of the heat. The best thing I can compare this to would be going up into a hot attic full of insulation in the summer. At best you could only stand to be up there for several minutes. We had now been in this house for about ten minutes and I was having some concerns about being overheated. I have to say, this is the hottest house I have ever been in.

I looked over at Officer Londo and could tell by the look on her face she was feeling the same way. After a few more minutes of talking with this mother, I finally told Officer Londo, "we need to wrap this up I feel like I am going to pass out." Politely, we answered a few questions the mother had and referred her to the crisis center for additional services. Then we got the hell out of there, that is what it felt like, hell. I got back to my car and into the ice-cold air conditioning. I could feel my sweat soaked uniform against my body. I spoke with Officer Londo, car-to-car for a moment. She told me she also felt like she was about to pass out.

To the opposite extreme, my winter uniform was all of my equipment and ballistic vest, a long sleeve t-shirt, long underwear, black turtleneck, a long-sleeve polyester uniform, thick black socks and boots, a heavy winter jacket with Thinsulate liner, gloves, knit uniform hat, earmuffs, neck warmer, face mask and hot packs. I didn't wear this all in my car because I had the heater on and would be roasted out. My jacket containing all of my hand and ear protection would lay next to my duty bag. On one call I would learn a very valuable lesson.

It was a cold winter afternoon shift and as night fell, the temperatures dipped below zero. It was an average night until Brown County Sheriff's department called for immediate help on Derby Lane. They were chasing a male on foot who was wanted on homicide charges and were asking for help on the perimeter. I was downtown and responded directly to the area and got out of my car to get on the outside perimeter. I ran up to the house with my shotgun at the ready, my adrenaline pumping and took up a position behind a big tree in the side yard. That's when it dawned on me, *where is my jacket?* It was sitting in my nice warm squad car which was parked a block away. At this point I thought two things, I hope they get this guy right away and thankfully I got out with gloves on.

As additional units arrived and took up various positions, I started coming to the realization this was going to take a while. I kept moving my feet around and had my turtleneck pulled up onto my face but after about fifteen minutes I realized there was no way I was going to survive this call if I didn't get that jacket and my winter gear. Over the radio, the dispatcher reported to all units on the scene that the male was held up inside the house on Derby Lane and the county was calling in their SWAT team.

I knew I had to take some action and fast because it would be another thirty minutes before they arrived. I had to act right, wrong, or indifferent, and now! I sprinted back to my car, grabbed my jacket and ran back to my position by the tree, hoping the bad guy wasn't watching me from the window and using this as his opportunity to escape. I didn't see any tracks in the immediate area, so I figured it was all good. I quickly put on my warm winter jacket and began getting my hat, face mask and neck warmer on. My hands were frozen even though I had gloves on. I added a couple hot packs to my gloves to warm them up. My only problem now was my feet.

I could hardly feel my toes and they were starting to feel like lead. I figured, *oh well, here goes nothing.* If the guy came out I would be chasing him in my socks, but if I could get my boots off and get some hot packs in them I would be set. I quickly sat down by the tree, stripped off my boots, added the hot packs and slammed my feet back into them. I grabbed my shotgun again and was all set. Thankfully I did what I did, because the SWAT team took an hour to get there and take over. I was outside for about two hours. I will tell you this, I never got out of my car in the winter without my jacket again.

CRAP, LITERALLY

There are certain calls that as much as you don't want to deal with, you must, and you must be courteous, respectful and polite in doing so. Officers typically refer to these calls as crap calls. But some calls are crap calls, literally. I had responded to a residence where two males had been outside on the front lawn duking it out. When I arrived with my partner, Officer Rivard (Cowboy), we were able to get the two untangled and with the help of several other arriving officers they were both taken into custody and placed one into each of our patrol cars. After talking to witnesses and family members, it was determined that both males were going to jail for disorderly conduct and battery.

    I was following Rivard to the jail. The male in my back seat was a bit intoxicated and asked me if I could stop so he could use the bathroom. I told him, he would have to hold it until we got to the jail. This is something that I am sure most people do not think about, but an officer cannot pull over at a gas station and allow a prisoner to use the bathroom. This would be an officer safety issue as the male would have to be un-cuffed to perform his duties. This would never happen. It would also be a huge liability in the event the person would assault someone else while in police custody. This male again asked me if I would stop so he could use the bathroom. I again told him he would have to wait until we got to the jail and I assured him upon arrival he would be allowed to use the restroom there. A few minutes went by and the stench of human waste began to fill my car.

    He crapped his pants in my backseat. I rolled the windows down and continued heading to the jail. Upon my arrival, I put on three sets of protective gloves and went to remove him from my back seat. As I grabbed his arm to assist him out of the car, I noticed urine mixed with brown poo in the bucket area of the rear seat. I got him to his feet and escorted him to the jail door. As I was walking with him, liquid poo was running down his legs and onto the floor of the jail garage. He had literally filled his pants and the sad part was, he didn't seem to mind.

    The jailers were less than happy with me because they had to deal with getting his clothes off and washed and giving this guy a shower. Honestly, there was nothing I could do to change the situation. Believe me if I could have, I would have. I returned to my squad and drove directly to the police garage to sanitize my back seat.

    My other shitty situation occurred very early on in my career. I responded to a disturbance in the 300 block of S. Oakland Avenue with Officer Shaw. He was the community officer at the time and knew all of the clients in the area. It was 21:00 and dark as I walked up to where he was talking to a couple of males on a porch. I stood by while they discussed some problems with a couple of the neighbors. Officer Shaw assured them he would put it on his list of troubled houses and he would deal with later them. We made our way back to our patrol cars and drove down the block to discuss this call and whatever else would be relevant to police work that night.

We had our windows down and we were talking car-to-car. It was a chilly fall night, so I cranked on my heat inside the car. I usually had it on the floor and windshield, so it wasn't blowing out of the vents directly on me. That is when I began to smell the aroma of cooking dog crap filling my squad car. I told Officer Shaw that I was pretty sure I had stepped in a pile of dog crap. He laughed and told me that he forgot to mention there were two dogs that lived at the house of the yard I walked through. I pulled my squad forward and got out. My work boot was caked with dog poo. I drove over to the west garage and used the hose to clean off my shoes and the floor of my front seat. That was a good lesson to learn early on, watch where you're walking!

Making a difference in the community

SHOP WITH A COP

Shop with a Cop is a program sponsored by local businesses that allows under privileged children to be paired up with cops to buy Christmas presents for their family members. I have always believed this to be an important event and participated in this program as much as possible. Sometimes it was difficult, participation is during your off time and cops don't get every weekend off. The schedule is five working days, three days off, five working days, three days off. This cycle gives you two weekends off every eight weeks. If you think about that for scheduling family events, that is not many weekends a summer; four if you're lucky. Devoting a Saturday morning to this cause was definitely worth every minute of it.

The day would start out at The Boys and Girls Club where you would be partnered with a shopping buddy. Your shopping buddy would bring a list of all of his or her family members with a couple of items on each person's wish list. Once all the kids were partnered up, we would get on buses donated by Lamers, and head to McDonald's for a donated breakfast of pancakes and sausage, juice, coffee or milk. Then it was off to Shopko to do the shopping with the kids.

At the back of the store by the Christmas trees was the photographer who would snap a photo of you and your shopping buddy. Once shopping was completed it was back on the buses to the Boys and Girls Club for the wrapping and tagging of the gifts. The whole event lasted about six hours and made you feel like you were making a difference, even if it was for such a short time. The first year I participated in Shop with a Cop my photo was on the front page of the Local Section of The Green Bay Press-Gazette. Ironically, this also happened on my last Shop with a Cop, totally unplanned. It was a nice little Christmas send off from The Shop with a Cop program.

OFC. SUSAN BICKETT

MICHAEL VARGUS

I was dispatched to a call on Dousman Street. It was a *check the welfare* type call for a male who had been drinking for days passed out inside his apartment. The caller thought this male was going to die from alcohol poisoning. I went on the call with Officer York. Upon arrival I knocked on the door. There was no answer. I tried the door handle and it was unlocked. Based on the call information, I entered the residence. I announced it was the police and again there was no response from anyone inside. This was a small efficiency apartment, an eat-in kitchen, a small bathroom off the kitchen and a living room area with a bed. As I entered the living room I saw a male laying on the sofa. On the coffee table in front of him was an oversized ashtray heaping with cigarette butts and a stack of beer cans a mile high. I went up to the male, he did almost look dead.

You never want to stand directly in front of an intoxicated person when you wake them, many times they wake up swinging. I nudged his foot a few times with no response, so I gave his foot a good kick. Slowly I saw some movement, I yelled very loudly that it was the police. He gave a few groans and started to come to. He was a frail looking man with long stringy hair that looked like it hadn't been combed in days. He had a week's growth of hair on his face. I watched as his eyes rolled around in his head until he was finally able to focus on me. His first words were, "What the fuck are you doing here?" except it wasn't that clear. It was more of a slurred garble of words, but I could still make out what he was saying. I thought, *holy cow this guy is fubar!* That is an acronym for *fucked up beyond all recognition.* I explained that someone had called to report he had been on a drinking binge. He self-admitted that he had been drunk for about a week.

I located his wallet on the coffee table under the stack of Budweiser beer cans. I asked him if I could look in his wallet for his ID. He said yes. As I thumbed through a stack of cards in his wallet, I noticed two things, he had an ID card from a Native American tribe and also a veteran ID card. These two forms of identification are significant when dealing with intoxicated individuals. Having that Native American ID card meant he had services available to him through the tribe. The veteran ID card meant he had served our country, which meant he had probably seen much in his tour and could be highly trained in firearms and hand to hand combat. Another variable when dealing with combat vets, PTSD. What this meant to me was I would have to deal with this guy with kid gloves. I took a very soft approach with him, telling him we were there to help him and careful to not say anything that would upset him. Intoxicated people are often times irrational and hard to deal with.

Things were going pretty well. We got him up off the sofa although he could not stand without our assistance. This guy was in bad shape. This was back in the day when Brown County Mental Health still took intoxicated people and that is exactly where this guy needed to go. The only problem now was convincing him this is where he needed to go. I told him I knew of a place where he could get some help and I wanted to take him there. After speaking with him for a while, he agreed to go with me.

Our department policy says that you handcuff everyone who you transport. When I took the cuffs out, that was the deal breaker. He insisted he was not going in cuffs. Sometimes as a cop you have to use your common sense. I could have told him he was going in cuffs and then we would have rolled around on the floor with him kicking and fighting us, risking injury to himself, my partner, or me. Another option was that I could bend the rules a little bit and agree to have him ride out there uncuffed. I did the latter.

Once I had him in the back of my squad and was driving out there, he began to think about that and asked me why I didn't make him go in handcuffs. I told him I trusted him and knew he was not going to hurt me. He started talking to me about the wrongs he had done in his past and that no one ever trusted him. When he started telling me different stories about how he had hurt people including cops in the past, I was thinking to myself, *man, I hope I didn't screw up by not putting this guy in cuffs!* That's when I told him that no matter what he had done in his past, God would forgive him. I told him about the grace of God; he would always be a child of God, no matter what he had done. I told him he still had time for redemption and he should think about that aspect of life. I got him to Brown County without a problem and when I left him there he thanked me for being so good with him.

But that is not where this story ends. About a month later I received a letter in my department mailbox. It was from him. It was a letter of thanks for saving his life and for trusting him. He told me because of the way I treated him and talked to him about God's redemption, he was getting help and had joined AA. That wasn't the only letter I would receive from him. Every year he would send me his anniversary coin from AA for being sober. At Christmas I would get a card with a letter updating me on his progress in life. As the years past, he moved back out to Cloquet, Minnesota where his tribe was located. He had become an alcohol and drug counselor and was helping others who were struggling as he had. What a reward for one act of kindness, that is what keeps a cop doing what they do every day.

Here's the most recent letter from Michael on March 09, 2016

My Dearest Samantha,

You will always be "My Dearest Samantha," February 10th is my 13th year Sobriety Anniversary. "But for the grace of God!" I haven't been in Green Bay since my dear friend Barbara passed away. She had emotional issues and lived with me for six years. I guess I sort of adopted her. I tend to be the Knight in Shining Armor and rescue "Damsels' in Distress" It's all God driven. I received my medallion at the Wednesday Calvary Lutheran Church meeting and when I spoke, I talked about you and the profound difference you made in my life and what you did that day. People spoke during the meeting about how inspired they were by my story about us. See...You have and will continue to touch and inspire people for years to come. You are the centerpiece of my recovery. You brought me to God.... AA....and a whole new way of life. I am eternally grateful!! Enclosed is my thirteen-year medallion. There were fifty people at the meeting and I asked them to put their dreams, hopes and prayers on it because I was going to give it to you. Hold it and carry it with you for Divine Protection as you "Serve and Protect" us as a police officer.

God Bless You Always,
Your Friend for Life,
Michael Vargus "Gray Wolf"

YES MA'AM

THE TONES ...AND OTHER SITUATIONS THAT CHALLENGE YOUR TRAINING

THE TONES

*T*HE TONES WERE AN ALERT TO ALL UNITS signaling something big was in progress; a gun call, knife call or a robbery in progress. It was a long high-pitched sounding beep that lasted 3-5 seconds. As a dispatcher I hated giving these calls, and as an officer I hated hearing the tones. When I started my career, the tones were only given about once a week. At the end of my career it was every shift, every day. I remember as a young officer hearing that sound and my heart would go into my throat and I'd think *Is this the day that I have trained for, read about and dreaded all at the same time?* Time would stand still for that brief moment while the dispatcher read off the location and the details that were known about the call; many times, even dispatch didn't have the whole story.

As a dispatcher you were always dealing with some hysterical person yelling into the phone for help. Usually they had no idea where they were, what had really happened or a good description of the bad guy. All the caller knew was they needed help and they needed it now. This was very difficult knowing the officers on the road would be asking questions about the call and you did not have the answers.

Once I became an officer I had nothing but respect for those taking the 911 calls and dispatching. That is a thankless job, so I thank you all for the job you do day after day. Thank you.

Now as a seasoned officer, the tones go out and the thoughts are more like *no big deal, another gun call, big whoop.* It's funny how in the beginning this was such an awful sound and now they mean nothing unusual to me.

EAST TOWN

I was working the day shift in the downtown district with my partner, Officer Leers. It was one of those Sunday mornings where nothing was going on, which was sometimes nice. This allows officers time to catch up on the backlog of paperwork that piles up or on follow ups, which are cases that get assigned back to you for continued investigation. Not every report goes to detectives, many times the road officer is responsible for the continued investigation and arrests. Quiet times between calls when you do not have to chase the radio is a good time to get things done.

No sooner did I get myself parked over by East High School and pull out my follow up folder, and the tones went out. A man with a gun, dang. The call was a domestic call. The soon to be ex-wife was reporting her soon to be ex-husband was at her apartment with a gun, threatening to shoot her. One of those ugly divorce calls, that always contain the line "I can't live without her." That is a bad line because it shows the desperation and the mindset of a person, they have nothing to lose. I was responding to the call, red lights and siren.

It was pretty easy to get through traffic because there wasn't any on a Sunday morning. The call was far east out on Chapel View Road and as I turned from Main Street onto E. Mason Street, Officer Leers was directly in front of me. As we made our way up the big hill by the old Kmart store, the dispatcher reported the male had a long rifle and had left the residence a short time ago in a red Chevy Silverado pick-up truck with Michigan plates. The words went out over the radio, and there was the truck heading westbound on E. Mason Street. The guy must have seen us coming because as we saw him he pulled into the East Town Mall parking lot, did a loop around the lot and then stopped and parked in the middle of the lot.

I pulled in and so did Officer Leers, but knowing he had a rifle we stayed pretty far back. The mall was not open yet. The only businesses that were open in the area were McDonald's and Perkins. It was winter, but it wasn't bitter cold. I still put my jacket on and had my .223 rifle racked and ready to roll; so did Officer Leers. The things that go through your mind at a time like this are unreal. *Was this the day I had trained my whole career for? Were we going to have to shoot this guy?* All it would take is for him to step out with his rifle and point it at us and we would take him out, if he didn't take one of us out first. I thought about my family but even more, I thought about Officer Leers' family. My family was all grown, but Officer Leers had little kids at home and a stay-at-home wife who took care of them. I was wishing I was in the position Officer Leers was because he was closer and more in the line of sight if the guy stepped out.

We had the radio channel dedicated to just this call; something that is done on weapon calls. You don't want to get interrupted by someone calling out with traffic stops or by other calls that would be going on. Officer Leers reported he could clearly see the guy did in fact have a rifle in the front seat with him.

As other officers arrived on scene, I was glad to see Officer King arrive behind me, he was a SWAT guy and one of the sharpshooters for the team. He took up a position on a large snow bank that was thirty feet high. He also had his binoculars and could clearly see the guy's movements in the front seat from his angle. Officer Knapp, also a SWAT team member working at the time of the call, went to headquarters and picked up the SWAT truck. He arrived with the truck within ten minutes. Additional SWAT members arrived and took up positions on top of the mall stores. We had this guy surrounded.

Officer Leers was able to contact the guy on the cellphone and began to negotiate with him, trying to persuade him to come out with his hands up and leave the rifle in the truck. This was the type of call you read about in the papers, suicide by cop. It would have been so easy for him, just step out with the gun pointed at us. I give a lot of credit to these SWAT guys, they train for this type of situations over and over again, and today it paid off.

After about a half hour of talking to this guy, Officer Leers got him to step out without the gun and the guy was taken into custody and brought to the Brown County Treatment Center for help. Thank you, SWAT guys.

TAKING A GUN TO A KNIFE FIGHT

People always ask, "isn't it scary to be a cop?" My answer to that is always, "I am never afraid or scared, because it is my calling to do this job." I guess in the back of my mind I always thought that God brought me here to do this, to serve others and to protect others. I always felt He was looking out for me and if it was His will that I would die this way, then that it what He wanted for me. But that doesn't mean I have never been tested that's for sure.

I never shot anyone, but I certainly had my gun out many times and in a matter of seconds, had the situation not changed, I would have fired if I was forced to do so. Thankfully, that was not my fate. The closest I came to ever shooting someone was at the Economy Inn back in the late 1990's. I was called there for a report of a man with a knife running around the hallways threatening people. People generally think that a knife is not as dangerous as a gun. If you had the training that officers have, you would realize that it is every bit as dangerous, if not more so. A person with a knife, twenty-one feet away from you, can stab and kill you before you can even get a shot off. Most people don't have that knowledge, but I did. Many times, officers can be hesitant when dealing with a person wielding a knife; it's not like a guy with a gun pointing at you, in which case you definitely pull the trigger. I arrived at the hotel as well as several other officers. I spoke to the desk clerk who was the caller of the complaint. He said the male in room 203 was high on drugs, intoxicated, and in the hallway with a large butcher knife threatening people. This called for immediate police action.

I went up to the second floor with the other officers. I did not see or hear any kind of disturbance going on and feared that maybe we were already too late, and people who had been stabbed were going to be laying all over the place. There was no one in the hallways. I went to room 203 with my partner. I listened by the door and could hear a television faintly through the door. After several minutes and having heard nothing else, I knocked on the door. We already had our guns out and pointed at the door. The door opened quickly and there he was, a man standing in his underwear holding a giant butcher knife over his head about five feet away from us. Yikes! That's way less than twenty-one feet. At that very moment we would have been justified to shoot immediately, but we didn't. My partner and I both backed up and I yelled, "drop the knife!" and to my surprise, he did. If he hadn't, I would be telling you a much different story. Instead we took the male to the Brown County Mental Health Center for treatment. All I can say to that guy is, "thanks for dropping the knife when I asked you to."

MOTEL 6

There is nothing quite like pulling up to a disturbance, grabbing your 12 gauge out of the squad car rack, getting out of the car and racking one in. It is a very distinct sound and to be honest, it captures people's attention really quick. I was good with the shotgun, very comfortable and natural with it. If that gun was an option for patrol today, I would still be carrying it. When we did have them in the squads, at the start of every shift you could hear that racking sound of guys checking their weapons to make sure they were operating properly. I loved that sound.

It was a summer day in July when I was sent to Motel 6 for a report of a male with a gun in one of the rooms. The details were sketchy, but someone reported a guy out in the parking lot waiving a pistol around and yelling at a female, then both people went into a room together. I was screaming across town from downtown toward Motel 6. I was telling people to get out of the way, honking my air horn and changing the tones on my siren all the way there; not that anyone could hear me swearing at cars or yelling to move over, but for some reason it is pretty common for officers to do inside their squads on the way to calls. The only thing about this practice nowadays is this is all recorded on your in-squad recording system. If something were to happen on the way to the call, like an accident, all the cop's swearing and yelling inside his car would be on tape for the entire world to hear. This was never the case early in my career. After learning the ropes and getting comfortable, my commentative driving reduced over time; I didn't want that showing up in some courtroom.

I was listening to the police radio for updates. Speaking of radios, that is another thing I never did in my squad, listen to the music radio. I mean really, a cop needs to multitask enough already. Adding blaring music on top of the regular police dispatch radio, driving in traffic, thinking about the call you're going on, didn't help. I know there would be some guys who would answer their police radio, key the microphone an extra click and it would pick up ACDC blasting out one of their famous tunes into the police radio and then click off. Sometimes the dispatcher would come over the air and say, "repeat, you had too much background noise," that was the universal comment to *shut your damn music off!*

As I was driving to this call, like I did on most all my calls, I was thinking about where I was going to park, what I was going to do and rehearsed what I was going to say on the call. At least as much as I could pre-think about before I got there. I arrived at Motel 6 pulled in on the east side of the building and parked. The room where the gunman went in was on the west side of the building. I grabbed my shotgun, got out of the car and racked one in; there was that sound! Except it did not capture the attention of the bad guy since he was on the other side of the building, but it did catch the attention of the Press-Gazette reporter who was already on scene with camera in hand. As other Officers arrived, and a perimeter was set up around the building, I was told by the Lieutenant to come around the back side of the building and get to a position of advantage on the room. I ran around the building and when I did, that photographer got me in an action shot that appeared in the Press-Gazette the next day.

The guy with the gun answered the motel door when the officers knocked. He was intoxicated and admitted to waiving around a loaded .38 in the parking lot. He said he was mad at his girlfriend and he was trying to scare her. Mission accomplished! The drunk, gun waiving man was now going to jail.

The photo for the Press-Gazette would be one of many of me that would make the papers over the years. It earned me the nickname of "newshound" to many of my fellow workers, family and friends. Every single time I would get a call from my mother who would tell me to "quit that damn job! It's too dangerous!" I would always diminish the true danger of any call I was on and tell her everything was fine, I was never in any danger, when really, I could have been shot on any one of them. It is what cops do every day without a second thought.

LOOK UP

The reality of suicide has always been a hard concept to stomach for me. In a line of work where people fight every day to stay in this world, it has always been hard for me to comprehend how many people fight so hard to get out. The people who leave notes or tell people are the ones who really don't want to end their lives but rather are crying out for help. It is often said that people who truly have their minds made up to end their life don't leave a note or tell anyone, they just do it.

I went on many suicide calls over my career, some successful and some not. One of the worst ones was on West Point many years ago. We were called by a distraught wife who was reporting her husband had not been seen since the night before. She said she called friends and family, but no one had heard from him. I was sent to take the missing person report. When I arrived at the residence, I met with the female in their living room. She told me they had both been intoxicated and had a verbal fight the night before. She told me she wasn't sure where he would have gone but was sure he walked off since both their vehicles were still in the garage.

I took all the information on the male for the report. Then I asked her if I could get their vehicle information to add to the report in the event he came back for a vehicle and left again. This information would be sent out on the missing person attempt to locate on the male. She showed me to the door off the kitchen that led to the garage. I turned on the garage light and entered the two-stall garage, walked to the back of each vehicle and copied down the license plates and vehicle descriptions. That is when I looked up to the rafters of the garage, and there he was. Hanging off in the dark corner of the garage. I actually jumped when I saw him.

He was obviously dead. I called for a rescue squad, another unit, and a supervisor ASAP. I went over to the male and checked his body, he was cold, stiff and deceased. I went back into the residence and waited for my cover, I did not tell his wife until they arrived. It is one of the hardest things to tell someone, ever. I will never forget the sound of the wife's wailing when we broke the news to her. Rescue arrived and cut him down and called the ME. I stayed with the wife and contacted some family members to come be with her. It is so hard to watch someone in so much pain, there is nothing you can do about it, not a thing. He didn't leave a note.

BABY AUTOPSY

After spending sixteen years on the road I joined the ranks of the detective division of the department. I had spent about two weeks in the position when I realized I had made a really bad mistake. I was assigned to the afternoon shift crew. Most of the detectives on that shift were people I didn't get along with, but I had wanted to try this job for as long as I can remember. Maybe I was a little burnt out from being on the road and chasing the radio or maybe it was the lure of knowing I always loved to hunt down the bad guy and get to the bottom of things. I got to the bottom of things in that division in a quick hurry. Most of the people I was working with spent a large part of their time trying to look busy and doing as little as possible. That part worked out well; it gave me plenty of work. The more days I spent back there working, the more the slackers resented me. They made it known that I was not welcome in their little unproductive world. Every day I would go in with a black cloud hanging over me, waiting for the bullying to begin. After my first couple of weeks, I had the opportunity to go back on the road. I went in and talked to my captain who told me he wanted me to stick it out for at least six months, he thought I hadn't given it a chance. I could see his point, so I stuck it out. During that six months I was given over one hundred counterfeit cases and investigated them all. I ended up taking down a major player and his team of puppets who were passing counterfeit money all over Green Bay. That was a sense of accomplishment. Other than that, it pretty much sucked.

One afternoon, I flexed my hours to come in early. The detective lieutenant called me into his office and told me I would be going to a baby autopsy. I was told that the child, a six-month-old, had died of suspicious causes and was currently at the morgue located at St. Vincent Hospital. I was assigned to go with Detective Graves who would show me the ropes. He was my least favorite detective and was as lazy as the day is long. I had worked with him on the road for many years, he was a slacker to say the least.

I want you to understand this, really get what I have to say here. No matter what you see in your entire life it will never, I mean never compare to watching this. For all you TV loving crime show analysts who think CSI, Bones or whatever other shows depict autopsies, I tell you they show nothing like the reality of the situation.

We got to the morgue in the basement of the hospital with the medical examiner and the coroner. We walked into the cooler. On the shelf was a small body bag about the size of a carry-on suitcase with a small lock similar to a suitcase lock on the bag. We followed the ME and coroner into the cold examination room which contained a large stainless-steel sink, countertop and island. The body bag was opened on this steel island. There he was, this most beautiful baby boy. I stood there mortified. Here was this little angel laying there eternally sleeping. He looked so perfect. That's when the Coroner started the Rotozip saw. I watched as the coroner and ME sawed the top of his head off and removed his brain. He then peeled his face off down to his nose area. I watched as he took a scalpel, opened his chest and removed all his organs and placed them on the stainless-steel countertop, then weighed and measured each one. I watched as he dissected a baby.

The ME and coroner were carrying on a conversation as if it were just another day. They talked about the baseball game the night before and all the sports their kids were involved in. I was standing there with Mr. Congeniality, and my insides were screaming for this to be over. I continued watching while they took their samples and whatever they needed and stuffed all the left-over pieces and parts back into the chest cavity and the brain back into the top of his head, set the skull cap back on the baby, put his face back on and put him back in the bag. The ME told me they are very delicate when doing these on people they know are going to have an open casket because it's important to the family not to butcher them up. At this point all I could think was, *get me the hell out of here!* Some people might have found this interesting and to them I give great credit. For me there isn't enough money in the world that would pay me to see dead babies day after day.

400 N. MONROE AVE

400 N. Monroe is an apartment complex specifically designed for the elderly, low income and disabled. I have been to this eight story building hundreds of times over my career. My last nine years I was a downtown car on the day shift, so I got to know the managers and most of the residents quite well. Mr. Walls was a tall, thin, charming man. He would give me a smile and a wave as he walked to the Marathon station to get his morning cup of coffee and the Press Gazette. He was somewhat introverted and didn't talk much. Most of the residents there either keep to themselves or are so outgoing you can't get them to be quiet.

I was called to the building by the manager, Jeb. The report was of a foul smell, like rotten garbage coming from Mr. Walls' apartment, who hadn't been seen in several days. Any veteran cop knows those two comments are never good. I responded with a supervisor, Lt. Wagner. I did not know this was going to be one of the worst calls I had ever been on. As we walked off the elevator on the fourth floor, I gave him a look and mentioned that it didn't smell too bad. We met Jeb, at the door of Mr. Walls' apartment. He told us he had already opened the apartment door to check on Mr. Walls; he was deceased in his bathtub. A dead guy in a bathtub, how bad can it be? Jeb used the pass key again and opened the door. The smell was like nothing I had ever smelled in my entire career. If I had a weak stomach I surely would have thrown up. My eyes began to water, and the stench was overpowering. Some of the guys carry Vicks Vapor Rub in their briefcases to put under their nose to mask the smell. I never did that but if I had some with me I would have for this call; it was retched.

I walked into the hallway and looked to my left into the bathroom. The overhead light was on. There was Mr. Walls, rotting in a bathtub filled with black, disgusting water. Mr. Walls used to be a white man, but now his skin was almost completely black. I wanted to close the door, get in my car and leave. But, we are the police; we can't leave. I had a feeling of utter disgust. I had a few questions running through my head; number one, why hadn't anyone checked on him before this, and number two, what person on this entire floor couldn't tell that smell was *dead body*? I was actually pissed off that Mr. Walls had laid in a bathtub soaking for three days. Damn, that was bad.

I looked around to see if there were any signs of foul play. There was an ice pick next to the bathtub. Who has an ice pick in their bathroom? I called in the detectives. After I described the scene to them it seemed to take an extra-long time for them to arrive on the scene. The ME and the funeral home guys actually beat them. Here is the thing you don't visualize, and Hollywood doesn't show you. How does that black, decaying man get out of that bathtub if he is dead? People like the ME, and the guys from the funeral home have to lift him out and place him into a body bag. We all put on rubber gloves and everyone takes a leg or arm. This corpse had been soaking for days. It was like pulling a chicken out of a kettle after being boiled for 3 days;

everything was coming off the bones. Once we had him out of the tub, we could see Mr. Walls had no signs of injuries to his body; other than what we just did to him by lifting him out of the tub. We had to drain the bathtub to ensure there wasn't any evidence in the water. This tub did not have a switch to flip to drain the water, someone had to put their arm into the tub and pull the drain by hand. The apartment manager Jeb volunteered to do the job. He placed a large black plastic garbage bag on his right arm and plunged his arm into the black water. The tub drained and there was no evidence located. The detectives finished taking their photos. The neighbors solved the ice pick question. We were told Mr. Walls was a paranoid man, he always had that with him as protection. That made sense.

I left the building and all I could smell was death on my clothes and my hair. Everything smelled of that foul, retched odor. Lt. Wagner told me to drive straight home, take a shower and change my uniform. I had never done this before; but then again, I had never been on a call this bad before. I did as I was ordered. Thank you, Lt. Wagner! This was my last dead body call. Thank God!

WE ARE NOT IMMUNE

Most people don't look at cops as normal people. I can understand that in some ways. We are held to a higher standard than the general public and let's face it, how many people do you know who would lay down their life for a total stranger. But the reality of it is, aside from being devoted to serving as an officer, we are just like you and your family. We all have our share of personal problems, relationship problems and even tragedy.

I had just attended afternoon shift roll call where I sat next to Officer Dellinger. He and I had been friends for a very long time and we shared many of the same family values. He was always joking around and giving people the business. Officer Dellinger had two daughters; one step daughter and one biological daughter. I always felt bad for the guy, he had shitty luck in relationships. His wife went off the deep end and was committed to a mental institution which meant he had custody of his teenage daughters. He was dating a gal from the 911 center who I also knew quite well.

The roll call was short and sweet. I joked with Officer Dellinger as we left the room that day. I was on the dispatcher that day, so I was heading up to the radio room and he was heading out on the road. I got into the room and as luck would have it, Tera, Officer Dellinger's girlfriend was at dispatch. Normally when you take over at one of the stations, the person you are relieving gives you a brief update on what is currently going on in the city. As I walked up she told me a fiery crash had just occurred out on Sturgeon Bay Road and University Avenue, units had just been sent and that is all she knew at this time.

As I sat down, the plate from the vehicle on fire came into the call from teletype. It came back to Officer Dellinger. Tera stood up and yelled out loud, "holy shit, those are Matt's kids!" and ran out of the room. I immediately called Officer Dellinger over the police radio to report to the shift commander. I did not want him looking up the calls once he was logged into the computer to see his name on the plate in that call. Then I called the shift commander and told him Officer Dellinger's kids were most likely in the burning car. The operations commander took Officer Dellinger and Tera out to the crash scene. It was his children in the car as well as another teenage boy. They did not get out and were all burnt alive.

Witnesses said the car veered off the roadway, went down a steep embankment, struck a tree and burst into flames. Several witnesses tried to get near the car, but the intensity of the fire was too hot to get close enough. Witnesses also said they could hear the girls screaming for help as the car was burning. My God, how do you ever live with that image? My friend and partner Officer Dellinger, would never be the same, who would after dealing with that? I went to the funeral; he had both girls' funerals together. I cannot recall a more utterly sad day than that. I talked to Officer Dellinger, he was numb. He told me he was struggling with not having any part of them left. Having some*thing* to mourn is a huge part of closure. I knew there would never be closure for him, but I still had to try.

The day after the funeral and now five days after the crash, I drove my squad car out to the crash scene. I parked along the roadway and walked down the embankment, following the tire tracks in the grass to a burnt black area in the grass at the tree. The tree was not more than fifteen inches wide and I thought to myself as I looked at it, *out of all the area here, that car had to hit that tree in the middle of nowhere.* There was also a chain link fence about one-hundred feet past the tree, and my thoughts were, *if they missed the tree, the fence would have caught them, and they would still be here.* But that isn't what happened. Instead they were gone, and my friend was suffering immeasurable pain and agony.

I got down on my hands and knees and began looking through the grass around the burnt area of the car, almost as if I had a premonition I would find something. I kept looking and there it was, a dark brown ringlet of hair, about four inches long and singed on both ends. This was why I was there. I snatched it up and placed it in a plastic zip bag. The chances of finding this could compare to actually finding a needle in a haystack. Think of all the people, cops, detectives, fire and rescue, ME, wrecker drivers, investigators, sight seers, and anyone else nosing around. How is it possible this lock of hair was not disturbed after five days? It was meant to be. I had to follow proper procedure and enter this in as evidence in the case, and I was glad to do it. This lock of hair would be locked up in evidence and would be there for Officer Dellinger when he was ready for it. I called him and told him about it. He was thankful and grateful I had done what he could not do, go to the scene and look like he would have looked, with a fine-tooth comb. Two years later, Officer Dellinger finally recovered the priceless lock of hair from evidence.

Another one of my fellow coworkers Officer Noble lost his daughter in a crash as well. This was a highly publicized case involving an intoxicated female who was drag racing on S. Oneida Street and ran a red light killing both Officer Noble's daughter and one of his daughter's friends.

Another one of my fellow coworkers, Officer Grant, lost his son to what was called an accidental shooting. Officer Grant's son, Jerry, was home alone for the weekend while the family was out of town. When they returned, Officer Grant found his son deceased in the home, shot with Officer Grant's own gun.

Bad things happen to cops too, really bad things. As parents, you are not supposed to bury your children. I cannot even fathom going through this and working. Imagine taking a week off and coming back to working the streets. I was on a traffic crash with Officer Grant shortly after he returned to work. Rescue had to be called for an injured driver. As we stood there waiting for them to arrive, I could hear their siren coming from several blocks away. I looked over at Officer Grant, he was crying. He told me when he hears sirens coming like that it reminds him of waiting for help on the morning he found his son. I told him I would work the traffic crash we were on and he could leave. He did and later apologized for his actions. No apology necessary. We are all human, even the cops!

YES MA'AM

THE UNBELIEVABLE ...AND OTHER SITUATIONS THAT MAKE YOU SHAKE YOUR HEAD.

THE TAMPON STORY

I HAD JUST PULLED INTO EXPRESS GAS STATION to use the restroom and change my tampon. This was always such a chore in uniform. You had to practically undress to get your pants down. It was also sort of gross doing this at gas stations. Finding a place to set your gun belt many times meant putting it on the floor in the bathroom, which is pretty disgusting when you think about the urine and germs on a public bathroom floor. Sometimes you could lay it over the sink but honestly that is not much cleaner. What I did learn is you go to the bathroom when you can; even if you don't feel like you have to. If you didn't take the opportunity, you could get caught on a call for hours. For a woman during that time of the month, that could spell big trouble.

I had just taken a tampon out of my duty bag and placed it in my top shirt pocket when I was dispatched to a house fire on N. Maple Avenue; the dispatcher said the location was totally engulfed. I had said and heard these words many times in my career, but seeing it is an entirely different situation. I was two blocks away; I looked in the direction of the call and could see smoke and flames coming over the treetops. I activated my emergency lights and siren and arrived on the scene in less than a minute. I parked in the alley, the fire trucks would be arriving and would need the space on the road. I got out of my car and started walking toward the fire. It was eerie. I was completely alone standing in front of the biggest bonfire I had ever seen. This had been a beautiful, old, two-story wood house built at the turn of the century. The flames were shooting hundreds of feet in the air. I could not even get close to the house, the heat was unbearable, and I was wearing polyester; not a good combination. I had instant respect for firemen from that moment on. I stood there watching this magnificent house burn. The flames were dancing out the windows and into the night sky. The firemen arrived and started putting out the fire.

Just like in the movies, it is the police officer's job to keep the crowds back, interview for witnesses and watch for a pyro who may have stuck around to admire his handiwork. I knew there was no one around when I arrived, however several neighbors had come out of their houses after seeing the red lights from the firetrucks flashing in their windows and of course the hundred-foot flames. I learned from several neighbors this was a vacant house that was being refurbished. One neighbor told me there was wood stripping chemicals on the side enclosed porch that could have accelerated the fire. I took down the names of the people I talked to and jotted their information into my pocket notebook. The pocket notebook is a patrolman's bible. You record all the names of people, birth dates, locations, things said to you in this notebook. It is something to refer back to when typing up your reports. That night my little pocket notebook would prove to be something else.

After the fire was put out, hours upon hours later, all the units on the scene, including my boss Lt. Timms, the fire inspector, fire captains, and arson investigators gathered in a circle under a street light to share information. The group was all men and one woman, me. Lt. Timms asked me what I had learned. I went to pull my notebook out of my top shirt pocket. As I made a swinging motion with the notebook, a tampon came flying out seemingly in slow motion with all eyes trained on it and landed directly in the middle of the circle. Instinctively about five guys immediately bent down to pick it up until they realized it was a tampon and did the backpedal. Never have I seen a group of tough firemen retreat so fast from anything. I could feel my face go completely red. There was a long moment of silence. As diplomatically as I could, I reached down to pick it up and said, "I got this, guys." Awkward.

THE CONCRETE DONKEY

My friends were always playing pranks on me as a cop. Sometimes they would see me on Dousman Street running radar and then turn around and zoom past or hang out the windows yelling crazy things at me. It was all in fun. After Christmas they would go around collecting Christmas trees that had been left at the curb for pick up and place them all in my front yard. When I woke up there would be thirty Christmas trees in my front yard. Sometimes I would get them back when I was out and about and saw their cars parked somewhere. I would place a yellow piece of paper under their windshield wiper to make it look like a parking ticket. After they got nervous they found a little message telling them to have a nice day.

I really had nothing to do with this particular story in the beginning. A group of my friends were out driving around when they came across a little concrete donkey with a broken leg. The concrete had chipped away from the rebar exposing about eight inches of rusty rebar; the rest of his legs were fine. The donkey was out at the curb in a pile of junk, so they took it. This was now the latest prop for their pranks. The donkey would be dressed up in different outfits, mostly football attire, and ended up in various friends' front yards as a gag for about a year. He even went to Madison and Manitowoc before he finally ended up back in Green Bay. My friend Lana took it home, cleaned it up, dressed it in her favorite team apparel and placed it in her basement as a cheerleader for the Miami Dolphins. After many years of rooting on the team Lana decided it was time to let her little donkey go, but not without one last spoof. The donkey was loaded into the truck and transported over to Patty's house and placed in the middle of her driveway.

At ten o'clock p.m. Patty went out to her driveway to get something out of her car only to find her car had been stolen and someone left an ass in her driveway. She immediately called the police. The officer came over and took the stolen vehicle report and confiscated the donkey as evidence. I knew nothing about this until later that night when Lana called me, worried sick the police were going to fingerprint the donkey and find her prints all over it. I swear I got such a good laugh out of this story and how funny it was that Lana didn't know Patty's car had been stolen and Patty thought the car thieves left the ass as if to be calling her one. The next day, I had to go in and talk to the detective captain and get Lana's ass out of evidence!

TEACH YOUR CHILDREN WELL

Kids learn from their parents. When a child is acting up somewhere and the parent sees a cop, sometimes you hear them say "If you don't start listening I am going to have that cop come and arrest you and take you to jail." WHAT? No, this cop isn't going to do any such thing. Why would you make a cop the boogeyman? Telling your kids that cops are going to take them to jail is only telling them that cops are bad. I was never a bad cop, ever.

I was driving through my district on a beautiful sunny afternoon. I remember I was having sort of a blue day, cops have those too. I was driving and thinking and driving some more. It's always good when the citizens see officers in their neighborhoods patrolling. I was driving down a residential road where there were people out on their porches and kids playing outside. I was traveling very slowly and waving to the kids as I drove by. That's when I saw him. This little man, a cute little Native American boy about the age of four was running toward the roadway, toward my car. I stopped in the roadway and rolled down my window. He stopped, took a crouched stance, and with his tiny little hand he flipped me the bird and then ran back into his house. I thought, *seriously! Did that little four-year-old just flip me off? Wow.* I drove away thinking, *there is the future of our country.*

I got a few blocks away and thought, *bullshit!* I turned around and went up to that house and knocked on the door. The child's grandfather answered, I knew him from many previous arrests; I knew the child's mother as well. I explained what the boy had done, even though I know it fell on deaf ears. At least it made me feel better. Kids don't learn that from watching TV.

WOMAN ON THE BRIDGE

It had been snowing nonstop since early that morning. The weather conditions had been deteriorating rapidly as the day continued. By the time I reached work the roads were hazardous at best. The mechanics already had chains on the tires of all the squad cars. The squads have always been rear wheel drive which is not the best for traction in the snow to begin with. The chains made it easier to get around, but it was still hard getting anywhere fast. The maximum speed with chains is about thirty-five miles per hour. I was working the afternoon shift and as the day wore on I worked traffic crash after traffic crash. Cops don't call them accidents because most crashes are not accidents. They are generally the result of driving too fast for conditions, following too closely, or inattentive driving. Of course, we don't tell people that, but the citations usually clue them in. It was tough going as I made my way around the city. By the time darkness fell, we were under white out conditions.

In cop time at 20:00 hours (or eight o'clock p.m. for civilians) the Department of Public works was doing some kind of work on the Main Street Bridge. We were notified by dispatch there was some type of malfunction and the bridge was currently stuck in the open position. Not only was it busy with the blizzard conditions, we also had to reroute traffic away from that bridge to either the Walnut Street Bridge or the Mason Street Bridge. I was assigned to the west side of the bridge with Officer Burkhart. Each of us placed our squad cars on N. Broadway and Dousman Street. This would block anyone from traveling eastbound onto the bridge. There were two other officers assigned to the east side to block traffic going westbound onto the bridge. This was not a bad assignment considering it meant we could sit in our warm squad cars as travelers came to this location and realized they could not get past us and continued on. This also meant with four officers tied up on this one call, the rest of the officers in the city were getting hammered with working more calls than usual. It was the luck of the draw to have been assigned here.

We waited for word on whether the bridge was going to be closed for an extended period of time, in which case barricades would be brought out, or just a short period of time, which would leave us here. I remember thinking to myself that there were two businesses that were open between us and the bridge, Titletown Brewing and Gallagher's Pizza. These parking lot areas had direct access to the bridge. The saving grace was the gates on the bridge were down and all the red flashing lights and warning signs were operating; for the few people leaving those businesses it would be obvious they could not get onto the bridge, or so I thought. This is one thing about being a cop that you learn rather quickly, *what is obvious to you is not always obvious to many members of the general public.* As I sat in my warm squad car with the heater on full blast trying to dry out my now soaked uniform and long johns, wet socks, and boots, I looked eastbound toward the bridge. I saw a vehicle covered in snow pulling out of the access road from Gallagher's and turn eastbound toward the bridge. The visibility was bad, I could barely make out two red tail lights moving away from me. I was waiting for the brake lights to come on. They never did, and the car vanished from sight. I couldn't help but wonder *what the hell just happened.* I quickly got on my radio and asked for another unit to come to my location STAT. I could not move my squad car from the position it was in because that would unblock the intersection and allow traffic to head for the bridge. I jumped out of my squad car and ran toward the bridge. I remember thinking, *my God did I just see what I think I saw, did a car really just launch off the bridge?*

My heart was pounding, thinking that someone had just plunged into the icy water and was drowning in a vehicle. And worse yet what was I going to do when I arrived there? My partner Burkhart was running with me and as we got closer, the vehicle came into sight. It had launched itself, like Starsky and Hutch off the stationary part of the bridge onto the inclined part of the draw bridge. The open bridge was at a twenty-degree angle leaving a gap of three feet the car had crossed. Now what? Both Burkhart and I jumped down onto the draw part of the bridge and ran up to the car, an older Chevy Beretta. Inside was a young female clinging to the steering wheel. She was petrified. As I opened the door I noticed the front windshield had not been cleared off at all. It was covered in ice and snow with only a tiny football shaped clearing made by the defroster to see through. This explained a lot.

We quickly assessed the woman's condition. She was not injured, very shook up, but not injured. We each grabbed an arm and escorted her back to the stationary part of the bridge deck. Once on the stationary deck we all took a moment to catch our breath, relieved this woman was safe and this hadn't turn into a tragic event. Just then the dispatcher came over the radio, "222A, is the woman off the bridge?" With great relief I said, "10-4" The words were no sooner out of my mouth and I heard the warning bells sound that the bridge was about to move.

Sure enough, the drawbridge was moving, the bridge had been fixed. I thought, *terrific, it will close, and the woman's car can be retrieved back to safety as well.* Then the bridge started to move but in an upward direction, raising higher and higher into the air, which meant her car was going higher and higher and the incline was getting steeper and steeper. Was this car going to get to a point where it actually would come back down on us? I didn't know, and I wasn't going to find out. I yelled, "run!" and all three of us, the woman, Burkhart and I started running west to get away from the area. Once we were at a safe distance, I turned around, the bridge was almost at a forty-five-degree angle. I watched as the woman's car slid backwards and then disappeared out of sight. Poof! It was gone. Yikes. Why would someone open the bridge when they knew the car was still up there?

Anytime there is any kind of "oops" in police work the first thing you do is call for a supervisor. I got on the radio to dispatch and reported "headquarters, send a supervisor to my location, someone opened the bridge and the woman's car is now in the water." There was a long pause, and the dispatcher came back on and asked, "can you repeat?" I again said, "someone opened the bridge and the woman's car is now in the water." Another long pause, then dispatch said, "I thought you said the woman was off the bridge." I said "10-4, the woman is off the bridge, but her car wasn't and it's now in the water."

We escorted the woman back to my squad car where she was placed in the back seat. We were freezing cold and wet. She was issued a citation for failing to clear off her windshield. I contacted a relative to come and pick her up. As it turns out, her car wasn't actually in the water. The bridge has a sort of catch basin under the draw area of the bridge that catches road debris when it is in the fully raised position, so in this case it caught the car. The next day the car was retrieved by a floating barge from the catch basin. It was completely totaled. After the internal investigation and the review of the radio transmissions, I was cleared of any wrongdoing, however this taught me a very valuable lesson about communications; make sure your dispatcher always knows what's going on. The city bought the woman a new Chevy Beretta.

Potty Talk
THE STOLEN MONEY

On this particular day I was working my downtown beat. There was a report of a theft in progress on the west side in zone 131, Bravo district. The dispatcher sent me to cross the river and cover Officer James. The dispatcher told us the victim had just had money stolen at the laundromat and the suspect was still in the building. The suspect was described as a large white female with brown hair, wearing gray sweatpants and a white sweatshirt. As I responded to this location, I kept my eyes open for a person fitting this description. I arrived at the laundromat before Officer James.

The victim told me she was doing her laundry with her purse sitting on the counter next to her laundry baskets. The female suspect was lurking around the same area and was uncomfortably close to her personal belongings. The victim said the female went into the bathroom and she saw her purse was open and realized that sixty dollars in cash, three twenty-dollar bills, had been removed from her wallet. She was positive the woman has stolen the money. I noticed there were cameras positioned all around the building. I went to the laundromat attendant and asked if I could view the video footage. I was told that the cameras were fake. This did not stop me from using them as leverage.

Officer James arrived, and I informed him of my findings. This was his zone and his call. I was there to cover him. He would do the report. Because this involved a female suspect who was now in the women's bathroom, I would make contact with the suspect at the door of the restroom. Officer James was with me in the event the suspect was uncooperative. I knocked on the door of the bathroom. This particular bathroom was a small room with one toilet and a sink. The door was locked. I announced through the door, "open up, this is the police." I could hear her shuffling around inside the room from behind the closed door. I again announced the police were demanding the door to be opened. When the door finally opened, there was the suspect in the described clothing. I told her we were investigating a theft of some money and she had been named as the suspect. She denied knowing anything about the situation. I patted her down, she did not have the cash in her pockets of her sweat pants.

Officer James stood outside the restroom while I searched the bathroom and the garbage can in the bathroom. I didn't find the money. I then told the female that I had reviewed the video footage and saw her take the money from the purse. She didn't know the cameras were fake and I hadn't seen any footage. I told her she needed to cooperate with me and I would find the money one way or another. It was at this point she told me she did in fact have the money on her and would get it for me. I could not leave her alone to do this as she was now under arrest. I would never allow a suspect to leave my sight, they could be planning their escape or arming themselves to assault me. She told me she had to go into the bathroom to get it. I thought, *how could I have missed it on the bathroom search?* Then I thought, *oh, it's probably in her bra.* That is where many women stash their cash and drugs.

I went into the bathroom with the suspect and she told me to close the door. I have to admit this made me slightly nervous because this woman was twice my size and we were in a small, closed area; but sometimes you do what you have to do to get the job done. I was expecting her to reach into her bra for the cash. Instead she pulled her sweatpants down to her knees and put her hand up into her vagina, out came the cash, one twenty at a time. I must admit, the odor coming from her vagina was pretty nasty. So was the cash. I quickly put on some rubber gloves and took the gooey, wet, stinky cash from her hand. She pulled her pants back up and I had her leave the bathroom in front of me. As we emerged from the bathroom I looked over at Officer James with a little smile. He asked me if she had had the money. I told him to put on some gloves. When he had, I dropped the cash into his hand. The odor was overpowering, and he looked as if he was going to hurl. I told him that I located the cash, up her vagina. His gag reflex kicked in. I handcuffed the suspect and placed her in his car. He took the cash and placed it in a brown bag; this cash was going to the bank to be destroyed. Here's a thought for you, we found this cash, but imagine the money that doesn't get found and goes back into circulation. Your mother was right, money is the dirtiest thing you will ever touch. Gross, wash your hands!

KICK THE BUCKET

Officer Sawyer and I were working the downtown district. Many times, in the morning we would receive calls for kids who didn't want to go to school. Officers would be sent to get the little darlings out of bed and drive them to school. It was one of my least favorite things to do simply because I think it should be up to the parents to get their kids up, dressed, fed and off to school. The police are not a babysitting and taxi service, but we do it anyway. One morning, we were sent to a house on Berner Street on the northeast side of town. The call was for one of our frequent truant juvenile delinquent gang bangers. (Yes, Green Bay does have gangs) I had been at this residence before for this juvenile, but Officer Sawyer had not.

When we arrived at the residence we were greeted at the back door by an irate Hispanic mother who was clearly fed up with the entire process of trying to get her son to school. I think the fact that she had four other younger children to get off to school and was a hardworking mother working the night shift had something to do with it as well. The residence was small, a two or three-bedroom, one-bathroom ranch style house with a small kitchen/dinette and a small living room. The kids were packed into this place, but it is all they had, and Mom tried to make the best of it.

The young man in question was Mom's sixteen-year-old son. He was supposed to be to East High School at 07:30. But, like most teenage truants, he went to school when he wanted to and left when he wanted to, and the time spent there was not for any type of learning but rather to meet up with his other gang friends and cause trouble in the school. Mom was asking for our help with him, just as she had for weeks now. Maybe this kid didn't want to walk in the winter weather or maybe he thought it was cool to get a ride to school from a cop, whatever the case, we would do what we could to help her.

The male slept in the basement of the house, which without an egress window was a housing code violation. These situations seldom get reported. This is a common practice for many struggling moms, with lots of kids. We walked down the steps into a dark basement. I flicked the light switch, but no lights came on. I pulled out my flashlight and shined it around the basement, four walls and a washer and dryer, and the curtains hanging in the far corner. They were actually blankets hanging from clothes lines suspended from the rafters, making a makeshift room. We walked over to the blanket and pulled back the corner announcing it was the police. I shined my light into the room and saw our teenager sitting on the edge of his bed, getting himself dressed. The room also had a dresser with a TV on top of it and an old sofa. He had a dimly lit lamp on the floor and what appeared to be most of the contents of his dresser.

I first tried the nice cop approach, asking him what was going on. When he answered, "none of your fucking business," I knew this was not going to go well. Maybe some persuasive talking would work. I explained we were called to the home by his mother because he refused to go to school, but it looked like he was getting ready and we would give him a lift. At first, he seemed to be actually thinking about going with us. He continued dressing, and I continued trying to get some dialog going with him. Once he was dressed and appeared ready to go, he sat back down on his bed.

I told him it was time to leave and we had other calls to go on, that's when he told me to fuck off. Officer Sawyer and I closed in on him to place him in handcuffs. He started fighting with us, swinging his arms and kicking us both in the shins. It was time to decentralize him to the ground. In other words, take him down and get him cuffed. In the struggle with him flailing around like a fish out of water, a white five-gallon bucket got knocked over and the liquid inside the bucket was now all over the floor. This kid continued to struggle and fight with us and we were now rolling around in what smelled worse than a port-a-potty at the fairgrounds. That's exactly what it turned out to be. The bucket was the kid's port-a-potty and we were now soaked in a months' worth of old urine.

We were able to get him into custody and another squad came by and took him to school. Both Sawyer and I came out of the basement and into the cold air, which froze the liquid stench to our bodies. I drove to headquarters and marked my squad as a biohazard and went to the locker room. I stripped down and placed all my clothing in a red biohazard bag and hit the shower. The only good thing I can think of for that call was, *thank God there was only number one in that bucket and not number two.*

Hanky Panky
INVERSED ON CHRISTMAS

I had often noticed how odd it is when someone retires from our department. There is no news release, no fanfare, and no ceremony like when you started. You work and slave for people who don't know you for so long. You give up family and friends, birthdays, anniversaries, holidays, special moments in one's life and devote it to people you don't even know; people who are home with their families, safe, warm and not giving a second thought to the sacrifice you make every single day. This is my Christmas Day story. It is the one single event in my police life that changed my police thinking forever. I have never let it go and I never will. There is nothing that will ever give me my family time back, nothing.

In our department, vacation time was picked by seniority. Everyone gets a first pick, all the way down the list from top to bottom, and then a second pick the same way, then a third pick. It is how it has always been and most likely always will be. Sometimes your days off would fall on a holiday which would be a lucky break because you wouldn't have to use your "pick" for a holiday. The wild card about working in Green Bay is the Packers. They run this city. When there is a Packer game, none of the rules apply. The Packers are the exception to all rules, no matter what. I didn't sign up to work games. The hard part is the NFL schedule isn't available on January first when you pick your vacations. There is always the possibility there will be a home Packer game on a holiday.

I didn't have off Christmas of 2005, so I took my first vacation pick for Christmas Day. Christmas is special to everyone, even cops. I took it as my first pick. It was something I needed, to be with my family. I know many people think it's no big deal, we make double time pay. Double time pay means nothing. It is time you can't get back and there isn't any money in the world that is worth that. This was my pick, I was sure to be off.

When the Packer schedule came out, there it was, a Christmas Day game at Lambeau. Why would the NFL do this? Worse yet, it was against the Bears. Really? How many ruined Christmas's did this bring to families? It's a frickin' game. I went directly to the operations commander just to make sure I would still have my first vacation pick off. I was assured vacation picks would not be touched.

Fast forward to Christmas Day. My older sister was having the festivities at her house that year. We were each assigned to bring a dish or something to add to the event. Sissy has seven kids, so I thought bringing the turkey would help out tremendously. I was off and so excited about the big dinner with all the fixings. I had the turkey thawed in the fridge just like grandma used to do. Christmas morning, I was up with the birds so to speak, three o'clock a.m. The Nesco roaster was on the counter and ready to go. Let the festivities begin! Let's get the bird started. I have Christmas spirit going on big time. The house was all decorated, carols were playing in the background, the tree was lit, presents were all wrapped and organized. This is it, finally after all these years of waiting to be senior, I was off on Christmas Day. I was in a euphoric state of mind. Work was the furthest thing from my mind.

I called my sister to make sure I had the bird at the right temperature for the family event and to ask if she needed anything else. She said she would call me back in a few minutes, she couldn't talk at that moment. There are two things I wish I had that day; a beer and caller ID. I was whistling around the kitchen without a care in the world. The phone rang back a few minutes later. My thought was, *it's my sissy telling me the last-minute plans.* Instead it was my operations commander. "Hello Susan, I am sorry to inform you, you have been inversed to work the Packer game today. Report to Lambeau Field at noon." There was a very long pause as the words I had just heard crushed my Christmas spirit. It was my duty of course.

I hung up the phone swearing like a sailor and wishing I would have had a mimosa or something alcoholic to drink while I was basting the bird. I could have said that I did but, in this life, integrity is really all you have. I would never let anything compromise that. I dropped the turkey dinner off at my sister's house, gave her a hug, and told her I was sorry. I asked her to hug and kiss my parents, siblings, nieces and nephews and I drove to Lambeau Field on Christmas Day. Merry frickin' Christmas!

Officer Gleason, a good friend of mine, and I were paired up as a walking team. This is a good assignment because you are not stuck in a stairwell on cold concrete freezing your ass off. I have had back issues in the past and standing there for three hours is quite possibly the worst thing you can imagine. The crowd thinks you are just watching the game and enjoying yourself.

The first thing Gleason said to me is "I can tell you're pissed." And the first thing I said to her was, "If I have to deal with one drunk person today, they are going to jail." I kept that promise too. The game was absolutely ugly. It was cold and dark out. I remember a couple of Chicago Bears fans asked if they could take a photo of "the two cute cops." Okay, it's Christmas, why not? We posed for the photo, this Bears fan with the two of us on either side. After the photo was taken, I realized there was some photo bomber behind us holding up a sign that said *we're with stupid.* It was pointing at me. We chased the guy through the stadium but never did catch him in the crowd. I am still waiting for that photo to surface at some point. Hopefully the guy taking the photo was too drunk to focus and it never turned out.

The whole day wasn't a total loss. As part of the assignment as a walking team, you get to go into the bathrooms to check for rowdy, drunk females. It is also a good way to warm up on a cold December day. My dad used to send me in there as a kid to warm up while he got another beer or two. That day the events in the ladies' room included walking in on several drunk females attempting to urinate in the bathroom sink. They had their pants down and were urinating all over themselves and the countertops. After throwing these classy ladies out came the best Packers Christmas Day story ever.

In the corner handicap stall, I saw two pair of feet facing each other. One pair was wearing women's fuzzy fur boots and the other one a pair of men's work boots, pants down around the ankles of each. I had a feeling there might be something more going on in this stall than going potty. The stall was rocking, and I came knocking. I announced myself as the police. Things seemed to cease fire and there was a moment of complete silence.

Apparently, they assumed being quiet would make the police go away. I waited until they got dressed. When they came out, I did locate a male and a female who were ten shades of red and caught in the act. I informed them that this type of activity was not allowed anywhere at Lambeau Field. They were being arrested for disorderly conduct, which is kind of the catch all for everything that goes on there. The fine was eight hundred and sixty-six dollars. Each. I handcuffed them, confiscated their tickets, and started taking them down to the booking area at the field. They were Bears fans and said they didn't understand the rules. I explained they were going to jail. The male said to me, "Can you go into the stadium and tell my wife I need bail money?" Merry Christmas to all and to all a good night! The Bears won the game 24-17. And no, I didn't tell his wife.

WE'RE ALMOST DONE

It was a sunny, summer, Sunday afternoon in the city and people were out everywhere enjoying a nice day. It was getting near quitting time on the day shift and I was circling the downtown area enjoying a bit of the nice day as well. I was thinking about what I was going to put on the grill when I got home and looking forward to a little family time on the deck, a cold beer in a pair of shorts and a t-shirt. When it gets near the end of a shift, most of the time the dispatcher will hold onto calls that don't need immediate attention. This helps the day shift get done on time, so the afternoon shift can come out and work the calls that are waiting.

I was on Main Street by the Embassy Suites when dispatch called my call number and sent me to a call at Leicht Park. It was a report of two people having sex out on the grass in the park. I thought about this call as I crossed over the Main Street bridge, *who would be doing this in broad daylight in the middle of the park? Surely the caller was mistaken as to what was being reported.*

I pulled into the driveway just east of the railroad tracks. I could see dozens of people out on the patio at Titletown Brewing Company having cocktails and looking out toward the park. When I pulled up into the parking lot, there they were, buck ass naked in plain view for all to see. A man and a lady going at it like they were the only two people in the world. I got out of my squad car and walked up to them. They either didn't notice me or didn't care, they just kept on going at it with gusto. I was about two feet away from them when I said, "Excuse me just what do you think you're doing?" To my surprise the male grabbed part of the blanket they were laying on and covered them up and said, "we are just about finished." What?!

Needless to say, his proclamation was accurate by about two seconds. My cover car arrived and both subjects were ordered to get dressed and to make it snappy. I issued them each a citation for disorderly conduct and sent them on their way. I did receive some clapping from the patrons of Titletown.

A PLUNGER?

I was working the downtown district when I received a call from probation and parole to go to a residence and check for a subject. There are several probation offices in that district and it is a common practice for agents to call in to the department to have officers go pick up one of their clients. Most often it is when someone on probation misses their appointment with the agent. The agents don't like that; it is a violation of probation. This call was just that. I was sent with Officer York to a halfway house located in the downtown area. This particular house takes in troubled young men and tries to give them an opportunity to turn their lives around. Each person staying there has their own room with a small bathroom, similar to an old-fashioned motel room. There is also a common living room and mess hall where meals are prepared daily for the tenants. They receive counseling and financial assistance from the staff. It really is a pretty decent set up for someone just coming out of prison, jail or even for a select group of the homeless.

I arrived at the house with Officer York. We went to see the pastor who runs the operation. Most often we do not get called here because he runs a pretty tight ship. I have known the pastor for many years and have a good rapport with him so as a courtesy, I checked in with him at his office on the way in. Pastor would also be able to help us get into the room, since the policy at this facility says that he can enter any room at any time per a contract that is signed by all tenants. We went up to the second floor with Pastor and knocked on the door. There was no answer. Pastor announced we were coming in and then opened the door with the key. The male who had missed his probation appointment was still laying in his bed sleeping. What an eye-opening way to wake up, two cops and a pastor looking over you. This call would turn out to be a real eye opener for all of us.

I explained to the male that his agent had contacted us, and he wanted us to bring him in, meaning to jail. This is how the agents handle this situation. At the agent's convenience they can go to the jail and interview their client as to why they missed their appointment. I always tell people on probation, if you enjoy your freedom, don't piss off your agent. As this male continued to shake out the cobwebs, he asked if he could go to the bathroom. Of course, we would let him, but he would have to leave the door open and Officer York would have to watch him with me close by in case he tried any funny business.

I opened the bathroom door and flicked on the light to enter the bathroom, that's when we saw it. An old-fashioned wooden handle plunger stapled to the floor in the middle of the bathroom, with a condom rolled down on the end of the handle. Seriously. I had to look twice at it to even believe what I was seeing. I looked at Officer York and he looked at me. This was one of those moments when you really have to exercise some control; you might be thinking something, but you damn well better not say it. Neither of us said a word. The look on the pastor's face was pure shock and dismay. He had plenty to say and didn't hold back. I don't recall his exact words, but I do know it included "you're evicted." I guess our subject should have never opened that bathroom door and held it until he got to jail.

SUBMARINE RACES

I had just finished training with my FTO's and was finally on my own. I was going to be assigned to the afternoon shift at the end of the month but first I went to the night shift. I had worked nights for several years in the communication center, but this was a whole different animal for me. I had never been out in a squad car *dealing* with the calls; I was always safe in my chair in the center *taking* the calls. Driving the streets at night is very different than during the day. Obviously, it is dark. The pizza delivery man can use a light to check addresses, this would not be a safe approach for a police officer. Locating addresses is something most rookies find very hard to do. Having grown up and living in Green Bay all my life I still didn't know the hundred blocks by heart. Many times, when I knew I was definitely a block or two away I would take my flashlight and give it a quick shine on a house just to get the numbers. All of our squads are equipped with spotlights but that is a dead giveaway shining that thing. It lights up the whole neighborhood!

I hated working the night shift. Everyone I dealt with was either drunk or high on drugs and the later in the night, the worse it got. People just don't know how to behave after midnight. I was driving around patrolling the west side neighborhood near Colburn Park. I was really just looking for anything out of the ordinary. The way to do this is not by parking at a gas station like many of the guys do; it's by making the rounds. I was driving down Loch Drive which is a winding street that borders the south side of the park.

At 03:00 I spotted a vehicle parked on the roadway in the dark shadows of the trees facing westbound. As I went by the car heading eastbound I lit up the car passenger area with my spotlight. I expected it to be empty, but it wasn't. All I saw was a naked ass moving up and down in the front seat, of course I knew there was most likely another naked ass on the bottom of that. I called out to headquarters with a suspicious situation and turned my squad car around. I activated my red and blue lights and my other spotlight, so I could fully see into the vehicle from behind. All I could see at this point were clothes flying everywhere as the male and female occupants were scrambling to get dressed before I got to the car. I stalled a bit as they were pulling clothing from the back seat which I am sure they whipped there in the heat of the moment never thinking they would be under pressure to locate them so quickly. I sort of chuckled about it, remembering days gone by with my steady. Then I snapped out of it thinking, *that is somebody's daughter in there.*

When they were finally dressed I approached the passenger side of the vehicle. It was obvious both male and female were extremely embarrassed. I first asked if everything was alright and both responded yes. I then asked them each for identification. Luckily for me they were both eighteen otherwise I would have been making some late-night phone calls to parents. I asked the female to get out of the car, so I could talk to her in private. Once I had her near the rear of the vehicle, I asked her if this was consensual activity or if the male was forcing this on her. I wanted to make sure this wasn't a rape in progress. It would be horrible for a cop to leave a victim with a suspect after coming upon the act in progress. That was not the case here. The female reluctantly told me this was her boyfriend and they each lived at home with their parents, so they had nowhere to go to get it on. I had her get back in the car and cancelled my cover car. I gave them each their identification back and sent them on their way. We used to call this going to the submarine races, I don't know what they call it nowadays. Oh, to be young again!

HANGING OUT

It was a glorious, gorgeous, sunny, summer Saturday. People were out enjoying the farmer's market downtown. Bay Beach Amusement Park was packed with people picnicking with family and friends. The city was buzzing with activity. A typical, enjoyable day of fun in the sun. At 13:00 I was dispatched to a check the welfare call for a male who was running on Radisson Street in his underwear. The notes of the call indicated the male was exposing his genitals as he ran down the street. I thought, *yowza, this is a very weird call to be going on!* I was happy my cover car was my supervisor Captain Flanders. If these allegations were true, it wouldn't be as uncomfortable since Captain Flanders was a male and the subject was a male. Maybe they could discuss this man to man instead of me trying to discuss this with the subject.

As I drove down Radisson from The Bay Beach Shell toward N. Irwin Avenue, I saw him. A thin, white male running and wearing nothing except what looked like underwear. I caught up to him and sure enough, he was wearing underwear; boxer shorts with an open fly in the front. I pulled up next to him and rolled my window down and asked him to stop. He did, and I got out to speak with him. I tried to be nonchalant as I attempted to take a peek as to whether or not *Jimmy and The Twins* were exposing themselves to the general public; but seriously how do you have a conversation with someone when you're supposed to be making eye contact but instead you're looking at his crotch? Awkward!

The guy immediately asked me why I am stopping him. What the hell do you say to that? *Well sir, we received a report that your junk was hanging out while you were running down the road.* Yup, I guess that's what you say, so I said it. The guy looked mortified; he was huffing and puffing because I just stopped his morning jog rather abruptly without a cool down.

Luckily Captain Flanders arrived, took the guy aside and spoke with him; which I am sure made this guy much more comfortable than me talking to him about his manhood. The guy was given a verbal warning by Captain and he was sent on his way. I got back in my car and pulled away, that's when the Captain came over the radio for all the other units in the city to hear, and said to me "1C1 do you have this caper covered?" to which I responded, "10-4," as I am sure every copper in the city was laughing out loud at the "caper covered" part of that transmission. Sometimes you just need a good laugh!

COPS SCREW UP TOO

No book would be complete without a couple of cop bloopers. I will start with mine.

I was working the afternoon shift and it was late in my shift when I decided to pull over a car on S. Ashland Avenue and Howard Street. This car didn't stop where I wanted it to and continued on down Howard Street and then onto S. Oakland Avenue where it pulled over to the curb. I always hated that; instead of being in a well-lit, high traffic area, I was now on a dimly lit street with no traffic. It is also a clue the driver could be planning something more for me than casual conversation at the window. I called out with the stop and asked for a cover car to roll my way just in case this didn't go as planned. I approached the car. There were two males in the vehicle, both were in their mid-twenties and seemed a bit put out that I had stopped them for no reason. I informed them there was a headlight out on the car.

Remember the hands, always watch the hands. When I asked the driver for his identification, he began digging between his legs which would not be where a normal person would keep their wallet. My immediate thought was, *oh no you don't! You're not going to shoot me here on this dark street and take off!* My reflexes kicked in and I drew my gun with my right hand and put my left hand inside the car to grab his arm that was moving about in his crotch area. I grabbed what felt like a tube, a tube of what, I had no idea, but I grabbed it and pulled it hard. The male screamed out in pain and yelled, "What are you doing? That's my cath!" I let go of it and shined my flashlight down into the car, sure enough the guy had a catheter with a colostomy bag attached to it; and his wallet between his legs. Oops, sorry dude I thought you were going for a gun. I ran both the guys through teletype and apologized up one side and down the other. And I never did that again.

The alarm call went out to several units. My partner Rivard and a couple other officers were sent way out on Nicolet Drive to a huge mansion of a house for a burglary alarm. Many times, these are false alarms and can be triggered by bad weather and other situations, but there is always that chance that it could be the real deal. On this particular night it had been raining when the officers arrived at the residence. A monster of a house with many levels, entries, and exit doors. When Rivard was walking up to the house he did not use the sidewalk but went through the yards leading to the house. There was a lot of mud in one of the yards. Upon arrival to the home he discovered the front door was wide open. Other cops had the house surrounded and Rivard and another cop were going to clear the house. That is, they were going to go systematically from room to room with guns drawn to make sure no one was inside the residence.

When they walked into the front door there was a grand living room with wall-to-wall white carpeting. Suddenly, Rivard bent down and untied his boots and took them off. Really. As it worked out there was in fact no one in the house and most likely the wind had blown the front door open. But had there been, imagine Rivard chasing some bad guy out of the house wearing nothing but socks. The guys gave him a lot of ribbing for this. I am sure he never did it again.

This one takes the cake. In the old days there was no such thing as laser lights for your gun, so at night you had to have your gun in your strong hand and your flashlight in the other. You would position the flashlight under your gun hand in an effort to support your gun hand and still be able to see ahead of you. It was awkward at best, but that is all we had until technology brought us the laser light. This was a great invention. The light could be attached to your firearm and would come on manually at the tap of your finger to the trigger. This would allow a stealth approach in certain situations that would not give away your position. When you tap your finger, you actually tap the sear which is on the trigger, but you do not fully pull the trigger to discharge a bullet. Cops were excited about this new way of being able to be more accurate on their targets. One of the golden rules for cops is *guns are only out on the range and in a controlled environment.* Unless of course you are on a deadly force call. One night, Lieutenant Brogan was sitting in the side lot and for whatever reason was testing his laser light. He pointed his gun at the car radio and pulled back on the sear to activate the light, but a little too much pressure was applied, and he shot the squad car radio. Oops!

PIGS

The old joke about cops and donuts gets pretty old after a while, but people think it's pretty funny. Every time someone would say something like this to me I would just laugh and say, "geez, I have never heard that one before." They would laugh right along with me, never realizing I had just dissed them for using the most overused line in policing. In all seriousness cops do like to eat, especially treats and free stuff. Anything that is set out either on the break room tables or in the roll call room is usually gone within the day, if not within hours of being set out. This is where everyone in the department gets rid of their overabundance of Halloween candy, Christmas cookies and candy or whatever leftovers in their house that need to go.

In the records division and detective division many of the people set out candy dishes with jelly beans or some sweet treat and each passing cop grabs a few or a handful. Cops have a twisted and warped sense of humor, here is a little proof. One day in the detective division someone brought in a large self-dispensing trail mix machine. This was like the bubble gum machines where you put your hand under the chute, turn the handle and a handful of delicious treats fall into your hand. The container, which was about two gallons in size, was filled to the brim with trail mix and set out at the start of the day. Every passing person would spin the handle and walk away throwing a handful into their mouths, while several of the detectives watched with smiles from ear to ear. The next day, the dispenser was completely empty, and someone had placed a note on it: "I hope you enjoyed the mixed birdseed."

HUMOR ON THE JOB

Something most people do not realize is that most cops have a very dry sense of humor and can actually be hysterically funny. Our morning roll calls, although meant to be informational, many times turned a bit of a stand-up show. I guess you could call it a little humor to start out the day and get us off in the right frame of mind, laughing in the face of danger. At the front of the roll call room was a huge chalkboard and in later years a whiteboard. These boards were for drawing diagrams of houses for officer entries or for posting something of importance for all the roll calls to see. With a little cop humor these boards turned into areas where you could post funny one-liners, or a series of comments directed at other cops for the sake of humor; they were damn funny. Of course, some round head ruined it for everyone by putting up inappropriate comments and diagrams. Administration had to put the kibosh on the boards because it could have been considered workplace harassment, even though it was all in fun.

Sometimes funny things happened out of pure accident, as was usually the case with my friend Officer Yago. Somehow, he was always in the wrong place at the wrong time. Even though each cop does not have an assigned car, they do have their favorites, either a favorite number or just the way a certain car rides, how old it is, or how the car is set up. Each car is just a little different. My two favorite cars were forty-three and sixty-eight for no reason other than I just liked them. I always had them cleaned up and filled with supplies. When I would pass the car off to the next shift, most of the guys knew I always had a clean car, filled with gas, and stocked with evidence collection items. My one habit was round wooden toothpicks. When I was driving around I would chew on them, sort of like a lot of guys use chewing tobacco. When I would go on a call, I had a rubber band around my visor and I would stick my toothpick in the visor rubber band and save it for later when I got back to my car. Sometimes I would forget it was up there and leave it in the car.

Officer Yago liked using my car. One day, I came on duty in the morning and had an email message from him:

> "Officer Bickett, please remove your toothpicks from your car at the end of your shift. This is the second time this week it fell out of the visor and onto my car seat. I didn't realize this and sat on it. Point up."

Oops! Sorry Yago, I didn't mean to poke you in the ass.

Officer Yago was also a DAAT (Defense and Arrest Tactics) trainer. Several times a year in addition to shooting on the range, we would also do hands on training involving these defense and arrest tactics. One of the tactics that had to be practiced was close quarters hand to hand combat. Officer Yago would dress up in a fully padded suit including a full-face mask helmet called Redman Gear. This gear offered him protection from the repeated blows and kicks he would receive throughout the training.

On this particular day, we had the full contact tactical training. Officer Yago was my trainer and was suited up in the Redman Gear. The object of the training was to pull the subject in close to your body and then administer knee strikes to the stomach area. Officer Yago was about my height. I placed my arms around the back of his neck and pulled him in tight against me. I then brought my knee up in one swift motion to strike him in the stomach, only I didn't strike him in the stomach, but instead gave him a direct knee to *Jimmy and the twins*. He went down like a sack of potatoes and didn't get up. The exercise was immediately halted, and his helmet was removed. He was out cold. The other guys in the class thought this was hysterical and were laughing pretty hard when he came to. I felt absolutely awful. Officer Yago made a joke about it saying at least he was already done having kids, but I could tell he was hurting. The one good thing about it was at least I had firsthand experience on how to take a guy out. Sorry Yago!

On the south side of police headquarters is an area marked for short-term parking of squad cars. There is about a half-dozen spots clearly marked *For Squads Only*. This is for the road cops to pull up and park, run into the station to use the restroom, do paperwork, pick up supplies, or see the shift commander. Often times when there is an event going on at the station, like training or seminars, the parking lot gets filled up with extra vehicles, leaving very few spots to park; sometimes people park their personal vehicles in the places reserved for squad parking only. One day, Officer Londo was running late to get into training and decided to park in the squad area. One of our more comical officers, Officer James, thought it would be funny to take tape and go all the way around the vehicle, taping the doors shut. He didn't just go around the car once, but dozens and dozens of times until the vehicle was completely covered in tape making it impossible for Officer Londo to get into her car without spending time unraveling the tape.

Usually Officer Londo had a pretty good sense of humor. However, that day she had to get out of there quickly to go pick up her kids. She was madder than a hornet, and while I am sure thinking back on this situation would seem pretty funny, at the time it was not. She didn't know who had done it. The parking lot is covered with video surveillance, the tapes were pulled, and Officer James was caught red handed. He was verbally disciplined and apologized for his actions. It's still pretty funny.

A COUPLE FENDER BENDERS

I don't think any police career would be complete without a couple of fender benders of their own. Let's face it, cops log thousands of miles in their career and are put in situations that require them to drive in a manner most people never have to. Drivers education doesn't teach you to drive over islands, curbs, go through ditches, drive over lawns, go into oncoming traffic, or park in the roadway to block traffic for the safety of others. Cops don't call them accidents. The vast majority of mishaps occur due to inattentive driving, not paying attention, or not being a defensive driver. Cops call them crashes, not accidents. Most crashes are avoidable if people would just pay attention and follow the rules of the road.

My first incident in a squad occurred in the first week I was solo. I had parked my squad westbound on Hillside at the corner of Bader. I was assigned to crossing guard duty and was out of my car, standing at the corner, helping small children cross the busy intersection. A school bus was traveling southbound on Bader Street, attempted to make a right turn westbound onto Hillside. I looked over just in time to see my squad being sideswiped by the bus. The driver cut the corner a little too sharply. This one was no fault of mine; my vehicle was legally parked.

The next little mishap involved a drive-up telephone. This was in the days that officers did not have cell phones. In order to dictate details, an officer would find a drive-up telephone booth, dial into an automated system and dictate into the phone the details of the event for the report. Yes, on a corded telephone! This particular evening it had been snowing for quite some time and the roads were slippery at best. I had just worked a disturbance on Humboldt Road and pulled into the I-57 Cenex gas station on Liebman and University where there was a drive-up phone booth on the west side of the parking lot. As I went to pull up to the phone booth, I did not realize the parking lot was a sheet of ice now covered in a thin layer of snow and I slid the front end of my squad car into the phone booth. There was minor damage to the squad and phone booth. The supervisor arrived and gave me a write up.

My next little incident happened at a Marathon Gas station on W. Mason Street. This is probably my most embarrassing mishap and looking back, probably my funniest. It was about 21:00 and I had just stopped at the gas station to use the restroom. I had pulled in facing forward, which is something I never do, and I am not sure why I didn't back in as I usually would. Probably because I really had to go. Cops usually back into parking spots. In the event of a hot call, the cop can get out of there fast and not have to monkey around with backing out and dealing with getting parked in.

I came back out of the gas station and got into my car. I went to back out not realizing there was a large concrete parking stop between the end of the parking lot and the east sidewalk, both my back tires went over the stop. I quickly hit the brakes and put my squad into drive. I hit the gas and nothing, just spinning tires. I got out of my squad to assess the situation. The frame of my vehicle was on top of the concrete parking stop and both my back tires were off the ground. How embarrassing.

Several guys were pumping gas and came over to help. They tried lifting the car up to free me from the parking stop. This was unsuccessful. Not wanting to call a supervisor and get an incident filed for this. I contacted several of the community police officers in the area to come over and assist me. I now had three citizens and three police officers trying to lift the back of my squad off the parking stop. Again, they were unsuccessful.

This was going to require a floor jack. I called the police garage to see if any of the mechanics could come with one. There was no one available. I could not believe I was going to have to call a wrecker to lift my car off this thing. I made the call and was patiently waiting while every gas station customer came by laughing at the stupid cop who backed over the parking stop. And of course, while I was waiting a supervisor just happened to be driving by and pulled in to investigate. Heavy Duty arrived and lifted me off the parking stop and the supervisor gave me a write up.

My next incident occurred on Ninth Street. I was at Ninth Street and S. Ashland Avenue when I was dispatched to a domestic disturbance way out on South Point Road. The dispatcher reported it was physical and was going pretty badly. I activated my red lights and siren and took off. I had just cleared the intersection of Ninth and Twelfth Avenue.

There were several cars in the westbound lane that were not moving over, so as trained, I pulled into the oncoming lane to pass them. I then pulled back into the westbound lane. I approached another car that wasn't pulling over, I got into the oncoming lane again just as the dispatcher cancelled me on the call and sent someone else who had just become available. I was committed to passing this car since I was already next to it when the driver decided to make a left turn southbound onto Spence Street.

The only problem was, I was there, and the driver turned right into my lane. I hit the brakes but there was no stopping on time and I struck the vehicle, went up the south curb and missed a huge tree by inches.

I immediately got out of the car to check on the other driver, who said she was not injured. I thought, *thank God!* The supervisor arrived and began talking to the driver, who was now reporting she was injured. A rescue squad was called, and she was taken to the hospital. The supervisor gave me a write up.

I was sitting at the East Pumps with Officer Yago. We were filling up our cars and talking about the nice July night. We had just pulled to a corner of the lot to continue our conversation when we were both dispatched to a burglary in progress on Van Deuren St. We both put on our emergency lights but no siren; we did not want to alert the suspects we were on the way to catch them.

I was following Officer Yago as we made our way down the back roads to the apartment complex where it was reported that several teenagers were entering the apartment building through a window. When officers get close to a call they shut off all their lights including the headlights, it's called *blacking out.* That is what we both did in this case. This can be tricky, especially when following someone because not only are you watching the squad in front of you, but you are also watching the area for any fleeing suspects. Officer Yago stopped his squad and I pulled in behind him. I was just about to get out when I saw a couple younger males running from the apartments.

Officer Yago saw them too and started to pull away in his squad, I assumed to go over the curb and go after them with the car. Well, that is not what he was doing. He was just pulling up a little closer to get out. I had already gunned my vehicle to follow him except he was now at a complete standstill, I tried to get on the brakes, but it was too late. I rear-ended him. We both got out of our cars, drew our guns and told the males we observed to get on the ground. They both did. I will never forget the both of them laying on the ground and the one guy said to the other, "wow did you see that? That was pretty fucking cool!" referring to me smashing into the back of Officer Yago's squad car. The two males were the burglars and were arrested. Neither Officer Yago nor I were injured, thankfully. The supervisor arrived and gave me a write up.

And last but not least. I was dispatched to a two-vehicle crash at N. Webster Avenue and University Avenue. The caller reported that both vehicles were in traffic and there were injuries. I had just left the station. It was raining like the dickens. I was traveling red lights and siren to the call but was proceeding cautiously because of the weather conditions. I don't know if you have ever noticed, but seldom do you see cops driving around in the rain. That's because it is dangerous. Most cops find a nice place to park until it lets up, this reduces the chance of accidents.

I was northbound on S. Monroe Avenue and had just cleared the intersection of E. Walnut Street as I came to Cherry Street. I had a red light, so I came to an almost complete stop to make sure traffic saw me, heard me, and stopped for me. They did and as I pulled into the intersection a westbound vehicle came around the two cars that had stopped in the roadway for me. It passed both of them and came smashing into the passenger side of my squad car. I was completely caught off guard. The impact of the crash spun me around and sent me over the northeast curb into a parking lot filled with cars. I smashed into two other vehicles before coming to a rest in the parking lot.

I quickly got out and checked for injuries, there were none. I told the drivers of the two stopped vehicles to stay put until my supervisor arrived, thankfully they did. My squad was smashed on all sides, but I was not hurt, that's the main thing. The supervisor arrived and charged the driver of the other vehicle with failing to yield right of way to an emergency vehicle. I did not get a write up!

I know this sounds like a lot of crashes but considering the number of miles cops drive and the conditions in which they drive in, it's really not. I was however, feeling kind of bad about having a couple of these back to back. One of my favorite supervisors, Lt. Timms took me aside to try to cheer me up. He told me, "cheer up. If you're not using all your fouls, you're not playing hard enough." I thought about that for a long time, and you know what, he was right. I guess I played pretty hard!

ARE YOU OKAY?

Early on in my career, I would go to a tavern occasionally for a couple of beers. One of my favorite places to go back then was Sue and Sally's tavern on S. Broadway. It was a place where I could unwind and be myself without being judged. Most of the locals in there knew I was a cop but didn't go into all the questions all the time, I liked that.

One particular night I was there shooting a few games of pool and relaxing when I heard a ruckus going on at the back of the bar near the back door. I usually don't get involved in girl drama and verbal disturbances, so I did not give it much attention and continued shooting pool. It wasn't too long after, these two girls went out the back door. I thought they had resolved their issues and that was it. Actually, they went out back to duke it out in the rear parking lot, literally. Someone came up to me to tell me the girls were fighting it out in the parking lot and they needed someone to break it up; I guess that would be me since I was the only cop in the bar. I hated this part about being a cop, but as a cop you can't just sit back and do nothing, so I went outside. Several people followed to see how I was going to break up this cat fight. I did not know these two and I wasn't sure if they knew me either. I walked up to them and announced that I was a police officer and grabbed the girl who was obviously winning the fight. Some of the onlookers grabbed the other girl and the physical fight was over, but now it was a constant barrage of name calling back and forth.

I tried calming the girl I had pulled off the other. All of a sudden there was a spot light from the street; we were all lit up. This silenced the entire crowd who were now frozen like deer in headlights. Officer Stancheck came over the PA system and asked, "Bickett, are you okay?" I gave him the thumbs up. He shut off his spotlight and drove away. I now gave both the girls a thorough ass chewing and informed them they were damn lucky the results of their actions didn't result in them getting arrested. They both agreed and went their separate ways. That was just a little bit embarrassing.

OFC. SUSAN BICKETT

AND THEN IT WAS OVER

*B*EING A COP HAS BEEN ONE OF MY GREATEST devotions to mankind and I would like to think that I impacted people in the most positive way possible. I have always wanted to make a difference and hopefully I have. No, I never rescued anyone from a burning car, or saved anyone from jumping off a bridge, no heroic saves. Not that I wouldn't have done it, but the opportunity never arose for me to. Many opportunities did arise for me to help those in need and I hope I handled them to the best of my ability. When I think about the thousands of people in this world that I have had contact with, I hope that most will think of me as a good, fair cop that strived to make this world a better place. This truly was and will always be my calling. It was a way I could help people, because honestly isn't that what life is really all about? I am grateful and thankful for the opportunity to have served with so many wonderful, caring people. All I can say is, what a ride!

I wanted to retire when I turned fifty, not because that was some magic number. I was tired, very tired. Even though I did not have the correct equations for the retirement formula, I still wanted it badly. Not because of the job, even though it was getting rougher for me to keep up my pace. I wanted it so badly because I was secretly doing two jobs, one at work and one at home. You never know what someone has on their plate, or what it's like to walk in someone else's shoes. I know that most of my coworkers had no idea of the struggle I was having for the last four years. It was pure hell.

In my mind, family comes first, and work comes second, but you need both to survive. In my case my immediate family needs were extreme, mostly health issues with my disabled partner and step daughter. It didn't end there, I have two disabled parents and one disabled sister; and all of them were relying on me for help.

On top of doing my daily jobs around the house and taking care of my family, I still had to be up for work at 04:30 and put in a full day of crime fighting. It became unbearable at times, but I pushed through it. I am not trying to be some martyr, I am just telling my story and how it felt; smothered would be a good word for it. Or maybe drowning. I felt like I was treading water every day, and then the next day, over and over again. When I turned fifty and knew I couldn't retire, I started paying myself a dollar for every hour I had to put in at work. I had piggy banks in my locker and every single work day I would deposit eight one-dollar coins into the banks. This was part of my coping mechanism, I felt like at least I was getting some kind of reward for putting in another day.

I started doing one of my favorite things to do as an officer, traffic stops. It was a way to make contact with the public and maybe make a difference in someone's driving habits, which in turn might save someone's life down the road. I was big on getting people to wear their seatbelts. Many times, just stopping them and "reminding" them to buckle up and telling them to slow down would be my mission of the day. I also did a lot of school zone stops. In my mind this is the single best stop that an officer can make. It slows down the speeder, it protects the children and it gives the officer high visibility to the community that you are out there doing your job. I did get quite a kick out of how many teachers I stopped in the school zones who were speeding to get to school; one I stopped twice in one week.

Work was getting tougher and tougher to stomach. We had a chief who was a control freak, a *my way or the highway* kind of guy. Don't get me wrong, I got along with him great, as long as I went along with him, which is kind of sad. Department morale was at the lowest I had ever seen it. This did not affect the slackers because they didn't give a shit, but it was now affecting the worker bees like me and many others. I always said, "when I stop having fun at this job, I will know it is time to quit." The fun had stopped. This chief had taken the fun right out of it.

One of my single greatest events that pushed me toward pulling the plug was the death of my dear friend, Heather Jeane. She was a jailor at the sheriff's department, but I knew her way before she had that career. We had been friends for about twenty-five years. She was diagnosed with stage four pancreatic cancer and within a year she passed away. She was fifty-one years old. This really put things into perspective for me and impacted my decision to get the heck out of law enforcement as soon as I possibly could and enjoy life. You need money to live but how much, really? And you have to *live* through it.

Living through it. Another topic that affected my decision. Thugs were killing cops at an alarming rate and the Black Lives Matter movement was in full swing. The media was making a circus out of some isolated events and in reality, was endangering every cop out there. I feel this media frenzy was fueling the assassination of cops. I didn't want to be any part of this anymore. I didn't want to go my entire career to have my decision-making abilities questioned by the media. I certainly didn't want it to end with a bullet in me.

I had thought about retirement for so long and watched so many go before me. It always seemed strange to me that a person can fight in the trenches, take a bullet for their fellow cops, share life with them, and when you retire, it all stops. You are replaced with another new recruit. On my last day of work, they gave me a plaque, a retirement badge for my wallet and we ate some cake. I cleaned out my locker and suddenly the fight, the drama, the worry, the replaying of events over and over in my mind, the sleepless nights, inversing, missed holidays, it was all gone, done, finished. All I could think was, *wow it's over. It's really over.* I walked out the door. It was over.

I have come to realize after being away from the madness for a few years now, that even though I don't go to that place anymore, I will never be the same again. I will never go into a hotel room without checking for every possible emergency route out. I have been made fun of for tying bed sheets together and attaching them to a fixed object in the room, just in case going out the window was the only way out. Every time I go anywhere I am always assessing the situation, the people, and my surroundings. That is never going away. People who haven't had to constantly look over their shoulder for years and years, will never understand what this feels like. It never goes away.

WEEDING FOR
A BEAUTIFUL GARDEN

The year I was sworn in Wanda Truttman Sibert's brother, James Truttman was killed by a drunk driver on E. Mason Street a few weeks before Christmas of 1998. Wanda is also the daughter of Sgt. Wayne Truttman of the Brown County Sheriff's Department who was shot to death on duty right before Christmas of 1973. In 2002 Wanda gave a speech at the Law Enforcement Recognition Ceremony. This is part of that speech that I have always tried to keep in mind as I was out on patrol. It seemed to give me strength in my daily work:

> Several years ago, I was talking with an officer who was approaching his fifth anniversary of service. He had begun to feel that the world was rapidly getting worse. It was hard to stay upbeat while wading through so much human misery. Viewing the saddest side of society had begun to blur the reality of what the rest of the world was like. He was unsure if he would ever want to bring children into such a place.
>
> I have thought of his comments often. In preparing to speak at a MADD banquet honoring outstanding police efforts, I wondered if there would be officers attending who might also at times have some of the same feelings.
>
> So, I told them about my garden: I am a gardener of beautiful flower gardens. People stop and tell me how they love to walk by my house and see the beautiful colors and smell the blossoms. I love to work in the garden- it feeds my soul.
>
> But here's the funny thing: When I am out making this beautiful, beautiful garden, I hardly touch the flowers-I am always pulling the weeds.
>
> I think that's what police work is. The flowers can take care of themselves: They grow, they bloom, they beautify the garden with little help from me. There are many good people like that! But officers work daily with the weeds: working at the soil line, trying to pull out plants that would-if left to themselves-choke out all but the toughest flowers.
>
> I have found that the key is to look up. When my back hurts and there is dirt under my nails, I find the hose, clean up, and walk to my bench, where I can view the garden as a whole. It is beautiful! The world is happy. I feel better.

I hope each of you has the chance periodically to clean up, step back and view the garden as a whole.

I am so grateful to you for giving daily service, essential to the happiness of my family, and so many others. We would be lost without your efforts.

As you drive this summer, and see the beautiful colors in our city, I hope you are reminded how we love you and need you. Thank you for so carefully tending the garden.

YES MA'AM

EXCLUSIVE PREVIEW

BLUE LIVES MATTER:
In the Line of Duty
By Hon. Steve Cooley & Robert Schirn, Esq.

Blue Lives Matter is a book that explores the line-of-duty deaths suffered by the law enforcement "blue" family. This book examines the deaths of eight police officers and one police canine in Los Angeles County. The chapters portray the fallen officers and the canine as true heroes who each made the ultimate sacrifice in service to their community. The cases include the murder of two officers solved over 40 years later; an officer murdered in front of his young son; two officers kidnapped and taken to an onion field where one officer is executed; an undercover officer murdered during a multi-million dollar drug transaction; an off-duty officer murdered by two gang members while riding his bicycle; and a cop-killer who fled to Mexico to avoid prosecution.

Co-authors Steve Cooley and Bob Schirn discuss each case in detail. Each chapter discusses the incident that cost the officer his life. The court proceedings are reviewed, including victim impact testimony of the effect of the officer's death on family members and fellow officers. A Lessons Learned segment in each chapter is designed to increase officer safety and awareness of dangerous situations.

Steve Cooley is a career prosecutor who served three full terms as the District Attorney of Los Angeles County. He was a reserve police officer for LAPD. He is uniquely positioned to discuss his involvement in each case and eminently qualified to provide perspectives and opinions on each case.

Blue Lives Matter: In the Line of Duty, and several other law enforcement titles, can be found by visiting us online:
www.TitleTownPublishing.com

Chapter 6
Deputy David March
Los Angeles County Sheriff's Department
"Changing the Law to Get a Killer"

INTRODUCTION (COMMENTARY OF STEVE COOLEY)

O N APRIL 29, 2002, I WAS NOTIFIED that a Los Angeles County Deputy Sheriff had been shot and killed in the city of Irwindale. Shortly thereafter, I learned that it was David March, an individual I had met about a year earlier, as he had attended a fundraiser in support of my candidacy for District Attorney. His brother-in-law, James "Kimo" Hildreth, was a District Attorney investigator who had brought him to that event.

I felt that it was important to go to the scene of the murder and did so later that afternoon. A modest but moving memorial consisting of flowers, candles, etc., was in place near the blood stains on the street.

A few days later, I attended the funeral for Deputy David March. I learned that he was born in March 1969 and that he was 32 years of age when he died. He was raised in the Santa Clarita Valley where he lived with his wife and daughter. After he graduated from Canyon High School, he worked security at Magic Mountain and worked briefly at his father's business. He had always wanted to be a peace officer, but his initial application to the Sheriff's Department was rejected. The mayor of Santa Clarita was Bob Kellar, a retired LAPD officer, and he took David March under his wing and tutored him for his second application to the Sheriff's Department. This time he was accepted by the Sheriff's Department and did well at the Sheriff's Academy. He worked in the County Jail for four-and-a-half years and then was assigned to the Temple Station where he was a patrol officer until his death.

The procession after the funeral to the grave site was several miles long. I was moved by the sheer number of people along the procession route holding flags and signs of support. At the funeral, I stood next to his father John March, who later became a dear friend. I promised him that we would not forgive, we would not forget, we would not give up.

John March later told me that at the funeral he observed a young male Hispanic standing next to the coffin weeping. John wanted to talk to him but was unable to because of the crowd. Six years later, John was at the yearly memorial at the site of the killing and was handed a cell phone by a deputy. The person on the phone said, "You don't know me, but I was at Dave's funeral. Dave arrested me eight years ago, he was at my trial, he visited me in jail, and he was there when I got out. He told me that I needed to straighten out my life, and he helped me do that. Now I am a youth pastor helping kids stay away from drugs and gangs." John thanked him and broke into tears of pride as he told his wife what the call was about.

JORGE ARROYO-GARCIA
EARLY YEARS AND CRIMINAL HISTORY

Jorge Arroyo-Garcia was born on November 3, 1976 in the Morelia, Michoacan area of Mexico. He entered the United States illegally in 1990. His last known school education was the seventh grade at McKinley Intermediate School in Redwood City, California.

Garcia was arrested as a juvenile on February 25, 1994 by the Drug Enforcement Administration. He attempted to exchange three pounds of methamphetamine for ten pounds of hydriotic acid, used to manufacture methamphetamine. He was convicted and committed to the California Youth Authority (CYA). At the time of his commitment to CYA, he identified his older brother, Hector Garcia-Arroyo, as his legal guardian and also named several aunts and uncles in the United States.

In the mid-1990s, Garcia lived with his brother, Hector Garcia-Arroyo, in Redwood City, California. In 1996, Garcia went to Baldwin Park in Los Angeles County, where he moved in with a friend. He remained in the Los Angeles area until April 30, 2002 when he fled to Mexico after the shooting death of Los Angeles County Deputy Sheriff David March. While in Los Angeles, Jorge Arroyo-Garcia was involved in the following criminal activity:

June 4, 2000 Arrest for Weapon Possession

On June 4, 2000 at approximately 1:20 a.m., Officer Batres of the El Monte Police Department was on patrol duty at the Valley Mall. He observed about ten to fifteen males standing near several vehicles from where he could hear loud music. Several males got into a white Chevy two-door pickup truck, which drove away from the mall. Officer Batres could hear loud music coming from the vehicle, which was in violation of the California Vehicle Code. He followed the vehicle and noticed that the truck's windows were tinted, which was also a California Vehicle Code violation.

Using his siren and loudspeaker, Officer Batres initiated a traffic stop. As he was making the traffic stop, he observed several of the occupants moving about inside the truck. Since he was working a one-man patrol car and since the detained vehicle contained multiple occupants, Officer Batres requested over the police radio for backup officers to respond to the location.

There were five male Hispanic young adults in the truck, with three occupants in the front cab of the truck and two seated in the rear passenger area. After backup officers arrived, Officer Batres approached the driver of the vehicle and asked the driver in both Spanish and English for permission to search the truck. The driver consented to a search, and the vehicle was searched pursuant to the consent. One of the backup officers found a Tech 9 assault-type weapon and a magazine containing 19 rounds wrapped in a T-shirt under the middle portion of the rear seat. Jorge Garcia-Arroyo was seated in the back seat directly above the area where the weapon was located. He told the officers that his name was Daniel Garcia.

Since the officers could not ascertain who was in possession of the gun, all five occupants of the truck were arrested and transported to the El Monte Police Department. At the station, each arrestee was interviewed. Jorge Arroyo-Garcia (whom the officers still believed was named Daniel Garcia) stated that he was the person who had purchased the weapon for $20 since it looked good, was cheap, and he didn't know if it was stolen. He further stated that the gun was wrapped in a T-shirt, and he placed it in the rear area of the truck.

By June 6, 2000, two days after his arrest, Jorge Arroyo-Garcia's true name had been determined. On that date, the El Monte Area Office of the District Attorney's Office charged him with one felony count of possessing a concealed weapon in a vehicle and one misdemeanor count of falsely representing himself to an officer. The 23-year-old Garcia was represented by the Public Defender's Office and remained in custody on $25,000 bail.

On June 23, 2000, before Judge Peters Meeks, Jorge Arroyo-Garcia entered a plea of nolo contendere, or no contest, to count one of possessing a concealed firearm in a vehicle. A plea of nolo contendere means that the defendant is not contesting the charges and, for purposes of the criminal case, is basically the same as a plea of guilty to the charge. Many defendants prefer a plea of nolo contendere because then they don't have to admit that they committed the offense. Judge Meeks sentenced Garcia to formal probation for three years with various fines and conditions including spending 364 days in county jail. The count two misdemeanor charge was dismissed.

With credits reducing his custody time, Garcia was released from county jail well before completing the full 364 days. However, he remained on formal probation, which required that he report to his probation officer. The Probation Department reported to the court that Garcia had deserted probation and, on March 21, 2001, his probation was revoked and a no-bail bench warrant was issued for his arrest.

Garcia was never arrested on the bench warrant. Apparently, he did not like being in custody, since he told several persons that he would kill a police officer rather than go to jail again.

November 18, 2001 Assault with Firearm

In 2001, Jorge Arroyo-Garcia was involved in a relationship with Maricruz Contreras Sanchez, and he moved into the home at 14344 Olive Street in Baldwin Park, California that she shared with her mother, sister, and brother-in-law. The relationship came to an end, and Garcia was forced to move out of the house. On November 18, 2001, Garcia telephoned Maricruz at her home and threatened her. She hung up the phone, and Garcia called back. This time Maricruz's brother, Refugio Contreras Sanchez, answered the telephone. Refugio told Garcia that Maricruz had nothing to say to him and hung up the phone. Garcia called again and told Refugio that he was coming over.

At approximately 7:52 p.m. on November 18, 2001, Refugio was walking in front of 14344 Olive Street when Garcia drove by the residence. Garcia was alone in a white Nissan Sentra and fired multiple shots at Refugio with a blue steel handgun. Garcia then drove off. Refugio was not injured in the shooting.

February 16, 2002 Assault with Firearm

On February 16, 2002 at approximately 8:07 p.m., Refugio Contreras Sanchez was driving through the Olive Square Market parking lot adjacent to his sister's residence at 14344 Olive Street. A black Nissan Maxima pulled slowly alongside Refugio Sanchez's vehicle. Jorge Arroyo-Garcia was driving the black Nissan, and he fired numerous shots from a blue steel handgun at Sanchez and his vehicle. Bullets struck his car, but Sanchez was not injured.

Refugio Sanchez reported both shooting incidents from November 18, 2001 and February 16, 2002 to the Baldwin Park Police Department. Detectives took photographs of Sanchez's bullet-stricken car from the February 16 incident.

As of April 28, 2002, Jorge Arroyo-Garcia had not been arrested or charged with the shootings at Refugio Contreras Sanchez, as the matter was still under investigation.

It is unknown whether Jorge Arroyo-Garcia knew that he was being investigated for shooting at Refugio Sanchez. However, he routinely carried a 9-mm semi-automatic handgun. Garcia also told several friends and associates that he would kill a policeman, if necessary, to avoid going to jail. This could be a deadly scenario for any law enforcement officer who might come in contact with Garcia.

THE SHOOTING DEATH OF DEPUTY DAVID MARCH
April 29, 2002 – Early Morning

During 2002, Jorge Arroyo-Garcia frequently drove the 1989 black Nissan Maxima bearing California license number 4BCZ512. The vehicle was registered to Martina Murillo, who was the wife of Jose Bustos Cabrera. Both Garcia and Cabrera were born and raised in the Morelia, Michoacan region of Mexico, and they were the best of friends. Garcia often slept in a white van at the rear of Jose Cabrera's residence.

On the evening of April 28, 2002, a male named Juan Gabriel Vasquez saw Garcia driving the black Nissan Maxima. He also observed that Garcia was carrying a black semi-automatic pistol in his waistband.

On the morning of April 29, 2002 at about 5:45 a.m., Jorge Arroyo-Garcia drove Carolina Rocha to work in the black Nissan. Approximately 90 minutes later, Garcia sat with Alfonso Castanon in the black Nissan for about 20 minutes in front of the Grand Home Inn on Valley Boulevard in El Monte. During this time Castanon observed a 9-mm handgun in Garcia's waistband. Garcia drove away from the Grand Home Inn at approximately 8:30 a.m. Between 9:00 a.m. and 10:30 a.m., he had breakfast at Cabrera's Family Restaurant, located at 625 East Live Oak Avenue in Arcadia. He was served breakfast by an acquaintance, Juan Gabriel Vasquez. At approximately 10:30 a.m., Garcia left the restaurant alone, driving the black Nissan.

Shooting Death of Deputy David March

On the morning of April 29, 2002, David William March was a peace officer working as an on-duty, uniformed patrol deputy for the Los Angeles County Sheriff's Department, assigned to patrol the Temple Station area in a one-man marked patrol car. Shortly after 10:30 a.m., Deputy March conducted a traffic stop of Garcia driving the black Nissan. This traffic stop occurred at the south curb of the eastbound traffic lanes at 242 East Live Oak Avenue in Irwindale. This location was just about a mile east of Cabrera's Family Restaurant at 625 East Live Oak Avenue in Arcadia.

At 10:38 a.m., as he was initiating the traffic stop, Deputy March entered the license plate number "4BCZ512" on the mobile display terminal (MDT) in his patrol car. Deputy March then approached the black Nissan on foot.

Jorge Arroyo-Garcia emerged from the black Nissan and fired five times at Deputy March with his 9-mm semi-automatic handgun. Deputy March was fatally wounded. Garcia immediately fled in the black Nissan.

Several civilians observed the shooting of Deputy March and the suspect leave in a black Nissan. Some civilians came to the assistance of Deputy March. One civilian, at 10:39 a.m., activated the emergency button on the MDT in Deputy March's patrol car.

Jorge Garcia – Flight to Mexico

After fleeing the scene of the murder of Deputy David March, Jorge Garcia abandoned the black Nissan on the street in front of 14143 Chilcot Street in Baldwin Park. This was on a cul-de-sac approximately 2.5 miles from the

EXCLUSIVE PREVIEW

location of the traffic stop and murder of Deputy March. Witness Sonia Martinez lived directly across the street from where the black Nissan was abandoned. She observed Garcia, who was alone, park and then exit the vehicle. Garcia then walked to Baldwin Park Boulevard and out of her sight. When interviewed by investigators, she positively identified a photograph of Jorge Garcia as depicting the person she saw exit the black Nissan.

At approximately 11:00 a.m., Garcia arrived on foot at the Buenos Aires Store at 14354 Olive Street in Baldwin Park. This store was situated in a strip mall approximately half a mile from the location where Garcia had abandoned the black Nissan. [Garcia had been a frequent customer of this store when he lived with Maricruz Contreras Sanchez, their house being a short distance from the Buenos Aires Store.]

Garcia made a telephone call from the Buenos Aires Store to Jose Bustos Cabrera, who was the co-owner of the black Nissan with his wife Martina Murillo. According to Cabrera, Garcia called him at home and said that the black Nissan had broken down and that he needed a ride. Alberto Reyes was at Cabrera's home when Garcia made the telephone call. Cabrera and Reyes drove to the strip mall in Cabrera's green Infiniti and picked up Garcia there. Garcia was shaken, crying, and perspiring. They drove him to the residence of Cabrera's cousin, Homero Mora Cabrera. During the drive, Garcia told Jose Cabrera and Alberto Reyes that he had shot and killed a policeman. Garcia stated that he had been stopped by the police because of the broken front lights of the Nissan Maxima. Garcia had exited the car when the officer approached him. The officer asked for a driver's license, but Garcia did not have one. When the officer began to search him, Garcia used his left arm to push the officer away and used his right arm to pull his gun from his waistband. He shot the officer several times and shot him again after he fell to the ground. He then fled in the car and abandoned it in a cul-de-sac street in Baldwin Park. Cabrera and Reyes observed that Garcia was still carrying his black 9-mm gun in his waistband.

Garcia asked Cabrera if he had any money. Because Garcia was armed and acting emotionally, Cabrera gave him his wallet. Garcia took $500 from the wallet and returned it to him. Garcia was dropped off at the residence of Homero Mora Cabrera, and Jose Cabrera and Alberto Reyes drove away from the location.

COOLEY & SCHIRN

Garcia remained at the home of Homero Mora Cabrera for several hours. Arrangements were made for taxi transportation of Garcia to Tijuana, Mexico for $200. A taxi driver picked up Garcia in front of Homero Cabrera's residence at approximately 9:40 p.m. on April 29, 2002. Garcia was driven to the international border where he was dropped off at a taxi stand on the Mexican side of the border.

INVESTIGATION OF THE MURDER OF DEPUTY DAVID MARCH

Sergeants Kenneth Gallatin and Steven Katz of the Homicide Bureau of the Los Angeles County Sheriff's Department were the officers in charge of the investigation of the murder of Deputy David March. At approximately 11:30 a.m. on April 29, 2002, they arrived at the scene of the shooting at 242 East Live Oak Street in Irwindale to take command of the investigation. Numerous law enforcement officers participated in the investigation that was overseen by Sergeants Gallatin and Katz. What follows is a general overview of the investigation that was conducted:

Deputy David March's black and white patrol car was at the crime scene. In the street by the patrol car there were five spent 9-mm shell casings. Also on the street was the front panel to the ballistic vest that was bloodstained. This vest had been removed by responding deputy sheriffs and paramedics at the scene to treat Deputy March for the wounds that he had received.

Deputy March's patrol car was equipped with a mobile digital terminal (MDT). This device is a computer that allows a user to access different data bases to check registration information on vehicle license plate numbers of stolen or wanted cars, driver's license status, warrants, and stolen property or guns. The MDT is also used to dispatch calls, i.e., to direct deputy sheriffs to specific locations where citizens have requested their assistance.

The last entry made in the MDT of Deputy March's patrol car was to check the status of California license plate number 4BCZ512. This license plate was for a 1989 four door Nissan Maxima registered to Martina Murillo at 918 Huntington Drive, Apartment K, City of Duarte, County of Los Angeles.

Officers went to the Huntington Drive location and learned that Martina Murillo had moved to 5019 Heleo Street, Temple City. Officers then went to the Heleo Street location. At this time in the investigation, any person with access to the Nissan Maxima was a possible suspect or person of interest in the shooting death of Deputy March.

Investigators located Martina Murillo and spoke to her on the evening of April 29, 2002. She stated that on the evening of April 28, 2002, her husband, Jose Bustos Cabrera, had loaned their Nissan Maxima to Jorge Arroyo-Garcia. The following day Garcia told her husband that he had shot and killed a police officer while driving their car.

The Nissan Maxima had been parked in front of 14143 Chilcot Street in Baldwin Park. On the afternoon of April 29, 2002, a Parking Enforcement Officer had cited the vehicle for illegal parking during street sweeping hours. When the officer heard that investigators were looking for the Nissan Maxima, she remembered the citation and the vehicle and told the investigators. The Nissan Maxima was located and impounded on May 1, 2002. It was examined by forensic experts who removed a drop of blood from its left rear tire. Laboratory analysis determined that the blood on the left rear tire of the Nissan Maxima was the blood of Deputy David March.

A detective from the Baldwin Park Police Department recognized that the Nissan Maxima had been identified as the vehicle involved in the attempted murder of Refugio Contreras Sanchez on February 16, 2002. Sanchez had identified Jorge Arroyo-Garcia as the shooter on February 16, 2002 as well as another shooting incident on November 18, 2001 in which Garcia had previously shot at him.

Within a few days after the death of Deputy David March, the investigation had clearly established that Jorge Arroyo-Garcia was responsible for the murder. However, the investigation had also established that Garcia had fled to Mexico. As long as Garcia remained in Mexico, he would not be tried or punished for the cold-blooded murder of Deputy David William March.

EXTRADITION

With Jorge Arroyo-Garcia having fled to Mexico, the Los Angeles County District Attorney's Office initiated the process of returning him to Los Angeles County to be prosecuted for the murder of Deputy David March.

The extradition of criminal suspects from one country to another is governed by the Extradition Treaty between the two countries on this subject. The United States – Mexico Extradition Treaty went into effect in 1980. It provided that neither country was bound to deliver its nationals for extradition, but this provision did not create a problem in most cases. The Treaty further provided that where the offense for which extradition is sought is punishable by death, a country may refuse to extradite unless the country seeking extradition assures that it will not impose the death penalty. Under the Treaty, the death penalty is the only punishment for which such assurances may be required. For many years, Mexico had extradited many suspects to California and other states without serious problems.

In October 2001, the Mexico Supreme Court ruled that the goal of penal law in Mexico was "rehabilitation" and that "a life sentence violates the Mexico Constitution." Mexico then extended this interpretation to the Extradition Treaty, deciding that it would no longer extradite a fugitive who is subject to life imprisonment with or without the possibility of parole unless assurances are given that guarantees a sentence of a determinate number of years. Under this interpretation, Jorge Arroyo-Garcia could remain in Mexico and avoid being prosecuted in the United States for the murder of Deputy David March.

EFFORTS TO CHANGE MEXICAN EXTRADITION POLICY (COMMENTARY OF STEVE COOLEY)

Even before the death of Deputy David March, the District Attorney's Office had been frustrated in its attempts to extradite some murderers who had fled to Mexico. One particularly aggravated case was the brutal murder in June 1999 of two young girls as they walked to school. The murderer, Juan Manual Casillas, had fled to Mexico; and the District Attorney's Office was seeking his extradition. However, Mexico refused to extradite based on the decision by the Mexico Supreme Court.

Jan Maurizi, my Director of the Bureau of Branch and Area Operations Region II, was an expert in extradition law. In the latter part of April 2002, just days prior to the murder of Deputy March, she went to San Antonio, Texas, to attend the U.S. Attorney General's United States/Mexico Conference on Extradition. She assumed that the Mexican authorities would announce a change in their extradition policy, but they refused to do so. Lt. Joe Hartshorne of the Los Angeles County Sheriff's Department also attended the conference. During the conference, on April 29, 2002, Lt. Hartshorne received a telephone call and stepped out of the room. He returned and told Ms. Maurizi with a heavy heart, "We just lost another deputy." He didn't have a name or any details –- just that a deputy had been shot and killed by an unknown suspect who had fled. Ms. Maurizi felt a wave of panic because she had a son who was a deputy sheriff working patrol at the time.

Even before the death of Deputy March, I had employed a multi-faceted approach to compel Mexico to extradite violent felons facing life sentences. But the brutal murder of David March gave that effort a new impetus.

I had appointed Jan Maurizi to coordinate many of the efforts in the extradition fight. She began a multi-year effort to change Mexico's policy on the extradition of violent criminals. She contacted the Office of International Affairs, the State Department, and met with members of the Senate and House of Representatives. She met with and briefed White House Counsel, and she gave presentations to law enforcement and victims' rights groups. Ms. Maurizi and I actively spoke on this issue on talk shows in an effort to raise public support and awareness for our cause. Popular local radio talk show hosts John Kobylt and Ken Chiampou were particularly supportive of this issue and keeping it alive.

One of the major elected officials who joined the effort was United States Senator Dianne Feinstein. In July 2003, she sent a five-page letter to Mexican President Vicente Fox urging him to act to resolve the problem. The letter included the following language:

> In California, for example, over 40 different crimes are punishable by possible life sentences and neither a judge nor a prosecutor can give

assurances of a determinate term for these crimes. As a result, Mexico's policy encourages people committing serious crimes in California to flee to Mexico and escape just punishment. Indeed, individuals in the United States with a criminal history have a pervasive incentive to kill an arresting police officer and head for Mexico rather than face possible prosecution and imprisonment in the United States.

In 2004, the District Attorney's Office, under the direction of Ms. Maurizi, launched the website "Escaping Justice.com." This website featured tragic stories of Los Angeles County crime victims and their relatives who were being denied justice because the suspects in their cases had fled to Mexico. Among the persons lending support to this effort were the parents and widow of Deputy David March. The website also sought the public's help in locating fugitive suspects, and it also served as a clearinghouse for information about the Mexican court decision.

Also, the District Attorney's Office sponsored and successfully lobbied for the passage of Assembly Bill 1432, which allowed re-prosecution of any fugitive who re-entered the United States after conviction or acquittal in a foreign jurisdiction. The bill was signed into law by California Governor Arnold Schwarzenegger in 2004.

Additionally, in August 2005, the District Attorney's Office helped congressional representatives draft a federal law that would have imposed sanctions for noncompliance with an extradition treaty. That legislation was enacted into law in October 2005. A month later, on November 29, 2005, the Mexico Supreme Court reversed its 2001 ruling. As a result, the extradition of suspects from Mexico reverted to its prior status. Mexico would now extradite its citizens to the United States upon receiving assurances from the requesting state that it would not seek the death penalty.

"COMPROMISE" EFFORTS
(COMMENTARY OF STEVE COOLEY)

The change in Mexico's policy was a successful conclusion to the heroic efforts of many persons to achieve justice in the murder of Deputy David

March. Now Jorge Arroyo-Garcia could be returned to the United States for trial and face a sentence of life in prison for his crime. This result was achieved despite the "compromise" efforts by persons one would expect to strongly support the District Attorney's position.

John and Barbara March, the parents of David March, remained strongly committed. They contacted government officials and often appeared on talk shows and on television to lobby for a change in the law. Terry March, the widow of David March, initially supported these efforts, but she eventually went on talk shows criticizing me for not giving in to Mexico's demands to have the trial and sentence handled in Mexico.

David Dreier, one of the most powerful congressmen in the House of Representatives, drafted a bill with the support of Sheriff Lee Baca. The bill proposed a federal law that provided for a maximum sentence of 22 years for killing a federal or law enforcement officer and then fleeing the country. Once a person was convicted under this federal law, state authorities would have been prevented from prosecuting that individual for the murder of the law enforcement officer. This proposed law was strongly supported by Sheriff Baca, who wanted closure to this long-standing and unresolved issue. If implemented, this law would provide a great incentive for cop-killers to flee the United States. Neither Congressman Dreier nor Sheriff Baca had discussed this proposed law with me or my office. I learned about it when they announced it at a press conference. When I heard about it, I exploded and issued a harsh public statement condemning it. Sheriff Baca criticized my comments, but I believe that my reaction helped scuttle this ill-advised proposal.

In 2004, California Senator Barbara Boxer was running for re-election to the United States Senate. In a debate with her opponent, she was asked about the extradition issue. She was caught flat-footed and looked, at a minimum, uninformed on the issue. She called me the following day and wanted to know why she had not been informed on the subject. The next day Jan Maurizi sent the Senator a thick packet of letters, memoranda, etc., that had been sent by the District Attorney's Office to Senator Boxer's office over a couple of years, none of which had been responded to. Senator Boxer's non-involvement was in sharp contrast to California's other U.S. Senator, Dianne

Feinstein, who played a supportive role in the return of Garcia to the United States for trial.

During my one and only conversation with Senator Boxer, I would have to describe her as functionally uninformed, rude, abusive, and boorish. In my view, she was one of the worst and most ineffective United States senators in California history. Her non-involvement in a matter as important as extraditing murderers from Mexico was just a stark example of her complete ineptitude.

WITNESS MARTINA MURILLO

On the late evening of April 29, 2002, the day of the murder of Deputy David March, Sheriff's investigators interviewed Martina Murillo. She knew Jorge Arroyo-Garcia as Armando Garcia. She stated that her husband, Jose Bustos Cabrera, and Garcia were born and raised in Morelia, Michoacan, Mexico. They were friends, and Garcia would occasionally stay with her and her husband because he was sometimes homeless. She and her husband owned a black Nissan Maxima that Garcia would occasionally borrow. On the evening of April 28, 2002, her husband loaned their black Nissan Maxima to Garcia. The following day, her husband told her that Garcia had told him that he had killed a police officer while driving the black Nissan Maxima.

On May 27, 2003, Detective Mark Lillienfeld of the Los Angeles County Sheriff's Department conducted another interview with Martina Murillo. She stated that a little over a year after the murder of Deputy David March, she and her husband Jose Bustos Cabrera were visiting her husband's relatives in Morelia, Michoacan, Mexico. There she met and spoke with Garcia. He told her that he was driving her Nissan Maxima when he was pulled over by a police car. Deputy March approached him as he sat in the driver's seat and asked him for his driver's license. Garcia told the deputy that he didn't have a license. Deputy March ordered him out of the Nissan and went with him to the patrol car. There he pulled out a gun and shot the deputy who fell to the ground. He shot him several more times in the neck area. Deputy March was shaking as he lay on the ground after being shot and was trying to reach for his own gun, so Garcia shot him in the head. Garcia then ran to the Nissan

Maxima and drove off. He eventually made his way to Tijuana, Mexico and ultimately to Morelia, Michoacan, Mexico.

This statement by Martina Murillo to Detective Lillienfeld on May 27, 2003 gave Sheriff's investigators and the District Attorney's Office information from a credible witness that Garcia was, in fact, hiding in Mexico. This would be crucial information in any subsequent extradition application to Mexico that Garcia was in Mexico to avoid appropriate prosecution and punishment under California law.

ARREST AND EXTRADITION OF JORGE ARROYO-GARCIA

Approximately three months after the Mexico Supreme Court reversed its ruling of October 2001, Jorge Arroyo Garcia was arrested by Mexican authorities on February 23, 2006 in a small town outside Guadalajara, Mexico. He was now subject to extradition to the United States if assurances were given that the Los Angeles County District Attorney's Office would not seek or impose the death penalty.

The actual request for extradition would be handled by the Office of International Affairs in the United States Department of Justice. It was up to the Los Angeles County District Attorney's Office to provide the Office of International Affairs with the proper documentation for the extradition request. Under the United States – Mexico Extradition Treaty, the United States Government had 60 days after Garcia's arrest to send to Mexico a formal request for extradition.

Bureau Director Janice Maurizi of the District Attorney's Office prepared a Prosecutor Affidavit of 19 pages that was sworn and signed on April 5, 2006 before California Superior Court Judge Steven R. Van Sicklen. Her affidavit and supporting documents included the following information as required by the extradition treaty between the United States and Mexico:

- Facts and personal information of the person sought that will permit his identification.
- Description of the offense and statement of the facts of the case.

- Text of the applicable legal principles of the requesting party on the disposition of the case regarding the essential elements of the offense, the punishment of the offense and the statute of limitations.
- Certified copy of the arrest warrant.
- Evidence that the laws of the requested party would provide for the apprehension and commitment for trial of the person sought if the offense had been committed within its jurisdiction.
- Assurances that the death penalty will not be imposed.

This Prosecutor's Affidavit contained eleven supporting documents that were attached to and incorporated into the affidavits as Exhibits A to K. These Exhibits included certified copies of the complaint and arrest warrant, a description of the relevant statutes, certified copies of Garcia's 2000 conviction, and the affidavits of Detective Mark Lillienfeld, Juan Gabriel Vasquez, Jose Bustos Cabrera, Martina Murillo, Sonia Martinez, Detective Johnny Patino, and Refugio Contreras Sanchez.

The Prosecutor's Affidavit was accompanied by a letter dated April 5, 2006 under my name as District Attorney to the Office of International Affairs in the United States Department of Justice. The letter provided assurances that the Los Angeles County District Attorney's Office would not seek the death penalty nor would a penalty of death be imposed in the case charging Jorge Arroyo-Garcia with the murder of Los Angeles County Deputy Sheriff David March on April 29, 2002 and other charges.

The Request for Extradition, including supporting documents, was transmitted through diplomatic channels, with the appropriate seals and ribbons, and translated into Spanish. After their delivery to the Secretariat of Foreign Affairs through the United States Embassy in Mexico, the "package" was sent to the Office of the Attorney General who sent the documents to the district judge in the Mexican jurisdiction where Jorge Arroyo-Garcia was being held.

After Jorge Arroyo-Garcia's arrest by Mexican authorities on February 23, 2006, he remained in custody until his Mexican appeals were exhausted and then extradited to the United States in early January 2007.

On January 9, 2007, a SWAT unit from Mexico took Garcia by airplane from Mexico City to Tijuana. In Tijuana, local and federal authorities took him into the United States. One of the peace officers who took custody of Garcia at the United States/Mexico border was Detective Mark Lillienfeld of the Los Angeles Sheriff's Department. Detective Lillienfeld had received Deputy March's handcuffs from his family, and he used the handcuffs in transporting Garcia to the Orange County Men's Central Jail. It was a symbolic act that the use of these handcuffs represented that Deputy David March had participated in the arrest of the man who had murdered him.

On January 11, 2007, Garcia was transported to the Pomona Superior Court where he was arraigned on the charges against him. Deputy District Attorney Darren Levine represented the prosecution, and Deputy Public Defender Grady Russell was appointed to represent Garcia.

GUILTY PLEA

On January 25, 2007, Detectives Mark Lillienfeld and Steven Katz transported Jorge Arroyo-Garcia from the San Bernardino West Valley Detention Center, where he was being housed, to Department M of the Pomona Superior Court for a court appearance before Judge Charles Horan. On the return trip to the Detention Center, Garcia made several spontaneous statements to Detectives Lillienfeld and Katz regarding the following:

Garcia discussed the possibility of pleading guilty to the charges against him. He specifically asked where he would be housed if he pled guilty to the charges, whether he would be able to marry his common law wife, and whether he would be able to receive visits from her while in state prison custody. Garcia asked whether he could use Detective Katz's cell phone to call family members in Mexico to discuss the possibility of pleading guilty to the pending charges. Detective Katz allowed Garcia to use his cell phone, but Garcia was unable to reach his relatives.

Detectives Lillienfeld and Katz reported Garcia's statements to prosecutor Darren Levine. Levine in turn contacted Garcia's defense attorney, Grady Russell, to advise him of Garcia's statements. Arrangements were later made for Garcia to phone and talk to his family members while in the presence of his attorney.

On March 2, 2007, Jorge Arroyo-Garcia was prepared to plead guilty to the charge against him involving the murder of Deputy David March. On that date, he appeared before Judge Charles Horan in Department M of the Pomona Superior Court. Below is a summary of the principals in the case and the charge to which he entered a guilty plea:

PEOPLE v. JORGE ARROYO-GARCIA
CASE KA056968

JUDGE:	Charles Horan
PROSECUTOR:	Darren Levine, Deputy District Attorney
	Crimes Against Peace Officers Section
DEFENSE ATTORNEY:	Grady Russell, Deputy Public Defender

COUNT AND SPECIAL ALLEGATIONS TO WHICH GARCIA PLED GUILTY:

- Count I (Penal Code section 187, Murder in the Second Degree)
- Penal Code section 190(c) (1) (Special Allegation of Killing a Peace Officer in the Lawful Performance of His Duties)
- Penal Code section 190(c) (4) (Special Allegation of Personal Use of a Firearm in the Commission of the Murder)

NOTE: *The special allegations in Penal Code section 190 (c) with a plea to second degree murder provided for a sentence of life imprisonment without the possibility of parole.*

As part of the guilty plea, Jorge Arroyo Garcia signed a five-page "Written Advisement and Waivers" and initialed 23 paragraphs contained in the document. Paragraph 19, initialed by Garcia, provided a factual basis for the plea, as follows:

19. *[initials] I offer to the court the following as the basis for my plea of guilty: On April 29, 2002, within the County of Los Angeles, I intentionally*

> killed a peace officer, Los Angeles County Sheriff's Deputy David March, while personally using a nine millimeter semi-automatic pistol.
>
> Further, I knew Deputy David March was a peace officer in the lawful performance of his duties when I shot and killed him.

Judge Charles Horan carefully questioned Garcia on each of the terms that he initialed in the "Written Advisement and Waivers" which was in effect a plea agreement. Garcia read the language in Paragraph 19 that he shot and killed Deputy David March to the court. Judge Horan then accepted Garcia's guilty plea to murder in the second degree with the special allegations.

After entering his guilty plea, Garcia made a lengthy statement in Spanish in which he asked for forgiveness by friends and family of the man he killed.

Judge Horan then sentenced Jorge Arroyo Garcia to life imprisonment without the possibility of parole pursuant to Penal Code section 190 (c). Two counts involving the attempted murder of Refugio Contreras Sanchez were dismissed.

In my role as District Attorney, I attended the court proceedings along with Sheriff Lee Baca. After the proceedings I made the following statement:

> Justice was done today. The man who gunned down Deputy David March nearly five years ago and left him to die on a street in Irwindale will be locked away forever. It is the same sentence he would have received had he gone to trial. Had it not been for the persistence and joint efforts of local, state, federal, and Mexican officials, this day would not have come, and Jorge Arroyo Garcia would still be a free man in Mexico. These criminals are being sought and will be caught. They will be returned to the United States—as Garcia was two months ago. They will be prosecuted. Justice will be served. Garcia is the first of several being returned from Mexico who will be sentenced to life in prison for his crimes. His guilty plea brings hope to hundreds of next of kin, victims, and survivors of crimes in which the perpetrator fled to Mexico to avoid prosecution.

EPILOGUE –
CALIFORNIA STATE PRISON AT CALIPATRIA

The Written Advisement and Waivers signed by Jorge Arroyo-Garcia was also signed by Deputy District Attorney Darren Levine and Deputy Public Defender Grady Russell. It stated in Paragraphs 5 and 6 that efforts would be made to have Garcia serve his sentence at the California State Prison at Calipatria and that authorities would not oppose legal visits by his family members. This prison facility is located in Imperial County near the Mexican border, and Garcia's incarceration there would facilitate prison visits by his family. This was a minor benefit for Garcia that helped insure his guilty plea and a quick and appropriate resolution to the case.

In a letter dated February 20, 2007 to the California Department of Corrections, Captain Raymond H. Peavy of the Los Angeles County Sheriff's Homicide Bureau requested that Jorge Arroyo-Garcia be housed at the Calipatria State Prison in Imperial County, California.

Jorge Arroyo-Garcia is presently serving his sentence of life imprisonment without the possibility of parole at the California State Prison in Calipatria.

EPILOGUE – CONCLUSION

On October 2, 2001, the Mexico Supreme Court issued its ruling that Mexican nationals subject to a sentence of life imprisonment could not be extradited to a requesting country. Almost immediately, the Los Angeles County District Attorney's Office took measures to overturn the effects of the Court's decision.

Sometimes it takes a dramatic or tragic event to provide a human face to a problem. The murder of Los Angeles County Deputy David March took place on April 29, 2002, which was approximately seven months after the Mexico Supreme Court decision. Suddenly, there was a real life event that made the court decision more than just a theoretical possibility.

The murder of Deputy March provided much of the impetus for efforts to have the Mexico Supreme Court reverse its 2001 ruling. The eventual sentence of Jorge Arroyo-Garcia to life in prison without the possibility of parole was the result of the efforts of many individuals, but a major rallying point for those efforts was the murder of Deputy David March.

EPILOGUE – DAVID MARCH CREDO

A few weeks before his death, Deputy David March underwent a department review of his performance. As part of the review, he was told to write his personal goals. He wrote the following:

"My goals in life are simple. I will always be painfully honest, work as hard as I can, learn as much as I can, and hopefully make a difference in people's lives."

After the death of Deputy David March, this became the official credo of the Los Angeles Sheriff's Department.

LESSONS LEARNED

This chapter has two lessons to be learned.

(1) Traffic stop: Just as Officer Martin Ganz in the previous chapter, Deputy David March was working a one-man police car when he conducted a fatal traffic stop. Deputy March detained Jorge Arroyo-Garcia for a traffic violation in a black Nissan. Several witnesses observed the shooting of Deputy March and stated that as he approached the driver's side of the Nissan on foot, Garcia emerged from the Nissan and fired several shots at Deputy March, fatally wounding him. In describing the incident to Jose Cabrera, Garcia stated that when Deputy March began to search him, he used his left arm to push the officer away and used his right arm to pull his gun from his waistband and shot the officer.

Under either scenario, Deputy March was vulnerable because he was working a one-man police car and made a traffic stop of a wanted person who was armed and dangerous and did not want to be arrested. Garcia made up his mind to shoot David March, and there was nothing the deputy could do to stop it.

(2) "We will not give up": The theme of the first chapter of this book was "we will not forget" the murder of a law enforcement officer. In that case, the 1957 murder of two El Segundo police officers was finally solved over 40 years later after the murders were committed.

The theme of this last chapter is that "we will not give up" in efforts to bring to justice the killer of a police officer. In every chapter in this book, the perpetrator was captured and convicted of the murder of the officer based on the coordinated efforts of law enforcement and the District Attorney's Office. The most challenging aspect in bringing to trial the suspect involved in the murder of Deputy David March was when the killer sought refuge in Mexico. It appeared that he might avoid arrest and prosecution for this brutal murder under statutory law and judicial fiat in existence in Mexico at that time. However, the Los Angeles County District Attorney's Office and local officials enlisted the assistance of the federal government. Pressure was put on Mexican officials who ultimately relented and allowed the return of the suspect to the United States where he was convicted of the murder of Deputy March. This case is the classic example of "we will not give up."

Made in the USA
Lexington, KY
17 December 2018